The Novels of
Harold Frederic

Drawing of Harold Frederic by Austin Briggs, after a photograph
taken by Frederic himself in 1896

The Novels of
Harold Frederic

by

AUSTIN BRIGGS, JR.

Cornell University Press

ITHACA AND LONDON

158145

First published 1969

Standard Book Number 8014-0535-1

Library of Congress Catalog Card Number 71-87014

PRINTED IN THE UNITED STATES OF AMERICA
BY VAIL-BALLOU PRESS, INC.

For My Mother
and Father

Preface

This book describes and analyzes the novels of Harold Frederic (1856–1898). It is an attempt to understand an eccentric achievement that has continually eluded proper definition. An admirer of William Dean Howells on the one hand and of Robert Louis Stevenson on the other, Frederic gave his allegiance to neither realism nor romance. He went his own way in his fiction, and the results were remarkably successful, from the early novels—so often praised as bitterly realistic—through the late ones—so often damned as trivially romantic.

Two works to which I am deeply indebted have cleared the way to an understanding of Frederic's fiction. The first is Paul Haines's unpublished dissertation "Harold Frederic" (1945), a study notable for the good sense of its critical judgments, for its thorough reading of Frederic's journalistic writing, and for its information drawn from interviews and correspondence with friends, acquaintances, and relatives of Frederic who are no longer alive. The second work, *Harold Frederic* (1961) by Thomas F. O'Donnell and Hoyt C. Franchere, admirably complements Haines's pioneer study in still further correcting the distortion of the literary histories, which portray Frederic as a harsh realist who chronicled a personal and angry revolt from the farm and the village. Throughout the pages which follow, I have relied heavily on the biographical research of Professor Haines and Professors O'Donnell and Franchere. I am grateful to Thomas O'Donnell for many kindnesses and favors as well, not the least of them good conversation about Frederic.

I am also indebted to another unpublished dissertation, "Harold Frederic: His Development as a Comic Realist" (1961) by Ralph Robert Rogers. I found this work stimulating and reassuring; it was a pleasure to discover that someone else had been struck by the comedy of works that so many others had treated almost as tracts. A graphologist who once analyzed a specimen of Frederic's handwriting detected evidence of a sense of humor "under the magnifying glass." Actually, no special lenses are required to appreciate the humor of Harold Frederic; a slight shift in perspective is sufficient.

Although I have made reference to Frederic's short stories, journalistic writing, and letters whenever it seemed useful to do so, I have concentrated most heavily on the novels themselves. Except for the excellent modern edition of *The Damnation of Theron Ware* published by Harvard University Press, I have used the first American editions of the novels. Almost all nineteenth-century American editions of the novels follow the same pagination.

Because so little scholarly work has been done on Frederic, I have deliberately included in my footnotes a great deal of information that will, I trust, be helpful to others working on Frederic. Those making use of my bibliography will wish to supplement it with the extensive "Critical Bibliography of Secondary Comment" on Frederic published in the second number of *American Literary Realism, 1870–1910* (Spring, 1968). Except for the few not listed there, contemporary reviews of Frederic's works are not listed in my bibliography and the titles of such reviews have been omitted from my citations. Although the bibliography compiled by the editors of *American Literary Realism* appeared after my research was completed, I was fortunate in having available the bibliography published by Robert H. Woodward in *Studies in Bibliography* (1960). I found Professor Woodward's listing of contemporary reviews of Frederic's work especially helpful, and I am still further in his debt for details he gave me about one of Frederic's letters.

Among the sources consulted, the collection of Frederic's papers in the Library of Congress was of prime importance, and I would like to express my thanks to the library for assistance while I was working there. The Colindale Branch of the British Museum and the Utica Public Library also provided valuable assistance. The librarians of the Hamilton College Library, especially those in charge of interlibrary loans, have been tireless in their efforts on my behalf. For permission to quote from manuscripts in their possession, I would like to thank the New York State Library and the libraries of Columbia, Cornell, Harvard, and the University of Southern California. I am also indebted to Harold Frederic's daughter, Mrs. Eliot Keen, for permission to quote from her father's letters.

This book was read in an earlier version by Professors Lewis Leary and Robert Gorham Davis, of Columbia. Paul Parker and Dwight Lindley, of Hamilton College, also helped me in substantial ways.

I owe a special debt of gratitude to two men. Edmund Wilson gave me encouragement to publish my book; his

vigorous interest in Harold Frederic provided encouragement of another but equally cheering sort. Edwin Barrett, of
Hamilton College, has given his services to my manuscript
beyond the call of friendship; there is scarcely a page in the
book that is not the better for his criticism.

The Danforth Foundation provided a Teacher's Study
Grant that enabled me to devote 1962–1963 to uninterrupted
research and writing. To the Foundation and to Hamilton
College for giving me a year's leave of absence, I am most
grateful. I would also like to thank Hamilton College for
assistance provided from a fund allocated by the Ford Foundation for research in the humanities.

The help and support my wife has given are beyond calculation.

A. B., Jr.

Clinton, New York
July 1968

Contents

The Novels of
Harold Frederic

1 / The Country Boy of Genius

When Harold Frederic died in 1898, it seemed certain that he would be long remembered. He was so entertaining a conversationalist that men went to his clubs just to hear him talk; he was a famous reporter in an age that liked to make romantic heroes of its reporters. The New York *Times* at his death expected that above all he would be remembered for his novels: "Everyone must read [them] who wishes to hold his own in popular literary discussion." [1] Gertrude Atherton recalled that "no American writer was ever more appreciated in England than Harold Frederic, and whatever he wrote was received by the press with the same consideration and distinction accorded to the leading British novelists. . . . The best men all read him, his books were seriously discussed, his next eagerly awaited." [2] Frank Harris expressed the views of many contemporaries

---

[1] "Harold Frederic," Oct. 20, 1898, p. 7.
[2] "The American Novel in England," *The Bookman* (New York), XXX (1910), 637.

when he called Frederic "one of the most extraordinary and fascinating personalities of our time." [3]

Frederic was forgotten, however, and forgotten quickly. His reputation survived only among isolated enthusiasts who either remembered or chanced to discover for themselves *The Damnation of Theron Ware,* and their attempts to revive a wider interest were in vain. "If reappearing were ever possible," thought some friends who tried to lure back Frederic's ghost at a midnight séance, "so strenuous a man as Harold would somehow shoulder his way past the guards." [4] But Frederic never answered the summons, and for decades it seemed that the brilliant reputation had vanished with the spirit, never to return. By 1960, John Henry Raleigh could report of *The Damnation* that scholars had allowed a minor classic of American literature to pass nearly into oblivion.[5]

[3] "Harold Frederic: Ad Memoriam," *Saturday Review,* LXXXVI (1898), 527. From 1884 until his death in 1898, Frederic was the London correspondent for the New York *Times,* in which capacity he reported on every kind of political and cultural news. In his *History of The New York Times, 1851–1921* (New York, 1921), Elmer Davis writes: "A feature of *The Times* which his readers could count on every Sunday was Harold Frederic's cable letter from London. In those simpler days only exceptional events in Europe were reported at any length as soon as they happened; the daily cables carried only a sort of skeleton of the news, and every New York paper depended on the weekly cable letters from London and Paris for general interpretative discussion of foreign affairs. In this field, of great importance in those days, Harold Frederic was in the eighties and nineties without superior, and his correspondence from London was one of the great features of *The Times*" (p. 164).

[4] Robert Barr to unnamed correspondent, June 8, 1900, quoted in Vincent Starrett, *Buried Caesars* (Chicago, 1923), p. 85. At the séance, held at Ravensbrook, Crane's former home, an attempt was also made to call back the ghost of Stephen Crane, who had died on June 5, 1900.

[5] Introduction to Thornton Wilder, *Heaven's My Destination* (Garden City, N.Y., 1960), p. 1.

In the 1960's, however, a new generation is discovering just how excellent *The Damnation* is; four publishers have issued editions of the novel,[6] and, in 1967, Raleigh noted that it was one of his students' favorite books at Berkeley.[7] With the publication of *Harold Frederic* by Thomas F. O'Donnell and Hoyt C. Franchere, readers curious about Frederic need no longer rely on comments like this, from a biographical dictionary: "His appearance indicated his nature—he had the long nose and narrow eyes of the fanatic, coupled with full, sensuous lips." [8] And for readers with a touch of their own fanaticism, there is the *Frederic Herald*, a newsletter published in Frederic's home town, Utica, New York.

The renewed interest in Frederic, however, is limited almost exclusively to one novel. Although *The Damnation* is unquestionably his best novel, four of the other seven are remarkably original and interesting. Two of them, *Seth's Brother's Wife* and *The Lawton Girl*, do receive some attention, usually as works of bitter realism, which they are not. The other two, *Gloria Mundi* and *The Market-Place*, are seldom mentioned even by Frederic enthusiasts. Harold Frederic deserves to be remembered for more than *The Damnation*, and he deserves a different reading than he has hitherto received.

The notion of half a century of neglect can be exaggerated. In the third volume of *Main Currents in American Thought*,

---

[6] For a summary of what Thomas F. O'Donnell says "may be safely called a Frederic revival—modest but steady," see his "Harold Frederic (1856–1898)," *American Literary Realism, 1870–1910*, No. 1 (Fall, 1967), pp. 39–44.

[7] "Readers and Writers: From Your Letters," *Frederic Herald*, I (Sept., 1967), 3.

[8] *Harold Frederic* (New York, 1961). Stanley J. Kunitz and Howard Haycroft, eds., *American Authors, 1600–1900* (New York, 1938), p. 288.

Vernon Louis Parrington did consider Frederic briefly, but so briefly that he did not even refer to *The Damnation*. Had Parrington lived to complete his work, perhaps he would have left more than a thirty-line paragraph describing Frederic's first novel. *Seth's Brother's Wife*, Parrington said, "is a drab tale of upper York State, as bitter as any tale of the western border," and, he concluded, "Harold Frederic quite evidently hates this countryside that bred him." [9] Over the years, it has generally been Parrington's view of Frederic that has found its way into print. Those surveys of American literature or culture that mention Frederic are in general agreement: Frederic was an exponent of a "forbidding" realism; he viewed the American scene with "moral confusion and dismay"; he was among the "ardent young rebels, . . . [in] the vanguard of the muckrakers, dismally aware of the passing of the old America"; he was a passionate novelist whose works "poured sullenly out of agrarian bitterness, the class hatreds of the eighties and nineties, the bleakness of small town life, . . . and the bitterness in the new proletarian cities"; and he was "burning with indignation against the conduct of his rural people." [10]

The fullest expression of Parrington's view that Frederic avenged himself in bitterly realistic novels upon the hated

[9] *The Beginnings of Critical Realism in America, 1860–1920* (New York, 1930), pp. 288–289.

[10] Robert P. Falk, "The Rise of Realism, 1871–1891," in Harry Hayden Clark, ed., *Transitions in American Literary History* (Durham, N.C., 1953), p. 438; Spiller *et al.*, eds., *Literary History of the United States* (New York, 1948), II, 1016; Henry Steele Commager, *The American Mind* (New Haven, 1950), p. 60; Alfred Kazin, *On Native Grounds* (New York, 1942), p. 16; Charles Child Walcutt, *American Literary Naturalism, A Divided Stream* (Minneapolis, 1956), p. 47.

countryside of his youth is to be found in Carey McWilliams' "Harold Frederic: 'A Country Boy of Genius.' " [11] The first substantial effort in the twentieth century to assess Frederic's significance, the essay turns to biography to explain why the novelist loathed the New York State of his upbringing. McWilliams' essay is particularly important because for almost three decades, until the appearance of O'Donnell and Franchere's book in 1960, it was the only convenient published source of biographical information about Frederic, with the exception of short and inaccurate entries in biographical dictionaries. Unfortunately, what McWilliams presents as fact is largely a mixture of misinformation and distortion. His description of Frederic's boyhood after his father's death is an example:

[At twelve, Frederic] was placed in the care of a neighboring farmer to serve as "chore boy.". . . It was a boyhood singularly barren of advantages but rich in impressions of a countryside that had only recently undergone vast transformations. . . . The road that had once been a proud turnpike, with hospitable taverns at every league, and the rumblings of great coaches and the horn of the postboy with echoes of its daily life and bustle, were gone. In their stead, a few gaunt old farmhouses, scowling in isolation, faced a dilapidated country road. It was this scene, coupled with his early hardships and goaded by glimpses of a romantic past, that bred in Frederic a mood of rebellion and contempt.[12]

What McWilliams has done here is to compose biography out of selected passages from Frederic's fiction and then use that biography to explain the fiction. In the paragraph above,

[11] *University of California Chronicle*, XXXV (Jan., 1933), pp. 21–34.

[12] *Ibid.*, p. 22.

the entire description of "the road that had once been a proud turnpike" has been transcribed, with one or two minor changes, from the opening paragraph of chapter 8 of *Seth's Brother's Wife*. The facts contradict McWilliams at every turn. Near the end of his first year in London, for example, Frederic was writing home to Howells that each successive month abroad left him "more tenaciously fond of all things American." [13] It was the narrator of "The Copperhead," not Frederic himself, who was sent away from home to work as a chore boy for a farmer. As Paul Haines and as O'Donnell and Franchere document the facts in their critical biographies, Frederic was eighteen months, not twelve years, when his father died, and his mother remarried two years later.[14] His education, better than that enjoyed by most boys of his period and class, ended with graduation from Utica Advanced Academy a month before his fifteenth birthday. Indeed, all the material assembled by Haines and by O'Donnell and Franchere demonstrates the impossibility of making a case for a childhood of impoverishment, an adolescence of rebellion, or an adulthood of contempt. Nor, when they turn to the novels themselves, do Haines or O'Donnell and Franchere find

[13] May 5, 1885, quoted by permission of the Harvard College Library.

[14] Paul Haines, "Harold Frederic" (unpub. Ph.D. diss., New York University, 1945). The reader interested in Frederic's life must consult Haines as well as O'Donnell and Franchere, who appear to have been severely cramped by the format of Twayne's United States Authors Series. Excellent as the biographical chapters of *Harold Frederic* are, they omit many important things contained in Haines. O'Donnell and Franchere, for example, do not give even a hint of the tremendous scandal that so damaged Frederic's posthumous reputation when formal charges of murder were brought against Frederic's mistress and the Christian Science healer whom she had called in to attend the dying author.

a realism that can be described as "bitter." Parrington's thesis, they conclude, "is wrong in detail and in its whole drift." [15]

When, at twenty-seven, "the unsophisticated country boy" was given the post of European correspondent for the New York *Times,* he met with remarkable ease the challenge of the sudden move from Albany into the political and literary circles of London. Throughout the late eighties and nineties—now off fishing with Sir Charles Dilke, now lunching on steak with Frank Harris while George Bernard Shaw lectured them on vegetarianism and ate macaroni—Frederic seems to have met "everybody," and with some notable exceptions "everybody" appears to have enjoyed his flamboyant company.[16] "Sophisticated" and "provincial" are relative. Frederic's term in Albany as editor of the influential *Evening Journal* must have taken some of the rough edges off the country boy before he sailed for England. Among the friends he made in the state capital (he was already a friend of Horatio Seymour of Utica, who ran against Grant in 1868) were two future Presidents of the United States—Grover Cleveland and Theodore Roosevelt—and one future presidential candidate—Alton B. Parker, who ran for the Presidency on the Democratic ticket in 1904.

The ferocious bear of a man from New York given to wearing soft silk shirts seemed exotic amid the boiled fronts of London evening society. Stephen Crane was surprised to find that even after fourteen years in England Frederic remained,

---

[15] Haines, "Harold Frederic," p. 256, quoted with approval in O'Donnell and Franchere, *Harold Frederic,* p. 153.

[16] *Current Literature* described Frederic as perhaps "the most popular of all London correspondents" ("Harold Frederic: Author of Theron Ware," XX [July, 1896], 14), but in 1919, Hugh Walpole noted that Joseph Conrad "spoke of Harold Frederic as 'a gross man who lived grossly and died abominably'" (Rupert Hart-Davis, *Hugh Walpole* [New York, 1952], p. 179).

"with no gilding, no varnish, a great reminiscent panorama of the Mohawk Valley." [17] To many members of the Savage and the National Liberal—clubs frequented by the most clubable Frederic—his accounts of milking cows in sub-zero dawns in Utica must have sounded grim. Although Haines is probably right in his contention that the many apocryphal stories of a hard youth may be "ascribed less to Frederic than to his listeners," [18] Frederic apparently relished and encouraged the misapprehensions of his audience. The game is an old one for Americans abroad, from Benjamin Franklin in Paris playing the Quaker in fur hat and unfashionable spectacles, to Joaquin Miller in London telling of buffalo herds in the streets of Boston and smoking three cigars at once, "as we do it in the States." [19]

[17] "Harold Frederic," *The Chap-Book*, VIII (1898), 358. See Charles Lewis Hind, *More Authors and I* (London, 1922), pp. 113–115, for a lively account of Frederic in London society.

[18] Haines, "Harold Frederic," p. 182. Perhaps it was such listeners Frederic had in mind when he lampooned the Englishman "Mr. Hump," whose special subject was the U.S. and who was reliably informed that Americans "had nothing but fried salt pork to eat for many months at a time" (*Mrs. Albert Grundy: Observations in Philistia* [London, 1896], p. 30). Frederic's friend Stephen Crane lamented that Englishmen "will believe anything wild or impossible you tell them and then if you say your brother has a bathtub in his house they—ever so politely—call you a perjured falsifier of facts" (Crane to James Huneker, Dec. ?, 1897, quoted in Stallman and Gilkes, eds., *Stephen Crane: Letters* [New York, 1960], pp. 159–160).

[19] See Van Wyck Brooks, *The Times of Melville and Whitman* (New York, 1947), p. 304. Frederic exaggerates the privations of his early years in his "Preface to a Uniform Edition," *In the Sixties* (New York, 1897), pp. vi-vii. He falsely claims that he was expelled from school at twelve and that later he was unable to join the Oneida Historical Society (which he helped found) because he could not spare two dollars for the membership fee. Clement Shorter says that "Frederic talked with such reckless bluntness that everything in his early

The attempt to make Frederic into an angry young man was misguided, but it was born of a laudable desire to establish his place in the literary history of the United States. In charting the rise of realism, as Everett Carter and Edwin Cady do in their books on William Dean Howells, it is reasonable to concentrate on placing Frederic in that tradition.[20] Such efforts, however, almost invariably sacrifice much of what is most original and distinctive in Frederic's work. Though unaware of either the myth or the facts of the biography, the reader who first looks into the works of Harold Frederic will find himself making connections between Frederic and other American novelists of the late nineteenth century. Reading *Seth's Brother's Wife*, he may note the Garland-like realism of certain passages, and in doing so he will be finding a place for a minor work. All well and good. Hamlin Garland himself felt a shock of recognition when he read *Seth*.[21] But the problem remains of what to do with all the things in *Seth* that are not Garland-like.

When tracing the development of American literary naturalism, it is also valid to point out the naturalistic elements in Frederic's work, yet it seems unreasonable to criticize Frederic for failing to develop into a naturalistic writer. Charles Child Walcutt, who sees him as a kind of naturalist *manqué*, objects

---

biography may be accepted with some hesitation" (" 'The Sketch' Regrets the Loss to London of Mr. Harold Frederic," *The Sketch*, XXIV [Oct. 26, 1898], 4).

[20] Carter, *Howells and the Age of Realism* (Philadelphia, 1954), pp. 237–244, *et passim*, and Cady, *The Realist at War: The Mature Years, 1885–1920, of William Dean Howells* (Syracuse, N.Y., 1958), pp. 211–212, *et passim*.

[21] Garland's review of *Seth* in the Boston *Evening Transcript* found the book "one of the most powerful novels of the year" (Nov. 11, 1887, p. 6).

that Frederic's technique is "better fitted for exploring people than for demonstrating the large scale operation of social forces." [22] The question arises whether a talent for exploring people is so small a thing in a novelist.

Understandably, even Frederic's most strenuous champions, those who have written doctoral dissertations on him, have generally assumed that their author's importance is best argued by placing him in what they consider to be the mainstream of American literature. Richard Chase's thesis in *The American Novel and Its Tradition* is a useful reminder here: "The history of the American novel is not only the history of the rise of realism." [23] "Pioneer realist"—or, far less reasonably, "pioneer naturalist"—may well be a title that casts glory on Frederic's name; but Frederic, being a pioneer, took his own path and was often to be found well out of sight of the chimney smoke of his nearest neighbors on the American literary scene.

Except, then, for occasional references to *The Damnation of Theron Ware* as a work of genius by a man whose other books are not worth reading, attention to Frederic has generally remained sharply focused on his realistic or naturalistic elements, a focus that usually restricts its view to *Seth, The Lawton Girl, The Damnation,* and the Civil War stories. Such a limited reading of Frederic's fiction is unfortunate. It almost completely overlooks Frederic's comic gift. It leaves to

[22] *American Literary Naturalism,* p. 48. See also Walcutt, "Harold Frederic and American Naturalism," *American Literature,* XI (March, 1939), 11–22.

[23] (Garden City, N.Y., 1957), p. xii. A notable and welcome exception to the general run of Frederic criticism is Everett Carter's introduction to *The Damnation,* in which he argues that the novel gives "evidence of shifts away from the realistic towards the symbolic and the mythical" ([Cambridge, Mass., 1960], p. xxiii).

obscurity his novels set abroad, in one of which—*The Market-Place*—Frederic came close to matching the greatness of *The Damnation*. And it deprives readers of the works set in America of the light that is cast on that fiction by the works set abroad, the "less typical" works.

Almost any effort to categorize Frederic's fiction is Procrustean, for Frederic "ran the gamut, utilizing nearly every form that his own age produced." [24] Frederic's range, in fact, is so wide as to be bewildering at first. There are novels of English high life, of the American Revolution and Irish Fenianism, of political skulduggery and stock market manipulation. There are novels of the village and farm that were greeted enthusiastically by Howells and Garland, a sophisticated novel of Bohemian London that was greatly admired by the *Yellow Book,* and Civil War stories that were the envy of Stephen Crane. Small wonder that *The Nation,* writing of Frederic in 1897, found it "most surprising" that "no one of his books in the least resembles another, except in neatness of execution and marked absence of the subjective note." [25]

If the wide range of Frederic's work were merely the result of confusion, one would not be greatly surprised, for the years in which he wrote invited confusion. Whether or not the nineties can be identified as "*the* critical period in American literature," there can be little doubt that the period was what Frank Norris called it, "a decade of fads." [26] The fetid nineties, the gay nineties, the mauve decade, the age of confidence, the yellow-romantic-electric-moulting nineties: the very habit of

---

[24] O'Donnell and Franchere, *Harold Frederic,* p. 161.

[25] Review of *March Hares,* LXIV (1897), 399–400.

[26] Italics mine; see Grant C. Knight, *The Critical Period in American Literature* (Chapel Hill, N.C., 1951); Norris, *The Responsibilities of the Novelist* (New York, 1903), p. 137.

assigning tags to the period suggests that it has some essential unity, but the unwieldy bundle these tags produce indicates the paradoxical, self-contradictory nature of whatever that unity may be.

There was perplexity and confusion all about the literary landscape of the nineties—in Mark Twain, lapsing into the gloom of his last period; in Howells, beginning to despair of the world's "ability to come out all right in the end"; [27] in Garland, failing to equal the achievement of *Main-Traveled Roads;* in Henry Blake Fuller, vacillating between novels of the Middle West and of courtly Europe; in Crane, searching out real wars after he had already made war real in *The Red Badge of Courage;* and in Henry James, "entered upon evil days" and struggling through a personal *"fin de siècle,* the unquiet passage from one literary period to another." [28]

It would be a mistake, however, to conclude that the range of Frederic's work merely reflects confusion. And, although the claims of his expansive public life and of the two households he maintained drove him at times almost to desperation for income to supplement his *Times* salary, it would be equally mistaken to conclude that Frederic's virtuosity betrays a journalistic hack eager to hit on the best-seller formula. Properly understood, Frederic's fiction reveals a surprising unity, a persistent and inventive elaboration upon a single and important theme. It is McWilliams, inaccurate and careless as he is, who suggests the true subject and unity of Frederic's fiction.

[27] Howells to Henry James, Oct. 10, 1888, quoted in Mildred Howells, *Life in Letters of William Dean Howells* (Garden City, N.Y., 1928), II, 417.

[28] James to Howells, Jan. 22, 1895, quoted in Percy Lubbock, ed., *The Letters of Henry James* (New York, 1920), I, 230; Frederick Dupee, *Henry James* (New York, 1951), p. 173.

Although he oversimplifies in contending that, with the exception of the novels of British life, Frederic had only "one set of characters, and wrote only one novel," his statement of Frederic's theme is most acute:

Frederic was concerned with the chaos that results when an untrained, uneducated, and unsophisticated person escapes from a provincial society and suddenly finds himself an heir to the culture, lore and wisdom of the ages.[29]

Recent critics of Frederic's work have, with considerable justice, treated McWilliams' " 'A Country Boy of Genius' " disparagingly or not at all—with one notable exception. Ralph Robert Rogers in his perceptive dissertation, "Harold Frederic: His Development as a Comic Realist," sees past the bias and misinformation in the essay and recognizes how close McWilliams came to hitting on Frederic's central theme.[30] Rogers expresses his agreement with McWilliams' thesis that *The Damnation*, like most of the other works, "is really concerned with the disastrous effects upon character that too often result from the sudden and violent awakening of an untutored mind," [31] but he disagrees strongly with McWilliams' assumption that throughout the fourteen-year residence in London, when all the novels were written, Frederic himself was a confused provincial. The Frederic hero is the provincial, the Pretentious Young Man; but the Pretentious Young Man is *not* Frederic the novelist. Instead, this hero is the young Frederic as viewed by the elder Frederic:

[29] McWilliams, "Harold Frederic," pp. 21, 30.
[30] Unpub. Ph.D. diss., Columbia University, 1961.
[31] McWilliams, "Harold Frederic," p. 30. Rogers calls this "the most important single pronouncement" made about *The Damnation* ("Harold Frederic," p. 146).

It might be said that in a dialectical sense there were two Harold Frederics, the innocent, uncultivated, romantic one and the experienced, sophisticated, realistic one. Although Frederic may have considered the conflict between his two inner hostile selves a matter of interest to himself alone, this same dialectical interplay actually provided the dramatic and intellectual texture for his novels.[32]

However well Harold Frederic may or may not have achieved a balanced personal adjustment between his two inner selves, rarely does the dialectic in his fiction reach anything like synthesis. As in traditional comedy—whether Shakespeare or Jane Austen—self-importance and illusion are buffeted and humiliated, but Frederic's sentimental egotists, Antaeus-like, no sooner hit the ground in a pratfall than they spring up, strong as ever and already convincing themselves that they are not such bad fellows after all. Most of Frederic's protagonists are just as silly and pretentious at the end of the novels as they are at the beginning. Only the hero of *Gloria Mundi* might be said to emerge freed of illusion, but *Gloria Mundi* is half of a larger dialectic; the other half is *The Market-Place*, a novel that concludes with its protagonist's resolution to rule England, hardly a sign of a chastened egotism. The critic who objected that *The Damnation* "leads nowhither" was right in a sense, as was the reviewer who found that in *Gloria Mundi* "nothing happens. One arrives nowhere."[33] The contrast between what men aspire to and what they achieve provides the comedy of Frederic's novels, not the contrast between what they aspire to and what they learn.

Frederic's heroes and heroines believe in progress, in im-

[32] Rogers, "Harold Frederic," p. 26.
[33] *The Nation*, LXIII (1896), 181; New York *Tribune Illustrated Supplement*, Nov. 20, 1898, p. 14.

provement, whether of the self or of society. From the first novel, with its reformers out to banish the political bosses of the Gilded Age, through *The Damnation*, with its hero dazzled by the brilliance of his own illumination, to the last novel, with its hero unable to see a limit to the expansion of his power, Frederic's fiction treats the bumptious hopes of characters filled with enthusiasm for the possibilities of their own development. Frederic himself does not share in these hopes. Had he lived to see *Man and Superman*, he would have recognized his own sense of man's endless—and comic—damnation in the argument of Shaw's Mephistopheles:

An epoch is but a swing of the pendulum; and each generation thinks the world is progressing because it is always moving. But when you are as old as I am . . . you will no longer imagine that every swing from heaven to hell is an emancipation, every swing from hell to heaven an evolution. Where you now see reform, progress, fulfilment of upward tendency, continual ascent by Man on the stepping stones of his dead selves to higher things, you will see nothing but an infinite comedy of illusion.[34]

Frederic expressed his own doubts about the reality behind such words as "progress" not only in his novels but in his notes. "People do not improve as the world grows older," he remarked. "They still fluctuate, as they always did, between imitating good models, and then forgetting why they did so." He saw "no earthly reason why [we] shouldn't all wallow back into blackest barbarism again. Think electric light [will] save you, do you?"[35] Such statements as these indicate how strongly Frederic sympathized with Father

[34] Act III; Shaw's play was published in 1901.
[35] Frederic Papers, Library of Congress, notes for *Gloria Mundi* titled "Progress"; notes for *The Damnation* titled "Intellectual Barbarism."

Forbes of *The Damnation:* "Let hurly burly spend itself. World goes on. Nothing matters." Frederic is not a Father Forbes, however, for he cannot commit himself even to disengagement. The " 'wise man' stands outside it all—watches it pass," Frederic writes, and then he characteristically adds, "but is that any more true wisdom than other?" [36]

The dialogue between the older and younger man persisted in Frederic's life as well as his work. Even his years—he died at only forty-two—cannot account for the frequency with which the word "youthful" comes up in contemporary descriptions of him. A man whose job it was to report the events of the immediate present, he seemed to be a New Man, seemed to embody all the freshness of the nineties. His was the period of *art nouveau*, the New Paganism, the New Fiction, the New Drama, the New Hedonism, the New Woman, and the New Spirit; and Frederic, in his riotous energy, his irreverence for convention, and his boundless enthusiasms, seemed one of the youths made to make the world new.

As one might expect from a man who lived virtually openly with two women at the same time, he was generous on matters of conduct. "Even among women," he once wrote, ". . . we must look for less rather than more [sexual self-denial] in the future." [37] From his early support of Cleveland in the United States to his support of the Irish cause when he was in England, he was a liberal in politics. His manners were so easygoing that to the end of his days he insisted on wearing clothes "that cried aloud amid the respectable gloom of everyday business garb in London." [38]

[36] *Ibid.*, notes on Father Forbes and notes titled "Religion vs. Science" for *The Damnation.*

[37] "Musings on the Question of the Hour," *Pall Mall Budget,* XXXIII (Aug. 13, 1885), 11.

[38] "Harold Frederic," *The Criterion,* XVIII (Oct. 29, 1898), 26.

Yet there was, as his friend Louise Imogen Guiney observed, a strong "trait of conservatism in Frederic's mind." [39] Most conspicuously, the conservatism expressed itself in a passion for history; the man who seemed so new was fascinated by the past. The passion dated back to his reading of books like Horace Walpole's four-volume *Life and Letters of George III*, which he claimed to have finished before he was six.[40] Whether or not he was such a prodigy, there is no question of his interest in history in later years. Linsky, the character in *The Return of the O'Mahony* who spends his twelve-year incarceration lost in a dream of ancient Ireland, and Vestalia, the girl in *March Hares* who earns her living by compiling genealogies, reflect the interests of their creator, who wrote medieval tales and whose knowledge of the British aristocracy, according to one awed Englishman, was superior even to that of Burke's *Peerage*.[41] Frederic was as a friend remembered him, a man of paradoxes, a large, loud, boisterous man, careless in his manners and dress, yet in his work a stickler for detail who wrote in the dainty hand of "a young girl who has learned copperplate engraving." [42]

"The country boy of genius" was a myth that Frederic himself helped to create by exaggerating the poverty of his upbringing and his lack of formal education, and by claiming that he had been raised on a farm when in actuality he grew

[39] "Harold Frederic: A Half-Length Sketch from the Life," *Book Buyer*, XVII (1899), 600.

[40] Frederic often spoke of his lifelong interest in history. He mentioned his early reading of Walpole, Mérimée's *History of Peter the Cruel*, and Hale's *History of the United States* in the interview quoted in Robert H. Sherard, "Harold Frederic," *The Idler*, XII (1897), 534.

[41] Aaron Watson, *A Newspaper Man's Memories* (London, 1925), p. 158.

[42] Arthur Warren, "Harold Frederic: The Reminiscences of a Colleague," New York *Times*, Oct. 23, 1898, p. 19.

up in a city of 20,000. The view of himself that he often promoted was that of the self-made man who owed nothing to the past. The story of his rise in the world, even without his embellishments, "would lend itself to any amount of gushing from the platforms of the 'Self-Culture' organizations," and Frederic loved to tell the story with a gushing, boastful pride, yet he was far from living in the eternal present of the Smilesian self-helpers.[43] His public image may have been the New Man for whom the past meant nothing and the present everything, but the man who reported European news for fourteen years and the man who wrote the novels often wondered whether the present weighed very much when balanced against the burden of the past.

Frederic's thinking about history led him to gloomy conclusions. His country had declined to a condition, he wrote to Cleveland, "as gross and wretched in its way as that under which Germany, and in fact all Continental Europe, weltered four hundred years ago." The Democratic victory in 1884, however, revived his hopes that the backward trend might be reversed. "All the greed and scoundrelism and prejudice of our political, race, and business sides," he assured the newly-elected President, ". . . are not able to stand up before the simple weight of an honest man and an upright cause." [44]

Ironically, at the same time that Frederic was beginning to hope that the New World might yet reform itself and follow

[43] "Harold Frederic," *The Criterion*, XVIII (Oct. 29, 1898), 26; one of the notes for *Gloria Mundi* in the Frederic Papers, Library of Congress, written in the elliptical style of so many of the notes, reads: "Notion improving men through their fears (*i.e.* Church) gone out. Now appealing to their greed and turning to universal education on Smiles' lines to help this out."

[44] Nov. 8, 1884, from the original in the New York State Library, Albany.

the path of progress, he saw the Old World for the first time. In the spring of 1884, at twenty-seven, he assumed his duties in London as the European correspondent for the New York *Times* and he found himself face to face with history as never before. His renewed faith in the possibilities of reform and progress, in the power of honest men or upright causes, was to be sorely tried by what he saw abroad. An anecdote of Thomas Beer's tells something of what Frederic found in Europe. An American woman asked Frederic and Henry James for advice on what to see during her visit to England. While Frederic sat impatiently by, James happily outlined a tour of the cathedral towns. Finally, unable to contain himself any longer, Frederic interrupted to recommend the slums of Liverpool and Manchester.[45]

What burst from him was surely not the Philistinism of *Innocents Abroad*, for Frederic, who had studied art as a young man with some thought of becoming a painter, was by no means blind to the beauties of Europe. Nor did he recommend a visit to England's slums because he had suffered the sudden and traumatic awakening that Herman Melville describes in *Redburn*. He had seen much of poverty, violence, and corruption in America—as a newspaperman sees it, day in, day out; nonetheless, Europe was disillusioning.

As depressing as anything that followed, as depressing even as the frightening reversion to barbarism he saw on his trip to Russia in 1891 to report on the pogroms,[46] was his visit to the

---

[45] *Stephen Crane* (New York, 1924), p. 153. Beer says Frederic once described James as "an effeminate old donkey who lives with a herd of other donkeys around him and insists on being treated as if he were the Pope. He has licked dust from the floor of every third rate hostess in England" (pp. 151–152).

[46] See Frederic, *The New Exodus: A Study of Israel in Russia* (London, 1892).

Continent less than a month after his arrival in London. In the summer of 1884, cholera broke out in southern France and quickly spread to Italy. Other correspondents were understandably content to write their reports of the catastrophe from secondhand sources, but Frederic courageously set out to see for himself the worst of the plague spots. He visited Arles, Toulon, and Marseilles. There he saw a misery such as one can scarcely imagine, a suffering that he found rooted in ignorance, superstition, and squalor.

"Down Among the Dead Men" was the name he gave to his articles on the epidemic, and the dead men were not merely those he had actually seen dead or dying, but the dead men of the past whose customs and beliefs had left Europe as exposed to the horrors of plague as in the Middle Ages.[47] The image, even the phrase itself, was to recur again and again in his fiction. The dead men came to stand for that force in the world and in human nature that makes a mockery of man's dreams of progress and reform.

Some of Frederic's young men and women are convinced that they will transform the world; others, that they are transforming themselves. Characteristically they think themselves to be new: New Men—from buccaneering tycoons to political reformers and utopian projectors; New Women—from "typewriters" to "Greek pagans." Living at the end of a century that has seen tremendous expansion and development,

[47] Frederic's weekly reports of the epidemic appeared in the New York *Times*, July 27–Aug. 24, 1884. The first really informative reports to reach the public, they made him famous overnight. English, French, and American newspapers quoted his articles and called him a hero (Haines, "Harold Frederic," pp. 110–111). "Down Among the Deadmen" is the title and refrain of a Jacobite drinking song still very popular in the late nineteenth century; the "deadmen" of the song are "dead soldiers"—empty bottles.

they think of their own lives in these same terms. Theron Ware drinks in Celia Madden's talk of her aspirations and her contempt for "old-fashioned ideas":

An involuntary thrill ran through his veins at recollection of her words. His fancy likened it to the sensation he used to feel as a youth, when the Fourth of July reader bawled forth that opening clause: "When, in the course of human events, it becomes necessary," etc. It was nothing less than another Declaration of Independence he had been listening to.[48]

All Frederic's protagonists have declared their independence, so to speak. The traditional view that Frederic was a bitter realist who recorded his hatred for the meanness of the small town and the farm in his American novels and deserted his true theme in his English works distorts and diminishes his achievement. The kind of realists to whom he is usually compared—E. W. Howe or Hamlin Garland—tell of men and women who begin with hopes and dreams and are beaten down by their environment to resignation or defeat. Frederic tells the comic story of what happens when young men and women are given the opportunity to realize their hopes and dreams. His farm boys become newspaper editors and lawyers; Theron Ware enters the society of the worldly and the educated; in *The Market-Place* a poor bookseller's boy becomes a multimillionaire. Unlike the realists who wrote out of an intense desire to expose or reform the painful conditions they felt had betrayed the promise of American life, Frederic found that his concern was with the question of just what that promise implied.

[48] *The Damnation,* John Harvard Library ed. (Cambridge, Mass., 1960), p. 263.

2 / *Seth's Brother's Wife*

In the preface to the uniform edition of his works, Harold Frederic explains how he began, almost casually, to write his first novel, *Seth's Brother's Wife*.[1] In 1885 he had been struggling with *In the Valley*, a historical novel, for almost a decade. Just as he was beginning to despair of ever finishing the book, his attention was caught "by the famous example of T. P."[2] Frederic's friend T. P. O'Connor had written a fictionalized reminiscence of his childhood in Ireland and sold it to the *Weekly Echo*. O'Connor had composed his story easily, "never touching the weekly installment until the day for sending it to the printer's had arrived, and then walking up and down dictating the new chapters in a very loud voice, to drown out the racket of his secretary's typewriter. This,"

---

[1] Unless otherwise indicated all information about the composition of *Seth* is drawn from "Preface to a Uniform Edition," *In the Sixties* (New York: Charles Scribner's Sons, 1897), pp. vii–viii.

[2] Letter from Frederic to Aaron Watson, quoted in Watson, *A Newspaper Man's Memories* (London, 1925), p. 164. Watson gives the date of the letter as December 12, 1883, which is clearly impossible, for Frederic did not arrive in England until 1884. The probable date of the letter is 1886.

Frederic recalls, "appeared to be a highly simple way of earning two hundred and fifty dollars, and I went home to start a story of my own at once." [3]

Frederic soon discovered that writing was not as simple as it had appeared. He brought his first chapter to Aaron Watson, the editor of the *Weekly Echo*. Watson read it over, told his friend that it might do in the States but was "too American" for an English audience, and advised him to substitute "comely" for some other word on the first page. Somewhat depressed by the fading away of the two hundred and fifty dollars, Frederic abandoned his new project—fortunately not for long. When he returned to *Seth's Brother's Wife*, he no longer hoped to make his fortune with it. Instead, he was determined to do what he had been unable to accomplish in ten years of struggle with *In the Valley:* learn "how to make a book."

A decade after the publication of *Seth* in 1887, Frederic confessed that he still found it easier to regard the work as he had originally, "almost wholly in the light of preparation for the bigger task that I had to do." Few readers, however, would agree that *Seth* is mere apprentice work or that *In the Valley* is "the real work." The two novels are more nearly just the opposite. Nothing in Frederic's earlier fiction, a handful of banal short stories, points to the brilliance and originality of

[3] Frederic's story about the inspiration for *Seth* is contradicted by his friend Charles R. Sherlock. According to Sherlock, *Seth* "had been planned in his [Frederic's] mind before he assumed his editorial connection in Albany," *i.e.*, before September, 1882 ("The Harold Frederic I Knew," *Saturday Evening Post*, CLXXI [1899], p. 616). There is no reason to distrust Sherlock's account, but it should be noted that many of the events in *Seth* are based on Frederic's experiences in Albany (see Thomas F. O'Donnell and Hoyt C. Franchere, *Harold Frederic* [New York, 1961], pp. 47–48).

Seth, and, in addition, little of *In the Valley* suggests those qualities either.

Anyone familiar with *In the Valley* should know that Frederic regarded the New York State of his upbringing with lasting affection. The warmth of that affection becomes obvious in the dedication with its tender reference to "the hills that watch over our beautiful river" and its solemn offering of the work in tribute to the memory of Horatio Seymour. Yet there have been many readers who have pictured Frederic as a bitter expatriate whose novels are acts of vengeance against the provincial community of his youth, and more often than not such readers have gone to *Seth's Brother's Wife* to support their view. Vernon Louis Parrington concluded from his reading of the novel that Frederic "quite evidently hates this countryside that bred him." [4]

Certainly the novel does appear to offer evidence of such hatred. For example, the following speech is delivered early in the narrative:

Oh, it must be such a dreary life! The very thought of it sets my teeth on edge. The dreadful people you have to know: men without an idea beyond crops and calves and the cheese-factory; women slaving their lives out doing bad cooking, mending for a houseful of men, devoting their scarce opportunities for intercourse with other women to the weakest and most wretched gossip; coarse servants who eat at the table with their employers and call them by their Christian names; boys whose only theory about

[4] *The Beginnings of Critical Realism in America, 1860–1920* (New York, 1930), pp. 288–289. On the same day that the "expatriate" cabled Scribner's his acceptance of the terms for publishing *Seth*, he wrote home about his forthcoming visit to the States: "I feel like jumping and singing like a schoolboy—so delighted am I at the prospect" (letter to Daniel S. Lamont, April 24, 1886, Cleveland Papers, Library of Congress).

education is thrashing the school teacher, if it is a man, or breaking her heart by their mean insolence if it is a woman; and girls
brought up to be awkward gawks, without a chance in life, since
the brighter and nicer they are the more they will suffer from marriage with men mentally beneath them—that is if they don't become sour old maids. . . . The trail of the serpent is over it all—
rich and poor, big and little. The Nineteenth century is a century
of cities; they have given their own twist to the progress of the
age—and the farmer is almost as far out of it as if he lived in
Alaska. Perhaps there may have been a time when a man could
live in what the poet calls daily communion with Nature and not
starve his mind and dwarf his soul, but this isn't the century
[pp. 32–33].[5]

These lines are spoken by Isabel Fairchild to her brother-in-
law Seth; when read out of context, they do speak of bitterness and revolt. But just after Isabel concludes her gloomy
prophesy of the fates awaiting country girls brought up to be
gawks, Seth interrupts: " 'You talk like a book,' said Seth, in
tones of unmistakable admiration. 'I didn't suppose any woman
could talk like that.' "

[5] All page references to *Seth* are to the first American edition (New
York: Charles Scribner's Sons, 1887). The novel appeared originally
as a serial in the newly-founded *Scribner's Magazine* from the first
number, of January, 1887, through November, 1887. It is doubtful
that *Scribner's* would have accepted *Seth* if the novel had been sub-
mitted after the new magazine had established its editorial policy,
which was disposed against realistic fiction. The firm of Scribner's
published *In the Valley* and "The Copperhead" both as trade editions
and as magazine serials, but it published *The Lawton Girl* only as a
trade edition. It is probable that the magazine was offered the novel
about a fallen woman and refused it because it was too raw. In 1895,
Scribner's refused *The Damnation* for serialization but offered to
publish it as a book (Spiller, *et al.*, eds., *Literary History of the United
States*, II, 953).

"You talk like a book": Seth's admiring tones notwithstanding, Frederic's intention here is ironic. In the first place, most of what Isabel knows of rural life she must have learned out of books, for she is a city girl who arrived in the country only a few days earlier. Despite Seth's embarrassed efforts to explain to her that she is not seeing the country quite "at its best here. . . . Things have kind of run down," Isabel takes as typical a farm that is the eyesore of its area, the local "badge and synonym of 'rack and ruin,' " (p. 7).

Even on the wretched Fairchild farm there is beauty for those who can see it. Isabel makes her little speech while she and Seth walk in the orchard. So busy are they that they fail to notice what Frederic calls attention to: "The apple blossoms close above them filled the May morning air with that sweet spring perfume which seems to tell of growth, harvest, the fruition of hope" (p. 32). Or possibly the spring perfume does reach them, possibly even in the century of cities Nature communes with man in her old-fashioned way. For all the feminist overtones of her speech, Isabel is a coquette whose feminine instinct must somehow tell her that no young man objects to being told that he is much too good for his surroundings—particularly by a sophisticated beauty who "talks like a book."

The argument that Isabel's attitude toward the country is not that of her author is supported by some notes on "Woman-Questions" that Frederic wrote when he was beginning work on *Gloria Mundi:*

Women make the Cities. Men are conscious of longing for farms, stock, gardens, etc., but women's thoughts are on shop windows, cabs, and calls. They pine and dwindle in country. Rarely honest liking for it. In deference to wives and daughters we go live in towns. . . . The horror of espionage in small towns, villages. How much does woman's eagerness to escape from this (which she understands so well and attaches so much weight to) account for her urban impulse? [6]

The warning to read Isabel's speech in the context of her character and her dramatic situation must be extended to other passages and scenes in *Seth*. Torn out of context, parts of *Seth* seem bitter and rebellious pages in the history of revolt against farm and village. Hamlin Garland wrote that "nothing in American fiction surpasses the grim beginning of Harold Frederic's novel." Out of context, passages treating political corruption can be used to place Frederic "in the vanguard of the muckrakers." [7]

But when one is quoting Frederic, one does well to bear in mind that particular passages of narration and comment seldom express Frederic's full view of things. Regarded as a nineteenth-century Dr. Johnson by many of his contemporaries and trained as an editorial writer, Frederic tended to

[6] Notes for *Gloria Mundi* on "Woman-Questions," Frederic Papers, Library of Congress. Frederic knew something of "espionage." For the last eight or nine years of his life, he maintained one household for Mrs. Frederic and their three children in London and another household for Kate Lyon and their three children just south of the city. "London suburban life is very merciful," he once wrote. "Nobody has any history there" ("Musings on the Question of the Hour," *Pall Mall Budget*, XXXIII [Aug. 13, 1885], 11). Frederic divided his time between the two households and apparently made no serious effort to keep his private life secret from his friends. An American who visited Homefield, the establishment set up for Kate Lyon, found it "a marvel, a miracle—the happiest home, it seems to me, I ever saw. . . . Harold told me that . . . his mind was calm, his conscience clear. His marital relations were pure, his children growing up in an atmosphere of love" (Lynn B. Porter to Cora Crane, Jan. 11, 1899, quoted in Lillian Gilkes, *Cora Crane* [Bloomington, Ind., 1960], p. 73).

[7] Boston *Evening Transcript*, Nov. 11, 1887, p. 6; Henry Steele Commager, *The American Mind* (New Haven, 1950), p. 60.

support whichever side of an argument he happened to find himself on. Those eminently quotable set pieces of comprehensive judgment (like Isabel's speech above) that are common in Frederic's novels are often very much like editorials—and in more than just their tone. As newspaper readers know, Tuesday's editorial is likely to be reversed, with equal conviction, in Friday's late edition.

Sometimes Frederic does appear to speak out openly, but what seems to be the narrative voice, speaking with the full authority of the author, usually turns out to be nothing of the sort. The long opening paragraph of chapter 5, for example, appears to suggest what is repeatedly denied elsewhere, that the Fairchild farm is representative rather than exceptional in its meanness and poverty. Carried off by the ringing authority and conviction of that opening, one is all too likely to fail to give due emphasis to the opening of the next paragraph: "Something of this Isabel felt" (p. 35).

The three main characters of *Seth's Brother's Wife* are those of the title: Seth Fairchild, his brother Albert, and Albert's wife Isabel, who is also cousin to the brothers.[8] As one might suspect from the title, the novel treats fraternal conflict within a love triangle. This subject had engaged Frederic's attention as far back as the time of the first story he is

---

[8] Keeping track of the family relationships in *Seth* is no easy task. Twelve Fairchilds are mentioned. Frederic often worked out on paper the elaborate family relationships of his characters. When Robert Barr saw the poster-sized chart which Frederic drew up for *The Market-Place*, he objected, "Good gracious! . . . How can people who don't exist have genealogical trees, or ancestors, or anything of that sort?" Frederic was indignant. "They don't exist! Who don't exist? They exist quite as much as my grocer" ("Harold Frederic, the Author of The Market-Place," *Saturday Evening Post*, CLXXI [1898], p. 396.

known to have published, "The Two Rochards," which he may have written when he was only seventeen.[9] And in its raw outline, the plot of *Seth's Brother's Wife* is as hackneyed as that of the juvenile "Two Rochards."

A virtuous young man, Seth, leaves the farm he has lived on all his life to go to the city to work on a newspaper. His eldest brother, Albert, a New York City bankers' lawyer with a greedy eye on an upstate congressional seat, takes up residence on the farm and begins to spend lavishly. After Seth has risen to the post of assistant editor, Albert tries to bribe him to keep the newspaper from bolting the crooked party ticket, but Seth remains true to his journalistic and political ideals. Albert is then foiled by a shrewd country politician, who outsmarts him, and by his own henchman, who fulfills poetic justice by putting a bullet through his boss's head. Seth helps solve the mystery of his brother's murder, resists once more the advances of his sister-in-law—who has been flirting with him all along—and proposes to his schoolteacher cousin Annie. In due course Seth and Annie have a baby girl, a reform candidate who has been Seth's mentor is elected to Congress, and the novel ends.

Such, in brief, is the story Frederic tells in *Seth's Brother's Wife*, a story that sounds as banal as a hero named Seth Fairchild. The novel itself, however, is far from what the conventional plot suggests. Here, as in his other fiction, Frederic makes witty use of what at first appear to be melodramatic situations, histrionic scenes, and stock characters. His technique is to put presumably predictable types in presumably predictable situations and then, in flashes of ironic illumination, reveal that the results were not predictable after all. The

[9] See Thomas F. O'Donnell, "An Addition to the HF Bibliography: 'The Two Rochards,' by 'Edgar,'" *Frederic Herald*, I (Sept., 1967), 4.

method requires readers with eyes sharp enough to see that the inconsistencies that Frederic's characters fall into are not the results of confusion in their author. They reflect his comic sense that people in real life seldom behave as they often do in books—as one expects them to.

One of the romantic conventions that Frederic plays with for comic ends is the duality between the brunette "bad" woman and the fair "pure" woman, between the passionate Hesters and Zenobias and the pale blondes who have less fun. Superficially, he appears to resolve the contest between the two types in the classic fashion: Isabel does lose Seth to Annie, a schoolmarm; Reuben Tracy, the hero of *The Lawton Girl*, chooses Kate Minster, not Jessica, the fallen woman who worships him and sacrifices her life for him; at the end of *The Damnation* Theron Ware stands beside his wife, not the uninhibited Celia. The novels, however, show little real sympathy with the old formula. Most of Frederic's liberated young women, in fact, have already fulfilled the prophecy to which Henry James referred in "The Future of the Novel" (1899): "It is the opinion of some observers that when women do obtain a free hand they will not repay the long debt to the precautionary attitude of men by unlimited consideration for the natural delicacy of the latter." [10]

Isabel Fairchild, the young woman who "talks like a book," is a prime example. An exotic—or at any rate a liberated city girl transported to a farm; an adulteress in intent if not in act; a woman brought to the brink of ruin by her passions: these are the roles the beautiful Isabel plays. But they are roles, for though life has provided her with a woefully limited stage,

[10] Leon Edel, ed., *The Future of the Novel* (New York, 1956), p. 41. James' essay originally appeared in Vol. XXVIII of *The Universal Anthology*.

Isabel is determined to live life as though it were opera. She is, Frederic says, "an artist." Having married young to gain what she calls "emancipation" from her family, she finds herself bored by a husband twenty years her senior. And as the novel opens she is trapped on a farm, more prey than ever to what John Fairchild (a third brother) identifies as the tendency of her "romantic mind to feed on itself" (p. 341). Nowhere is this tendency more evident than in her epistolary flirtation with Seth after he leaves the farm for the city. He soon begins to find writing to his sister-in-law a "nuisance"; the best he can manage, usually after a good dinner or an evening spent viewing a romantic play, is a sentimental "force of sweet rhetoric." The lonely Isabel, however, treasures every line as "deeply, deliciously, personal" (p. 191). Although pathetic and even tragic possibilities lie in such self-delusion as Isabel's, Frederic never allows them to develop. If the portrait sometimes suggests Madame Bovary, it usually contains comic touches that, if broadened, would bring to mind that other and different Emma who also confused life and literature—Twain's Emmeline Grangerford.

Much as it might gratify her theatrical instincts, Isabel is neither a tragic figure nor a wicked one. On those occasions when she takes herself most seriously, Frederic is always at hand to upstage her and spoil her planned effect with an incongruous detail or an ironic aside. The scene in which Isabel sits in a pretty blue chair with just the right cast of light coming in through the window behind her is one instance (it is here that Frederic calls her an artist). As she sits, listening to Seth read, Isabel may well imagine herself as Francesca and Seth as Paolo. But the props are wrong. Rather than the story of Launcelot, Frederic has Seth read "Jeff Brigg's Love Story" off the front page of the Sunday newspaper.

Frederic himself has frequent recourse to the theatrical metaphor in characterizing Isabel. Standing close to Seth, her hand clasped in his, Isabel says that his leaving the farm after a visit is "as if the tomb door were swinging back on me again." Then, Frederic says, "she broke down altogether, and, with the disengaged hand, put her handkerchief to her eyes." The little touch about the disengaged hand might go unnoticed, but the next comment is less oblique: "Seth had never seen a young and beautiful woman in tears before, off the stage" (p. 178). Even Seth, obtuse as he so often is, eventually comes to see in what sense Isabel really does "talk like a book." Thinking that he has murdered her husband (for love of her, of course), Isabel meets Seth with sobs and moans and shudderingly presses kisses on hands she believes stained with fraternal blood. Seth hardly plays the part she expects: "Come, come!" he says; "You are acting like a tragedy-queen on the stage" (p. 288).

Isabel, not Frederic, would divide up womankind into the good and the bad, and generally she finds the latter role the more interesting. "Am I a wicked woman?" she asks herself late in the novel. Significantly, she debates the issue standing before her mirror, studying herself "with an almost impersonal interest" (p. 369). She really does feel a good deal of remorse, though she alternates between blaming herself and others for her actions, but she never settles the question of her wickedness. Instead, she is suddenly distracted by the thought that although she has maliciously separated Seth and Annie they will eventually patch things up, marry, and—worst of all—forget her! And so she goes off to bring the young lovers together. She plays at sacrifice, Frederic makes amply clear, not to expiate any guilt she may feel but to make sure that Seth and Annie do not, in fact, forget Isabel. The scene is all she could wish. She gives her blessing to the couple with the light of a candle "glowing upon her throat and lower chin and nostrils and full, Madonna-like brows. Her face was at its best with this illumination from below. She would have been a rare beauty close before the footlights" (p. 396).

Seth Fairchild is nearly as contradictory as Isabel. He is the hero of the novel almost by default, for, as John Henry Raleigh observes, "the ambiguous hero was one of Frederic's fortes," and Seth is as ambiguous as one could wish.[11] At first Seth is likable enough but a little dull. Until Isabel shows up and begins talking about the dreariness of rural life, he is the patient youngest son, resigned to caring for the plowing, the stock, and the old folks while his two brothers enjoy wider horizons. And with Isabel comes her husband—Seth's eldest brother—to take over the family responsibilities and send Seth off to "a chance in life," an editorial assistant's job on the Tecumseh *Chronicle*, a big city newspaper. It is at this point in the novel, when Seth arrives in the city and reaches "The Threshold of the World" as the chapter title puts it, that he really captures the reader's interest—and Frederic's as well, one suspects.

Seth's arrival in Tecumseh is neither prompt nor auspicious:

It was half-past six of a summer afternoon (for a failure to make connections had prolonged the sixty-mile journey over eight hours), and the sun, still high, beat down the whole length of the street with an oppressive glare and heat. The buildings on both sides, as far as eye could reach, were of brick, flat-topped, irregular in height, and covered with flaring signs. There was no tree, nor any green thing, in sight [p. 106].

[11] "*The Damnation of Theron Ware*," *American Literature*, XXX (1958), 212. Raleigh's article is reprinted as the introduction to the Rinehart Edition of *The Damnation* (New York, 1960).

Neatly placed as it is, immediately after a long account of one of Seth's last days in the country, a day of fishing and lazing in a lush pastoral landscape, this high evening sun, glaring down on the city streets, casts its harsh light all the way back to Isabel's rosy picture of the good life in the city.

Like Red Crosse Knight, Seth emerges unscathed from his first encounter with the World. Armed with "the cardinal rule of traveling countrymen," he sternly rebuffs the efforts of station porters to help him with his luggage (transparently the attempts of "brigands intent upon robbing him" [p. 105]). But, like Spenser's clownish young man, Seth's weak spot is pride, and his vanity is badly mangled in his next engagement, this time with a platoon of giggling young factory girls who hoot after him, "Hop-pick—ers!" Dick Whittington and his cat arriving in London; Ben Franklin and his two loaves of bread arriving in Philadelphia; Seth Fairchild and his carpet bag arriving in Tecumseh: the situation is classic, and in Frederic's eyes classically comic.

Seth begins to wonder at "the general imprudence" of his coming to the big city and presuming through his newspaper work "to teach its people daily on all subjects, from government down, while he did not even know how to gracefully get his bag off the street" (p. 106). Like the Frank Courtneys, Harry Vanes, Robert Rushtons, and countless other Alger heroes before him, Seth has come to the city determined to be strong and steady, to be slow and sure, to strive and succeed. He discovers, however, that although "his head was full of negative information, of pit-falls to avoid, temptations to guard against. . . . on the affirmative side it was all a blank" (p. 107).

Having carefully prepared the reader to anticipate one more version of the success story that follows the rise of the good younger brother who makes his way in the city after serving out his time on the farm, Frederic turns his story upside down and relates the story of the good country boy who goes to ruin in the city, turns from Horatio Alger to the Prodigal Son. The conception is witty, and it is all the wittier for Frederic's ironic treatment of urban debauchery. Many an upstate New York farmer and villager, Frederic says, dreams wistfully of Tecumseh's "gilded temptations, its wild revels of sumptuous gayety, its dazzling luxuriance of life, as shepherd boys on the plains of Dura might have dreamed of the mysteries and marvels of Babylon" (p. 266). For the sake of the occasional shepherd boy who made the trip, one dearly hopes that Babylon turned out to be better provided than Tecumseh. There may be real dens of iniquity here, but Seth does not find them.[12]

Bismarck's, the German beer hall Seth is shown to on his first night in the city, is totally bereft of even the glitter of "the really gorgeous saloon from a Chicago standpoint" that so bewitched Theodore Dreiser. Nor does it glow with the hellish radiance that blazes in the private dining rooms frequented by Frank Norris' abandoned young San Franciscans. Although Bismarck's has music—piano, harp, and flute—and gaming—dominoes—it lacks not only swings with velvet ropes but, apparently, accommodations of any sort for ladies of any sort. The talk is interesting, however, and Seth has a fine time until he falls asleep, drugged by an evening of dissipation consisting of a couple of Liederkrantz sandwiches, some pickled lamb tongue, and three-and-one-half steins of bock.

In his first year on the paper Seth achieves none of the suc-

---

[12] There apparently are, in fact. Seth sees one of the Lawton girls in Tecumseh, "a girl who had gone utterly to the bad" (p. 147). The oblique reference is most likely to the title character of *The Lawton Girl* in her career as a prostitute.

cess that he assumed would be his once he escaped from the farm. At first his disillusionments are merely funny: the proof-reader's marks he laboriously copies out are so precise that the printers cannot read them; "our Martyr President Abraham Sinclair" appears in an article he has gone over in galley proof; he overlooks "mayonnaise" for "*moyen âge.*" By the time he learns the routine of newspaper work he has lost all ambition to do anything but follow routine. The nature of his work inevitably enlarges his mind somewhat, but it is "a formless, unprofitable expansion" (p. 141). Seth does not become vicious or depraved, Frederic says, nor does he become indolent. He spends his days on "the relentless treadmill" of *The Chronicle*, his evenings in the cigar smoke of Bismarck's, performing the duties of the former "decently and inoffensively," and pursuing the pleasures of the latter in much the same dull way.

The forty-odd pages describing Seth's adventures in the city are as realistic as the first forty pages of the novel, which tell of Seth's life in the country, but they are realistic in a different way. Those who would make a tract of *Seth* have focused their attention on Frederic's "labor of elementary truth-telling about farm life" [13] while overlooking almost completely Seth's labors in the city on tasks "almost as unintellectual and mechanical as the plowing and planting he had forsaken" (p. 132). In their search for signs of angry revolt in this and Frederic's other works, such readers have missed the greater and more characteristic achievement of Frederic's ironic and comic insight into the American character and its ample mythology of success and failure, country and city, virtue and vice.

Frederic watches Seth's descent into a rut (not an abyss, as

---

[13] Alfred Kazin, *On Native Grounds* (New York, 1942), p. 16.

would soon become the case in many novels) with an amused detachment that is all the more remarkable when one realizes the extent to which *Seth* is a self-portrait.[14] When moralizing censure falls on Seth it comes not from Frederic but from the editor and the owner of *The Chronicle*. Between themselves the two men loftily discuss the pedestrian work of young Fairchild, who devotes his spare time to Bismarck's rather than to improving his mind. The reader who thinks that in this conversation he has at last found out Frederic's position is, as usual, in for a surprise. Frederic closes the scene as follows: "Then the proprietor and the editor locked up their desks, went over to the Club, and played pyramid pool till midnight" (p. 142).

Eventually, Seth does make a success of newspaper work, or, more accurately, he regains his ambition when the Fates

[14] "Harold Frederic," the obituary editorial in the Utica *Observer* of October 20, 1898, p. 4, testifies to the similarities between Frederic's duties on the *Observer* and Seth's on the *Chronicle*. Haines shows that Frederic also drew deeply upon his experiences in Albany for *Seth* ("Harold Frederic" [unpub. Ph.D. diss., New York University, 1945], pp. 85 ff.). Although Frederic's ascent in journalism was not quite as meteoric as Seth's, it was phenomenal nonetheless. At nineteen he began as a proofreader; at twenty-two he was news editor of the *Observer*; at twenty-three, editor in chief. Then, two weeks after his twenty-sixth birthday, he became editor of the important Albany *Evening Journal*. His friend Charles Sherlock recalls that the stir Frederic immediately began to create in the capital left him—characteristically—"more struck by the humor of the thing" than anything else ("The Harold Frederic I Knew," p. 616). Part of the joke was that Frederic, a reform Democrat, was now running the most influential Republican daily in upstate New York, sitting in a chair held for decades by the paper's founder, the redoubtable Whig-Republican Boss Thurlow Weed. Frederic's enthusiasm for Cleveland, says Allan Nevins, soon began cropping out in "reputedly Republican editorials . . . like veins of gold in a cold quartz ledge" (*Grover Cleveland* [New York, 1933], p. 133).

open up a position of responsibility for him by seeing that a senior editor of the paper is mangled by a runaway horse. Seth is greatly assisted in reforming himself by Richard Ansdell, a fire-eating idealist out to reform just about anything he can lay his hands on. Most of the time Ansdell is curiously exempt from the irony to which the other characters of the novel are subject. To be sure, Frederic does reflect upon Ansdell's intolerance of opposition and his contempt for wrongdoing which often leaves only "a microscopic line between his attitude and fanaticism" (p. 188), but, generally speaking, Ansdell is "the embodiment of Principle." [15]

There is a great deal of talk about political reform in Seth, by no means all of it from Ansdell, for the private dramas of the novel are played out against the public drama of a congressional contest, a struggle "between the good and bad in politics," as Frederic described it to Daniel Lamont, President Cleveland's private secretary.[16] O'Donnell and Franchere devote the greater part of their discussion of Seth to its political side. They conclude that Frederic's purpose is to show that "the integrity and the moral fiber of an American community win out over 'the greed and scoundrelism and prejudice and folly' of an age," and argue that the novel follows "the story of the growth of morality, both public and private." [17] There

[15] Ralph Robert Rogers, "Harold Frederic" (unpub. Ph.D. diss., Columbia University, 1961), p. 52.

[16] April 24, 1886, the Cleveland Papers, Library of Congress. See also Robert Woodward, "The Political Background of Harold Frederic's Novel Seth's Brother's Wife," New York History, XLIII (1962), 239–248.

[17] O'Donnell and Franchere, Harold Frederic, pp. 79, 81. Theodore Roosevelt praised Seth, but later he protested against Booth Tarkington's exposure of political venality in The Gentleman from Indiana (see Van Wyck Brooks, The Confident Years [New York, 1952],

can be little doubt that Frederic did not intend *Seth* to be a muckraking exposé; otherwise he would hardly have sent to the White House a special presentation copy of the novel along with a letter reminding the President of how events in *Seth* paralleled Cleveland's own career in the crucial campaign of '82.[18] But somehow Frederic's reading of human nature would not let him embody in the novel even the cautious optimism he sometimes felt as a political observer.

It is a part of the history of human progress [writes Frederic in *Seth*] that grand moral movements, once they have fulfilled their immediate purpose, swing backward to the establishment of some new abuse. The net gain is, no doubt, century by century, continuous. But to those who look for episodic interest rather than epochal meaning the march of the race must often seem crab like [p. 192].

Albert, Seth's venal brother, says the same thing—only more vividly—when he discusses the Fairchilds' dissipation of the family reputation and fortune that old Senator Seth had built out of nothing before the Civil War:

---

p. 329). The letter in which Roosevelt commends *Seth* to Henry Cabot Lodge contains the amusing declaration, "Thank Heaven Henry James is now an avowedly British novelist" (Feb. 15, 1887, quoted in H. C. Lodge, ed., *Selections from the Correspondence of Theodore Roosevelt and Henry Cabot Lodge, 1884–1918* [New York, 1925], I, 52).

[18] Frederic's letter to Cleveland of November 11, 1887, speaks of "some political phases [of *Seth*] which may suggest other recollections not unpleasant" (Cleveland Papers, Library of Congress). Had these other recollections received public notice, the sales of *Seth* might have been boosted considerably. Paul Leicester Ford's *The Honorable Peter Stirling* (1894) "became a best seller after a hint that it derived, a bit remotely, from the career of President Grover Cleveland" (Grant Knight, *The Critical Period in American Literature* [Chapel Hill, N.C., 1951], p. 95).

If you have a state of society where sudden elevations of this sort occur, there will inevitably be corresponding descents—just as lean streaks alternate with fat in the bacon of commerce. The Fairchilds went up—they come down. They have exhausted the soil [p. 56].

Whatever Frederic's hopes for political reform under Cleveland were, his faith in the possibility of reform within the individual was dim indeed.[19] One might adapt Albert's homely simile and say that in Frederic's view "the lean streaks alternate with the fat in the bacon of human nature." Frederic may well have begun *Seth* intending to trace the growth of public and private morality, but before he got very far into his novel his deep instinct that such growth is seldom either sturdy or regular took control. Before the novel was over, he provided a whole series of revelations and reversals that not only leave the line between the "good and bad in politics" indistinct, but also wash away almost all clear distinctions between good characters and bad, heroes and villains.

The finest of these comic reversals occurs in a long scene played first between Seth and Isabel and then between Seth and Albert. The scene, in fact, offers a series of reversals that are worth examining in some detail, so beautifully do they illustrate Frederic's disposition to set up conventional confrontations between innocence and corruption, and then proceed with great skill to confound expectation. After listening to some blunt reminders of what a young man owes to an older brother who has generously helped him, Seth has reluctantly returned to the farm to discuss with Albert whether

---

[19] Against his interest in Cleveland's efforts at reform should be weighed Frederic's refusal to accept Cleveland's appeal to enter politics, a refusal based on the assumption that politics were dirty (see O'Donnell and Franchere, *Harold Frederic*, pp. 50–51).

the *Chronicle* will support Albert's political ambitions. Albert is absent when Seth arrives, and Seth soon finds himself reading "Jeff Brigg's Love Story" to his cousin Isabel. (He feels more comfortable thinking of his sister-in-law in that relationship.) One thing leads to another—with Isabel doing most of the leading—and before Seth knows quite how, his arms open for an embrace and he finds "my darling" on his lips. At this moment, Albert arrives home, right on comic cue.

Albert sends Isabel promptly off to bed, not exactly as she expected to go, and closely examining his brother's face, finds himself well-satisfied with what he finds there. The ensuing dialogue is brilliant. Albert reminds Seth once more of what fraternal obligation is, delivers a short lecture on the theme that honesty, whether in journalism, medicine, law, or politics, is "a purely relative term," and throws open the doors on several skeletons in the closets of Seth's superiors on the *Chronicle*. As for political reform, Albert tells Seth about a book he has read purporting to describe "An American Politician": "In almost every scene in the book where he appeared, he was drinking tea in some lady's drawing room, declaiming to the fair sex on how he was going to reform politics." Albert lists Ansdell among "the men who go to afternoon teas in America" (p. 223).[20]

Seth returns with fervent words on "rule of the machine" and "the dry rot of venality," but Albert rightly identifies his talk as the rhetoric of the editorial page. Neither Albert nor Frederic, however, is willing to leave merely implicit the in-

[20] Presumably the novel is Francis Marion Crawford's *An American Politician* (1885). Sneers like Albert's against reformers were common at the end of the century. Frederic's fellow Utican Senator Roscoe Conkling characterized the G. W. Curtises of this world as "the man-milliners, the dilettanti and carpet knights of politics."

congruity of Seth's lecturing a brother on public morality five minutes after making love to that brother's wife:

I don't think you are a knave [Albert says]. To be that requires intelligence. You are a fool,—a conceited, presumptuous, offensive fool. You set yourself up to judge *me*; you arrogate to yourself airs of moral superiority, and assume to regulate affairs of State by the light of your virtue and wisdom—and you have not brains enough meanwhile to take care of yourself against the cheapest wiles of a silly woman, who amuses herself with young simpletons just to kill time.

Poor Seth feels the prick of the knife in all this, but he does not know how helpless he is, stretched out on the altar of his own vanity. His reply is perfect, a reflexive, rhetorical moo: "A man who will speak that way of his wife is a coward and a scoundrel! And if it is my cousin Isabel he means, he is a liar to boot! If you were not my brother—." Albert does not miss the upturned throat; before he leaves the house, he has the last word: "If I were not, what then?" (pp. 229–230).

Frederic's method in the scene traced here is characteristic. At the moment Seth rejects the base in politics, he is most vulnerable to the charge that he is base. Given the situation that Frederic develops, all of Seth's fine words about honesty in public life and honor in private life become just that—fine words. Technically, Seth has made his moral choice in rejecting his brother's plea for journalistic support in the Congressional race, but Seth's victory, like the victory of Reuben Tracy at the conclusion of *The Lawton Girl* or like the illumination of the Reverend Theron Ware, is most ambiguous.

After Albert leaves, Seth again is tempted, and again he resists, and again his moral victory is ambiguous. Reflecting in his bedroom on the evening, he is troubled. "I have never known before what suffering was," he thinks, and does not begin to think any more clearly when Isabel tiptoes down the hall to tell him that she is still awake. Between gusts of self-recrimination he stands by his door, listening and wondering whether she will return to his room. Finally he decides he had better take a walk and manages to get down the front stairs and out of the house rather than down the hall and through Isabel's door, which she has left ajar.[21]

In the cool night air, Seth wanders aimlessly and thoroughly befuddled. His night's experiences are not over yet, however, for Frederic caps the evening with still one more comic invention. About to return home, Seth meets Annie Fairchild, his school-teacher cousin. When Seth was only a farm boy, it had been generally assumed that someday he would marry Annie, but once he became a newspaperman, Annie, though still "a dear, good girl," seemed—"what shall I say?—rural." Then it appeared to Seth "simply suicide to marry a wife whom I perhaps would have to carry up with me, a dead weight" (pp. 170–171). To readers of *The Damnation* the accents of the "liberated" Theron Ware as he condescends to his wife Alice are all too clear in Seth's remarks.

Yet as Seth resisted Albert's pleas for the sake of the good

[21] As Walter Blair says, Frederic "was not averse to treating sex in a fashion which might distress young ladies" (*The Literature of the United States* [New York, 1947], II, 285). Considering that *Seth* was written in the mid-eighties it is remarkable that Frederic did not force Isabel to confess herself a wicked woman and punish her to boot. The day after the events described above, Isabel does little to redeem herself: believing that he has murdered her husband, she offers to provide Seth with an alibi by swearing that he spent the night with her. In "The Martyrdom of Maev" (1890), Frederic's Irish heroine ruins her reputation but saves her young man from criminal charges by falsely claiming that he was with her until late at night.

in politics, so he resists Isabel for the sake of the "dear, good girl." Wandering about in the moonlight, Seth discovers that the rural dead weight looks positively angelic. Typically, the rhetoric of the language betrays the hollowness of the conversion: "An Idea—a great, luminous, magnificent Idea—unfolded itself before his mental vision." After a good deal of disjointed talk about his need for stability, for a "balance-wheel" as he unromantically puts it, Seth blurts out his great Idea to Annie: "I want to pledge myself to you, to swear that you are to be my wife" (pp. 251–252). To Annie's credit, she declines the proposal, though only for the time being. Seth, in the classic tradition of romantic fiction, turns out to be the prize for virtuous conduct (though he is scarcely the proper judge of it).

After the series of chapters that send the hero virtually blindfolded and spinning from situation to situation, *Seth's Brother's Wife* loses a great deal of its comic momentum. The humbling of Isabel remains: she has yet to learn that Seth was not out till all hours killing her husband for love of her, but instead was proposing to Annie in the moonlight. The whole business of Albert's murder and the resultant mystery, however, is far from comic; it is in fact conceived as melodrama. But Frederic's comic sense never deserts him completely. Even Albert's murder cannot relegate the Comic Muse to a minor role for long. At the very moment the reader is asked to shudder at the spectacle of Albert's cold and broken corpse, he is distracted by a pair of rube vaudevillians—a lugubrious undertaker and a county coroner in the Dogberry tradition. Just as the vast extent of the late Albert's political schemes is being fully exposed, it is also revealed that the villain has left the bulk of his vast fortune to his brothers—the greatest share by far to Seth.

The finer ironies of the closing chapters, however, are re-
served mainly for the public rather than the private sphere of
action. It develops that the real opposition to Albert's political
ambitions has come not from aroused public morality, nor
from crusading newspapers, nor from reformers (tea-drinking
or otherwise). Richard Ansdell does finally win the congressional nomination and election, but he does so only with the
leave and assistance of one Abram K. Beekman, known to all
of upstate New York as "the Boss." Beekman is introduced
late in the novel and may very well be an afterthought on
Frederic's part. It is entertaining to imagine Frederic reading a
novel about "An American Politician" like the one that so
disgusted Albert and sitting down to produce Beekman. Afterthought or not, Frederic has painted a superb portrait of the
tall, chin-whiskered politico who has worked his way up
through local politics to a position of great, if obscure, power
"by that process of exhaustion which we call the survival of
the fittest," as Frederic wittily puts it.

From his first appearance Abe Beekman is fascinating. "His
face was thin, hungry, with a plaintive effect of deep lines, and
his great blue-black eyes were often tearful, like a young
robin's, in their intent watchfulness" (p. 270). This memor-
able figure with the face and form of a Lincoln and the watery
eyes of a fledgling is probably the only sympathetically por-
trayed machine politico in American fiction until Edwin
O'Connor's Skeffington, and Frederic never permits himself
the kind of sentimental liberties that occasionally mar O'Connor's portrait—in 1887 a good many hurrahs were yet to
come. An odd amalgam of homely democratic virtue and
ruthless bossism, Beekman stands for neither the wonderfully
monstrous corruption of Senator Ratcliffe in Henry Adams'
Democracy, nor the monstrously wonderful virtue of Tark-

ington's Gentleman from Indiana. He stands for—he is—a
perplexing fact of American life.[22]

From the start Frederic makes it clear where Beekman
stands in the struggle between Albert Fairchild and Richard
Ansdell. A just despot to faithful followers, Beekman has an
"oriental" way of punishing disloyalty and opposition, and
Albert has made the mistake of trying to circumvent Beekman. Albert has also made the mistake of assuming that politics
is all money. Beekman's assumption is scarcely high idealism:
"I'm not in politics fur what I kin make aout of it," he explains. "I'm in because I like it; because it's meat 'n' drink to
me; because I git solid, substantial comfort aout of it. There's
satisfaction in carryin' yer eend; there's pretty nigh as much
in daowning them that's agin yeh." As for Ansdell, the
Boss does not worry much about a "high-toned, kid-gloved,
butter-wouldn't-melt-in-his-maouth kind o' man like what's-
his-name." Reforms spurts," says Beekman, "don't winter
well. They never last till spring. The boys lose their breath
for a few months. But then they git daown to work agin,
and baounce the reformers to the back seats where they
belong" (pp. 272–274). And so, not knowing that Albert is
out of the race for the sufficient reason that he is dead, Beekman decides to throw the district nomination to "what's-his-
name."

[22] Although Frederic was an anti-Conkling man from his earliest
days in journalism, Beekman, as well as Albert, talks surprisingly like
Conkling at times. One can easily imagine Beekman saying, "Parties
are not built by deportment, or by ladies' magazines, or gush" and,
still more easily, "A government is a machine; a church is a machine;
an army is a machine . . . the common-school system of the State of
New York is a machine; a political party is a machine" (Conkling,
quoted in Richard Hofstadter, *The American Political Tradition*
[New York, 1951], pp. 162 and 171). Despite the millions in graft
and bribes which passed through his hands, Conkling, like Beekman,
apparently was not in politics for money.

Beekman, in many ways a preliminary sketch of Brother Soulsby in *The Damnation*, makes possible a perfect comic resolution to the political matter of *Seth*. His role in the novel surprisingly and explosively confounds conventional expectations. On the one hand, he provides an ironic variation on the honest countryman who gives the rich city slicker his comeuppance; on the other, he plays hob with the tale of the young reformer who defeats the powers of political corruption. Frederic saves his parting shot until the last page but one. There he discloses that the Honorable Richard Ansdell, "the embodiment of Principle," is shortly to marry the gayest widow in Washington—who is, of course, Isabel Fairchild.

For a first novel, written by a young man not yet quite thirty who had published almost no fiction, *Seth's Brother's Wife* is an impressive performance. To those most concerned with following the rise of realism (the grimmer sort of realism, that is) the interesting pages of *Seth* will remain its early ones. Yet even in the bleaker pages of the novel Frederic's view was likely to shift suddenly and catch the humorous side of things. Into the gloomy picture of a farmhouse funeral, for example, Frederic could not resist introducing the comic discomfiture of soft little Father Turner, the Episcopal priest whose side whiskers reminded Isabel of baby brushes. Nor could he resist catching the neighborhood farm women at the funeral service as they furtively scraped their feet on the parlor carpet to test its nap.

The pages of *Seth* that capture the darker side of rural life are important, but it seems clear that those pages are neither the most notable nor the most characteristic of the work. Although it is possible to see in Frederic's first novel early stirrings of the movement toward the kind of realism that was soon to become dominant in American fiction, it is more reasonable to see the novel as continuing a tradition of comic realism that had already been vigorous for some time.

Frederic had the perception to see that "what the world knows as American humor" is "the grim, fatalist habit of seizing upon the grotesque side" (p. 35). Yet he somehow managed to see life as humorous without finding it so terribly grim after all. He was, in an old-fashioned sense of the word, a humorist—one who delights in viewing the humors of others. The character in *Seth's Brother's Wife* who comes closest to functioning as a moral center for the book is John Fairchild. John, Frederic says, "had in almost unmeted degree that habit of mind which welcomes statements of both sides of a controversy" (p. 351). Harold Frederic had that same habit of mind, no small virtue in a young man starting out to write novels.

3 / In the Valley

Although *In the Valley* was completed and published after *Seth's Brother's Wife*, it is in a sense Harold Frederic's first novel.[1] In the "Preface to a Uniform Edition," Frederic himself begins the discussion of his works with his historical novel. He speaks of years and years of frustrating struggle to do something with an idea that seemed "to have been always in my mind,"[2] an idea he traces back to his earliest recollections, his grandmother's tales of the American Revolution that she had heard from men and women themselves alive in the Mohawk Valley of the 1770's. By the time he was twelve, Frederic continues, he had completed "several short but lurid introductions" to a narrative about the Battle of Oriskany. By the centennial anniversary of Oriskany in 1877, Frederic says,

---

[1] Before it appeared as a book in 1890, *In the Valley* ran serially in *Scribner's Magazine* from Vol. VI (Sept., 1889) through Vol. VIII (July, 1890).

[2] Unless otherwise stated, all information pertaining to the composition of *In the Valley* is drawn from the "Preface to a Uniform Edition," *In the Sixties* (New York, 1897), pp. vi-ix.

he had the plan of his work in mind;[3] how complete a plan is not clear, but by 1883, he was able to tell the whole story of the novel as it finally appeared.[4] Still, the book just would not get written.

By 1885, Frederic had accumulated masses of "notes, cross-references, dates, maps, biographical facts, and the like,"[5] had made repeated false starts, including one draft of more than twenty thousand words, had consumed "nearly ten years in fruitless mooning," and seemed no closer than ever to completing his novel. "I did not know how to make a book of any kind," he ruefully concludes, "let alone a historical book of the kind which should be the most difficult and exacting of all."

And so it was that Frederic set aside his historical novel to work on something "easier," a "contemporary story." Once *Seth's Brother's Wife* was written—before it was quite completed, in fact—Frederic was back to work on *In the Valley*. Now the writing went smoothly and rapidly, and Frederic's

[3] For the celebration of the anniversary, Frederic wrote an essay, "The Mohawk Valley during the Revolution," published in *Harper's New Monthly*, LV (1877), 171–183.

[4] "I . . . heard Harold Frederic tell the absorbing story of 'In the Valley,' as he wrote it several years later. This was in the spring of 1883" (Charles R. Sherlock, quoted in Nelson Greene, ed., *The History of the Mohawk Valley* [Chicago, 1925], IV, 711). In 1896, Frederic said that the story and spirit of *In the Valley* "soaked into my mind eleven years before I wrote the first chapter" ("Chronicle and Comment," *The Bookman* [New York], III [1896], 383).

[5] Notes for Frederic's novels often were "as bulky as the novel itself," said Arthur Warren ("Harold Frederic: The Reminiscences of a Colleague," New York *Times*, Oct. 23, 1898, p. 19). Although Warren exaggerates, the notes and outlines that survive in the Frederic Papers in the Library of Congress are indeed bulky.

expectations soared to extravagant heights, even to hopes that the work might become "in American literature what Henry Esmond is in English." [6] In a letter to his editor at Scribner's, written before the book was even finished, Frederic lays down his "statement of faith" that the work "is to be the best thing of the kind ever done by an American." [7]

Apparently the completed novel did not disappoint its author. Frederic's letter to Cleveland urging him to read the *Scribner's* installments of *In the Valley* contains the astonishing admission that "I myself have so great a liking for its political side that if I could be sure that every young man in the United States would read it, I should feel like working day and night to provide every one of them with a free copy." [8]

[6] Letter to John Howe, 1886, quoted in Thomas F. O'Donnell and Hoyt C. Franchere, *Harold Frederic* (New York, 1961), p. 58. Over a decade later, Frederic wrote about *The Virginians* in terms that suggest his own efforts in *In the Valley* to differentiate between social, political, and national groups. He praises Thackeray for painting "the minutest shades of temperamental differences which distinguish American colonists from Englishmen, and even Whigs from Tories" ("On Historical Novels, Past and Present," *The Bookman* [New York], VIII [1898], 332). The high praise for Scott and Stevenson in the article stands in contrast to the view that Frederic gave his full allegiance to the realists. Scott, as Everett Carter says, "was the *bête noire* of the realists" (*Howells and the Age of Realism* [Philadelphia, 1954], p. 31).

[7] Letter to Edward L. Burlingame, Oct. ?, 1886, quoted in Roger Burlingame, *Of Making Many Books* (New York, 1946), p. 5. Frederic did have his moments of doubt. Three months after this letter, having in the meantime sent off the first half of *In the Valley* and as yet receiving no acceptance from Scribner's, Frederic wrote: "I could not help construing your silence to mean that it was no good. . . . You will let me know . . . as soon as possible, won't you?" (January ?, 1887, quoted in Burlingame, p. 6).

[8] Nov. 13, 1889, Cleveland Papers, Library of Congress.

Not quite every young man in America showed interest in *In the Valley*,[9] but Frederic cannot have been much cast down by the critical notice his work received. "When Mr. Harold Frederic's 'In the Valley' appeared we reviewed it favorably as a perfect specimen of an American historical novel, and similar treatment was extended to it generally by the press," wrote *The Athenaeum*; on both sides of the Atlantic critical opinion of *In the Valley* was indeed favorable at its publication in 1890 and even beyond the turn of the century. *The Dial* found it to be "one of the most remarkable of American novels," and Stephen Crane, who was in Frederic's debt for a handsome review of *The Red Badge of Courage*, ranked *In the Valley* as "easily the best historical novel that our country has borne." Although the novel continued to find enthusiastic readers for many years and although such critics as Carl Van Doren and Granville Hicks have praised it, modern readers generally find *In the Valley* dreary going.[10] In his letter to Cleveland of November 13, 1889, Frederic said, "I know that you don't read novels—but this is grave enough to be something else." [11] Most present-day readers find it altogether too much "something else."

One of the few nineteenth-century critics who disliked *In*

[9] "We have never worked harder over any books than we did over 'In the Valley' and 'The Lawton Girl' and yet their sale was not proportionate to our efforts" (Charles Scribner to Harold Frederic, n.d., quoted in Burlingame, *Of Making Many Books*, p. 117).

[10] *Athenaeum*, review of *The Damnation*, CVII (1896), 378. Review by William Morton Payne, *The Dial*, XI (1890), 239. Crane, "Harold Frederic," *The Chap-Book*, VII (1898), 359. *In the Valley* was the best American historical novel and, Crane continued, "perhaps the only good one." Van Doren, *The American Novel: 1798–1939* (rev. ed.; New York, 1940), p. 215. Hicks, *The Great Tradition* (rev. ed.; New York, 1935), p. 159.

[11] Cleveland Papers, Library of Congress.

the Valley was William Dean Howells. He found it "a fresh instance of the fatuity of the historical novel as far as the portrayal of character goes." [12] Although a great deal of *In the Valley* is fatuous, Howells revealed bias as well as insight in his remark; the artistic success of "The Copperhead" (1883), Frederic's novella set in the Civil War period, is evidence enough that historical fiction need not be an exercise in amateur theatrics. The failings of *In the Valley* have little to do with any intrinsic defect in the historical novel as such.

The faults of Frederic's novel are Frederic's, and they are several. The prose of the first person narrative is sometimes almost bad enough to justify Kenneth Roberts' objection that *In the Valley* is "written in a sort of pre-Cambrian." [13] The dialogue, usually so strong in Frederic's fiction, is frequently weighted down with an eighteenth-century rhetoric more appropriate to the neoclassic essay than the daily conversation of colonial New York. And as for the characters, Frederic himself later confessed that "their personalities always remained shadowy in my own mind." [14]

Saddest of all is the plot. In *The American Historical Novel*

[12] *Harper's Monthly*, LXXXI (1890), 800. The review brushes *In the Valley* aside to go on to an enthusiastic discussion of *Seth* and *The Lawton Girl*. More out of respect for a newly found brother realist than any real regard for *In the Valley*, one suspects, Howells did temper his condemnation of the work slightly: "We do not mean to say that it is not very well written, and all that; it is uncommonly well written." Commenting on Howells' remark, Larzer Ziff rightly notes that *In the Valley* was an example "of how Frederic's realism was advancing in depth beyond Howells', and of the way in which the complex, disunited America in which he grew up demanded of him historical and political explanations before moral judgments could be made" (*The American 1890s* [New York, 1966], p. 218).

[13] *I Wanted to Write* (Garden City, N.Y., 1949), p. 333.

[14] "Preface to a Uniform Edition," p. ix.

Ernest Leisy credits *The Spy* with having set the plot for the countless novels of the American Revolution that followed Cooper's: "A dashing, noble, rebel officer loves the daintily feminine daughter of a staunch landed loyalist. . . . There follows a conflict between love and duty." Finally, "the rebel exposes the villainy of his loyalist rival, converts the father to the justness of his cause, and wins the beauty. This plot pattern," Leisy says, "was used over and over again by most of the novelists for half a century."[15] Not fifty, but almost seventy years had elapsed between *The Spy* and *In the Valley*, yet the threadbare pattern Leisy traces is clearly to be seen in Frederic's novel of the Revolution.

Even if Cooper's plot had not been so thoroughly hackneyed by the time of *In the Valley*, it would have served Frederic but poorly. Frederic's fiction simply does not dramatize the historical truth as he sees it. His fiction calls for deeds of derring-do, for displays of freedom-loving heroism and goodness in conflict with Tory wickedness. His sense of the history of the Revolution, however, is far beyond such Whiggish simplification. The plot of brave New York patriots creating a brave history does not jibe with Frederic's instinctive feeling that the real story is of men shaped primarily by events. As

[15](Norman, Okla., 1950), p. 10. It is a mistake to assume, as some have, that Frederic was trying to cash in on a popular fashion with *In The Valley*. The tremendous interest in historical fiction which ran through the first decade of the twentieth century began, Leisy says, in the mid-nineties (p. 15). The revival was already stirring when Frederic published *In the Valley* in 1890, however; the same year saw the establishment of the Daughters of the American Revolution and the Colonial Dames. The most interesting connections to be made with Frederic's novel are not with such romances as *Janice Meredith* and *Alice of Old Vincennes*, but with works like Beard's *Economic Interpretation of the Constitution* and the revisionist novels of Howard Fast.

fiction, *In the Valley* presents a personal conflict between a hero and a villain; as history, it presents civil conflict between ordinary men fighting for complicated motives of national origin (what Frederic calls "race"), class, economics, and prejudice.[16]

If, like Scott at his best, Frederic had chosen for his hero a man relatively disengaged from the conflict he witnesses, *In the Valley* might have been a far more solid achievement. Instead, he chose to combine in a single character a partisan protagonist and a narrator who must at times speak for Frederic's dispassionate and far from simple view of events. Unfortunately the kind of patriotism and heroics the young Frederic so relished in the novels of Erckmann-Chatrian got in the way of the elder Frederic's mature understanding.[17] Later Frederic learned how to avoid the difficulties that confounded him in *In the Valley*. In most of his Civil War stories he set his scene far from the actual battlefield and made his narrators not brave soldiers but young boys, more acted upon by the events they so clearly and naively relate than acting in those events. And in two of the Civil War stories that do offer heroic protagonists, one of the heroes is a Copperhead and the other a deserter.

[16] Although the word "race" appears frequently in Frederic's novels, it never has any of the unpleasant implications it so often has in the works of such contemporaries as Frank Norris.

[17] Frederic expresses his strong admiration for the French authors in the "Preface to a Uniform Edition" (p. x). In his unpublished "Story of Peter Zarl" (Frederic Papers, Library of Congress), he went so far as to use the Alsatian setting and Napoleonic period of many of the Erckmann-Chatrian romances. Frederic's respect for the popular writers has frequently excited surprise or condescension; it might be worth noting that Henry James found *L'Ami Fritz* "a real masterpiece" ("Notes," *The Nation*, XXIV [1877], 14).

The difficulties that Frederic encountered in *In the Valley* can be attributed largely to the fact that although the novel was completed by the thirty-two-year-old London correspondent of the New York *Times*, it was begun by a romantic twelve-year-old schoolboy who liked to stride around Utica dressed in a garibaldi shirt and a Kossuth hat. Frederic's use of the trite romantic conflict between two young men, one loyalist, one rebel, and both in love with the same daughter of a loyalist, becomes more understandable when one considers that he used the same plot in "The Blakelys of Poplar Place," published when he was twenty, and that the characters of Douw Mauverenson and Philip Cross were already sketched out in "The Two Rochards," the first story he is known to have published.

The highly confusing lineage for Douw and Cross that one can trace from "The Two Rochards" through "The Blakelys of Poplar Place" to *In the Valley* suggests the degree to which Frederic's characters in the historical novel did indeed remain "shadowy" in his mind. In "The Two Rochards" the fair Paul Rochard is a gregarious and elegantly dressed young man of "Antinous-like beauty" who is "a voluptuary, a finished roué." His elder brother, Philip, is the master of a mansion named the Poplars and is served by a deformed Negro slave.[18] The antithesis of his brother, Philip Rochard is a somber melancholiac devoted to his books and, with the exception of his young wife, whom Paul seduces, his own company. A Philip and a Paul reappear in "The Blakelys," and again Philip

---

[18] Utica *Observer*, Sept. 30, 1876, p. 2 and Oct. 7, p. 2. The story, published under the name "Edgar," was discovered by Thomas F. O'Donnell, who identifies it as Frederic's because of the many similarities between it and "The Blakelys of Poplar Place" ("An Addition to the HF Bibliography," *Frederic Herald*, I [Sept., 1967], 4).

is the elder brother and the master of a house called the Poplars, and again he is dark and dour and soberly dressed. Now, however, Philip is the villain, a dark-featured Tory, "all business and books." He is served by a henchman named Rab. The heroic brother, Paul Blakely, resembles Philip Rochard: Tall and fair, "with eyes as blue as a June sky," he sports "the finest clothes in the valley." [19]

The villain of *In the Valley* is also named Philip and also has a henchman named Rab, but now it is the villain who is fair-haired, blue-eyed, and dashing, who dresses elegantly and looks down on trade. The hero, Douw Mauverenson, resembles the victimized Philip Rochard in his dark features, his plain manners and dress, his deformed Negro slave, and the loss of his ladylove to Philip Cross; he likewise resembles the villain Philip Blakely in his looks and dress and manners and his interest in trade, as well as the loss of his ladylove.

The convoluted lines of relationship among the characters traced here suggest that Frederic worked within romantic convention only with a certain confusion. He is unable to decide whether virtue or vice is to be assigned to dark-featured and plain-mannered seriousness, whether fine clothes and manners and fair good looks bespeak good or evil. Later he would unite the opposing qualities of his paired characters in single characters such as Theron Ware or Joel Thorpe. His interest in the simple external conflicts between the dark and the fair would give way to a mature concern for the complex internal struggles of individuals who contain within themselves both innocence and guilt, weakness and strength, good and evil. Unfortunately, when he set the plot and characters of *In the Valley* he committed himself to the conventions of his

[19] Utica *Observer*, June 30, 1877, p. 2.

juvenile fiction, conventions that appear to have but poorly represented his sense of reality.

Douw Mauverenson is akin to the "untrained, uneducated, and unsophisticated" heroes of whom Carey McWilliams speaks.[20] He is only distantly related, however, for compared to the provincial young men of Frederic's other novels, Douw has had a good many advantages. Although he is reared on the frontier of colonial New York, he is reared amid good books by a step-father who is a gentleman. As Mr. Stewart's ward, Douw is welcome even at Johnson Hall, seat of Sir William Johnson, the great lord of the Mohawk Valley. What little gentle and educated society there is in the valley is English, however, and Douw is Dutch. Although his public actions in the war show resourcefulness and courage, Douw Mauverenson in his private life is no more dashing or romantic than his name. In the manner of Cornelius Littlepage's swipes at Jason Newcome in Cooper's *Satanstoe*, Douw occasionally bursts out against the Yankees, "who know how neither to rest nor to play" (p. 188),[21] but he is something of a puritan himself. His priggish animadversions against lowcut gowns and the indelicacies of *Roderick Random* as well as his distrust of the punch bowl justly earn him the nickname "Cousin Sobriety."

The isolation that Douw is to suffer later is suggested early in the novel when he and Philip meet for the first time as children and play French and Indian War. When Douw objects to playing the hated French attacker, Philip's rebuff is harsh: "You're a Dutchman. . . . All foreigners are the same. . . . You wear an apron, and you are not able to even speak

---

[20] "Harold Frederic: 'A Country Boy of Genius,'" *University of California Chronicle*, XXXV (Jan., 1933), 30.

[21] All page references to *In the Valley* are to the first American edition (New York: Charles Scribner's Sons, 1890).

English properly" (p. 27). Douw soon leaves his apron and his accent behind, but as the Revolution draws near, the English community looks upon him more and more as the outsider, the foreigner, the Dutchman. In the eyes of his childhood friends his Dutch loyalties and rebel sympathies inevitably link him with the ignorant and the common. No gentleman, no one but a Dutchman, his foster-father says, would turn his back on gentlefolk to make his own way "tricking drunken Indians out of their peltry, and charging some other Dutchman a shilling for fourpence worth of goods" (p. 150). Hardest of all for him to accept, the heroine of the novel, the woman Douw loves, begins to change. Daisy begins to coil her braids about her head like a crown, to wear silks and laces, and to treat Douw's aunt, Mr. Stewart's housekeeper, like a mere servant; in short, she begins to act the fine lady. It comes as no surprise to anyone when Daisy announces that she will wed Philip Cross, who has recently returned from England to settle in the territory with a large patent and is already taking his place as a leading member of the landed and indolent gentry.

Although Daisy is not very interesting in her own right, she is clearly related to Frederic's more interesting heroines. She turns from Douw to Philip much as Kate Minster in *The Lawton Girl* turns her attentions from Reuben Tracy to the sophisticated Horace Boyce. Daisy is also reminiscent of Isabel Fairchild in the boredom that drives her into Philip Cross's arms, and she dimly foreshadows those restless New Women who figure so largely in Frederic's later fiction. It is difficult to say whether Frederic himself was conscious of Daisy's similarity to characters like Kate and Isabel, Celia Madden and Edith Cressage. Perhaps he was, for when he wrote *The Lawton Girl* he made Kate Minster the great-granddaughter of a colonial beauty bearing the odd name of Desideria Mauverenson, Daisy's real name.[22]

The similarity between Douw and the naive young protagonists of Frederic's other novels, it must be reasserted, is incomplete. When he is finally forced to leave his home, Douw visits Albany. There, although singled out as a country "Cousin Sobriety," he is welcomed and accepted by a Dutch society quite as gentlemanly as the English society in which he was brought up.[23] "Heretofore," Douw realizes, "I had suffered not a little from the notion . . . that gentility and good-breeding went hand in hand with loyalty to everything England did, and that disaffection was but another name for vulgarity and ignorance" (p. 189). In such novels as *The Damnation of Theron Ware*, of course, questions of vulgarity and ignorance would not be so easily settled.

One expects to be able to trace a line of development in Frederic, as in other artists, from the early to the late work. But it is surprising that Frederic seems to double back from this second novel to his first, *Seth's Brother's Wife*. Almost all of Frederic's modern-day critics, following the lead of Howells, have celebrated *Seth* as the triumph of a novelist finding himself as a realist, and have dismissed *In the Valley* as the failure of a realist temporarily seduced by historical

[22] Frederic thought of his characters as one big family, so to speak. Not only are Douw and Daisy the great-grandparents of Kate, but one of Douw's sisters is the grandmother of Judge Wendover in *The Lawton Girl*. The yacht which sends Theron Ware's thoughts cruising around the world with Celia is identified as belonging to a Barclay Wendover.

[23] An unresolved difficulty of which Frederic does not seem aware is that Douw's rebel cousins and friends in Dutch Albany stand allied to the same ideal of an aristocratic landed gentry as do Philip Cross and the other upstate Tories.

romance. Although such a view does have some truth in it, it also has the unfortunate consequence of obscuring the similarities that do exist between the two novels. Completed and published after *Seth* and decidedly an inferior and very different work, *In the Valley* is nevertheless a prime source for *Seth's Brother's Wife*. Putting aside the very different ways in which Frederic treats his materials in the two novels, one is struck by how alike those materials are. As we have seen, Frederic had the story of *In the Valley* well in mind many years before he completed that novel or began *Seth*. When he temporarily abandoned *In the Valley* to work on *Seth*, the story and characters he used turned out to be variations on the story and characters that he had just laid aside.

In *Seth's Brother's Wife* Frederic returned to the theme of fraternal conflict that had interested him as far back as "The Two Rochards." The theme is also dimly present in *In the Valley*, for Philip is also a kind of adopted son to Mr. Stewart. Albert Fairchild, Seth's brother, corresponds in a number of ways to the three Philips of "The Two Rochards," "The Blakelys of Poplar Place," and *In the Valley*. Like Philip Rochard, Albert discovers that his bored young wife has fallen into the arms of his younger brother. Like Philip Blakely, Albert is "all books and business" and manages to get title to a family farm that is at least as much his brother's as his. Both Philip Blakely and Philip Cross are served by slouching henchmen, and Albert too has an unkempt right-hand man. In this case it is a farm hand rather than a half-breed, but Milton Squires, who looks fifty though he is not yet thirty-six, is obviously cut from the same pattern as the Rab described in *In the Valley* as "a young-old man" (p. 251).

Like Philip Cross, Albert Fairchild is a snob and an aristocrat, for Albert's grandfather had been a United States

Senator and the richest farmer in the county. *Seth* takes place in the nineteenth century rather than the eighteenth century of *In the Valley*, so Albert's political aspirations are not feudal, but in his Gilded Age view of things there is little difference between Senator and Squire. Albert's ambition to buy himself a seat in Congress is essentially Philip Cross's ambition to set himself up as lord and master over the German and Dutch farmers settled in the Mohawk Valley, and the citified Albert's underestimation of the resourceful rural temper is as ill-advised as Philip's patrician contempt for the mob. Albert turns out to be no match for Boss Beekman, who, like Douw, is Dutch, "that silent, persistent, quietly-masterful race" (p. 270). And, most striking of all, Albert and Philip Cross meet violent deaths in what appears to be the same ravine.

Other parallels can be drawn between *Seth's Brother's Wife* and *In the Valley*—between Douw's aunt and mother and Seth's Aunt Sabrina, for example, or between Daisy and Annie or Isabel. But enough has been said to indicate that Frederic set aside the manuscript, not the material, of *In the Valley* to work on *Seth*. The similarities between the two works suggest the causes for Frederic's letdown in *In the Valley*. It was one thing to treat Seth and Albert Fairchild in a contemporary setting and expose them as something more than simply hero and villain locked in conflict between "the good and bad in politics," but it was another to treat patriots and Tories of the American Revolution in the same ironic fashion.

Despite his historical sense that New Yorkers had fought the Revolution for issues that were local and basically narrow and conservative, careful as he was to note that in his valley, men did not fight for "the more abstract and educated discontents of New England and Virginia" (p. 116), Frederic could not escape his patriotic feeling that the War for Independence had been heroic and noble. Not quite twenty-one, he had listened to his idol Horatio Seymour appeal at the centennial of the Battle of Oriskany for someone to restore to "the general intelligence of our people" the priceless "records of the past." [24] *In the Valley*, which is dedicated to Seymour's memory, was Frederic's reply to that appeal, a reply that was almost an act of piety.

If Frederic had shown his characters torn by their own inner conflicts, *In the Valley* might have turned out to be a better novel, but it would scarcely have been a fitting tribute either to the revered memory of Horatio Seymour or to deeply felt local pride and patriotism. "All four of my great-grandfathers had borne arms in the Revolutionary War," Frederic once said, "and one of them indeed somewhat indefinitely expanded his record by fighting on both sides." [25] Everything that is known of Frederic indicates that he inherited the greater share of his temperament from the one forefather; but when he was writing *In the Valley*, for once the undivided loyalties of the other three held sway within him.

Frederic's talent for perceiving the ambivalent motivations that often drive men is not completely in abeyance in *In the Valley*, however. Most obviously, it is to be seen in the erratic career of Douw's foster father. Born Thomas Lynch, the son of a man believed to be a by-blow of James Stuart, Duke of York, he has fled to the New World after following the Young Pretender into the disaster of the Forty-five. In the forests of the Mohawk Valley, though perversely adopting the

[24] Seymour's speech of August 6, 1877, is recorded in Samuel Durant, *History of Oneida County* (Philadelphia, 1878), p. 129.

[25] "Preface to a Uniform Edition," p. vi.

name Stewart, Lynch has turned his back on all the Pretenders, on all the follies and dreams over which he has wasted his youth. When he first appears in the novel he is outside his log cabin clearing timber, the very model of the democratic frontiersman. But age encroaches on him, and Europe penetrates even to the frontier. By the eve of the Revolution, Stewart is heart and soul for the King, the Old Pretender of the New World, so to speak. In his foster father, Douw explains, there "came up a second growth of old-world, medieval notions—a sort of aristocratic aftermath" (p. 68).

Such ambivalence is to be found not only in Stewart but in Douw and Philip as well. Through most of the novel the two young men present a complete antithesis: the one as the heroic representative of the New World, the other as the villainous representative of the Old. In a curious way, however, Frederic suggests that Philip is not simply an external force against which Douw must struggle, but is part of himself. Midway in the novel, having just learned of Philip's engagement to Daisy, Douw picks a fight with his rival on a narrow path overlooking a steep gorge. As they strip down for a combat that may well end in death, Douw notices that "by some strange freak of irony" it is one of his own greatcoats that Philip wears (p. 166).

When Douw and Philip meet for what is to be their last encounter, the Battle of Oriskany has been fought and the conclusion of the novel is near. Douw finds Philip badly wounded. From the moment they confront each other there is something strange and new in their relationship. "The look in his eyes," Douw recalls, "was both sad and savage—an expression I could not fathom. . . . The speechless fixity of this gaze embarrassed me" (p. 379). His embarrassment is caused partially by the recognition that the helpless Philip knows that Douw's first thought is to show no mercy. But it is more than that; Douw suddenly finds that he does not know how he feels about Philip. Though torn by contrary desires, Douw finally decides to abandon vengeance and return Philip to Daisy.

Douw's rescue of his mortal enemy and rival in love sounds melodramatic in the extreme. Frederic's treatment of the trite situation, however, is not at all trite. Far from being sentimental, the rescue is one of the finest things in *In the Valley* and shows the novel Frederic might have written if only he had not begun with a simple opposition of hero and villain. It is clear that Frederic knows Douw's sacrifice of his own interests to save Philip can be considered preposterously quixotic. He puts a rough, hard-drinking woodsman on the scene not only to help the wounded Douw get Philip to safety, but also to speak for the kind of instinct and reason that Douw might have yielded to on finding his enemy helpless at his feet. In some respects the woodsman is noble in the style of Natty Bumppo,[26] but Enoch Wade can be very savage: "I nailed you right under the nipple, there, within a hair of the button I sighted on," Wade explains to Philip; "I'd

---

[26] Frederic was such an avid student of his state's history that he must have read Cooper; *Satanstoe*, in fact, appears to have directly suggested features of *In the Valley* and "The Blakelys." Yet Frederic never mentioned Cooper's name, and throughout *In the Valley* he writes as though he is the first novelist to use New York history. Should Frederic's failure even to acknowledge the existence of the most famous of his country's historical novelists be attributed simply to the general antagonism to Cooper in the latter nineteenth century? Or was Frederic personally displeased by Cooper's outspoken social views, views diametrically opposed to those expressed in *In the Valley*? Curiously, none of the contemporary reviews of *In the Valley* mentions Cooper.

have potted you just as carefully if we'd been perfect strangers" (p. 381). When Douw announces that Philip is to be saved, Wade's response is characteristic: "The hell you say!" (p. 390). As much as anything else, it is the "cool brutality" of Wade's talk that brings Douw to his humane decision. And, similarly, Wade's assumption that the natural thing to do is to abandon Philip to scavenging wolves or the scalping knives of Indians makes it impossible to find Douw's decision anything but natural.

The entire journey away from the battlefield and by canoe down the Mohawk, traveling only by night, has a curiously unreal quality. Douw repeatedly speaks of the experience as "dreamlike" and "nightmarish." At first the two men almost cease to have names for each other, each becoming merely "my enemy." Every time he thinks of Daisy, who has long-since regretted her choice, Douw is tempted to kill Philip after all, but, he says, "I tore my mind forcibly from the idea, as one looking over a dizzy height leaps back lest the strange, latent impulse of suicide shall master him" (p. 401). The figure Douw uses here is curious. Obviously enough, the dizzy height recalls his struggle with Philip at the edge of Dadanascara Gorge earlier in the novel and anticipates what is to come, Philip's fatal fall into the same gorge; but why should Douw think of the impulse to kill Philip as suicidal?

Douw has begun to see into Philip, to realize that Philip is not simply his opposite, a villain to be hated, but is a man like himself. "Under other circumstances he might have been as good a man as another" (p. 403); as good a man as myself, Douw might have added. There are, Douw begins to see, two Philips, "two distinct men" (p. 402). The reconciliation between Douw and Philip is by no means total. Frederic asks no such incredible magnanimity of his hero. Indeed, when Douw finally reaches Daisy, he wonders whether perhaps he has not played the fool in saving his beloved's husband. He receives little reassurance from Daisy, for in a welcome reversal of her role of pure and perfect womanhood she greets the news that Douw has rescued her brutal husband with a dismay that leaves no room for praise of Douw. When Douw reminds her of duty and honor, the best she can reply is, "Yes, I ought to see it" (p. 414). When Philip conveniently dies a few minutes later, Daisy seems relieved.

Even if qualified, there is a reconciliation at the conclusion of *In the Valley*, and Frederic feels it to be very important. So that the reader cannot miss the point, Frederic includes in his final chapter Douw's epilogue account of the two children Daisy bears him. The first is "a dark-skinned, brawny man-child whom it seemed the most natural thing in the world to christen Douw." The second, by a process more plausible in symbolic than genetic terms, is "a fair-haired, slender crea-ture" who soon grows into a "beautiful, imperious little boy" (p. 424). To this child, they give the name Philip.

Tired as the device may be, the rescue of Philip is clearly something more than convention. In bringing Douw and Philip together, Frederic was trying to bring his fiction into focus with history. Unfortunately, he introduced Douw's recognition of Philip's humanity into the novel too late to save the work from considerable confusion. Even the reader who fully appreciates what Frederic was trying to do in the conclusion must find *In the Valley* muddled. On the one hand it tries to present the Revolution as something more compli-cated than a conflict between high and low principles, yet on the other it gives the burden of the narrative and the leading action of the novel to a high-principled patriot who opposes a base Tory.

At one point in the novel, Douw enjoys a long conversation with a Major Dayton, who is introduced purely for the sake of the talk, surely Frederic's own. Dayton, Douw says, "was one of the first to arouse in my mind the idea that, after all, the Tories had their good side and were doing what seemed to them right, at tremendous cost and sacrifice to themselves" (p. 279).

You seem to miss the sad phase of all this, my friend [the Major explains]. Your young blood feels only the partisan promptings of dislike. Some day—soon, perhaps—you will all at once find this youthful heat gone; you will begin to walk around men and things, so to speak, and study them from all sides. . . . Rid your mind of the idea that because a man tries to understand a thing he therefore defends it. But I can see how they [the Tories] would defend it to their own consciences—just as these thrifty Whig farmers hereabout explain in their own minds as patriotic and public-spirited their itching to get hold of Johnson's Manor. Try and look at things in this light. Good and bad are relative terms; nothing is positively and unchangeably evil. Each group of men has its own little world of reasons and motives, its own atmosphere, its own standard of right and wrong [pp. 280–281].

When Douw finally came to battle, "when the stress came," he says, "all this philanthropy fell away," and it is dramatically appropriate that it should. Still, it is a pity that Frederic himself forgot Major Dayton's advice through so many pages of *In the Valley*.

An article by Robert Barr gives weight to the idea that Frederic's temperamental allegiance was not to his three patriot forefathers but to that fourth colonial grandfather who expanded the family record "somewhat indefinitely" by fighting on both sides in the Revolution. Shortly before the end of his life, Frederic outlined to his friend Barr a plan for a new novel. He began by explaining that one of his ancestors was a Hessian brought over by the British to fight in the colonies, "a hired man, as it were, of war. He shot for pay, and not for patriotism." Frederic proposed to write his novel from the point of view of that hired man, "a big swaggering bully." On the one side would be the colonists, "fighting for liberty." On the other the British, "equally honest and determined in the faith that they are putting down disloyalty." And in the middle, "here is our hired man, who despises both sides."

Frederic knew full well how unique an historical novel written from such an irreverent point of view would be:

All the books that have hitherto been written on that struggle are partisan, either British or American, and so far as they are parti-san, are valueless. . . . I shall clear my mind of all sympathy with America, and all prejudice against Great Britain; I shall turn back the clock a century, and be that hired man while I write. I shall give an impartial account of the incidents I take part in, but have no particular interest in, not caring a Continental which side licks, and give my views of these two sets of idiots, speaking the same language and industriously cutting each other's throats, both alike foreigners to me.[27]

The novel outlined to Barr offers convincing evidence that Frederic knew where both the weaknesses of *In the Valley* and his own vigorous strength as a novelist lay. Judging from Frederic's magnificent portrait of Joel Thorpe, the "big swaggering bully" of *The Market-Place*, one can guess that the hired man would have been hair-raising. And doubtless the hired man's narrative would have "walked around men and things and studied them from all sides," as Major Dayton puts it, would have explored the territory that was the subject of Frederic's best fiction, Major Dayton's "little worlds of reasons and motives."

[27] "Harold Frederic, The Author of the Market-Place," *Saturday Evening Post*, CLXXI (1898), 396.

4 / *The Lawton Girl*

Harold Frederic's remarks on *The Lawton Girl* are the most illuminating of the few statements he offered on his own fiction:

"The Lawton Girl" suggested itself at the outset as a kind of sequel to "Seth's Brother's Wife," but here I found myself confronted by agencies and influences the existence of which I had not previously suspected. In "Seth's Brother's Wife" I had made the characters do just what I wanted them to do, and the notion that my will was not altogether supreme had occurred neither to them nor to me. The same had been true of "In the Valley," where indeed the people were so necessarily subordinated to the evolution of the story which they illustrated rather than shaped, that their personalities always remained shadowy in my own mind. But in "The Lawton Girl," to my surprise at first, and then to my interested delight, the people took matters into their own hands quite from the start. It seemed only by courtesy that I even presided over their meetings, and that my sanction was asked for their comings and goings. As one of many examples I may cite the interview between Jessica and Horace in the latter's office. In my folly, I had prepared for her here a part of violent and embittered denunciation, full of scornful epithets and merciless jibes;

to my discomfiture, she relented at the first sight of his gray hair and troubled mein, when I had brought her in, and would have none of my heroics whatever. Once reconciled to the posture of spectator, I grew so interested in the doings of these people that I lost sight of a time-limit; they wandered along for two years, making the story in leisurely fashion as they went. At the end I did assert my authority, and kill Jessica—she who had not deserved or intended at all to die—but I see now more clearly than anyone else that it was a false and cowardly thing to do.[1]

Clearly this is not Frederic's admission of unsurmounted difficulties, not a confession that he lost "control" of the novel in the ordinary sense of the term. Frederic's account of how his characters took matters into their own hands is filled with wonder and delight. The two examples from *The Lawton Girl* that he cites show how right Frederic was to be grateful for his loss of authority. The death of Jessica, through which he reasserted his authority at the conclusion, is undeserved—grotesquely so in fact. And the scene between Horace and Jessica which they conducted on their own is one of the finest in the entire novel.

Frederic's account of how his characters became independent of him was his own declaration of independence. The authority he felt himself losing in *The Lawton Girl* was really no authority at all, but rather subservience to dictates tyran-

---

[1] "Preface to a Uniform Edition," *In the Sixties* (New York, 1897), pp. viii–ix. *The Bookman* (New York) reported an interview with Frederic as follows: "He says that when a book is finished he feels sorry, for the pleasure of a novelist's life is living with his characters. . . . The people go out into the world, and he . . . has to begin all over again and create a new set of friends" ("Chronicle and Comment," III [1896], 384). Frederic's characters "were always very real to him," observed the novelist Robert Barr ("Harold Frederic, the Author of the Market-Place," *Saturday Evening Post*, CLXXI [1898], 396).

nical and fatal to an artist: worn conventions, the moral expectations of the general reading public, and his own weakness for, in his word, "heroics." Although the recognition that killing his fallen woman was a cowardly thing to do came too late to save either Jessica Lawton or the conclusion of the novel, it did come in time to keep Frederic from ever retreating again. In acting as Jessica's executioner, obedient to the law that girls who suffer a fate worse than death must suffer the lesser fate as well, Frederic was abdicating the authority properly his. Was he executioner, or just another victim of the Iron Madonna?

In *Mrs. Albert Grundy: Observations in Philistia* Frederic repeatedly satirizes the woman reader, yet he does it with indulgence and even affection. One reason that Frederic's fiction is so remarkably free of the reticences, indirections, and inhibitions that marked the novels of his day is that he felt little of the fear and impotent hostility that is expressed in H. H. Boyesen's "Iron Madonna who strangles in her fond embrace the American novelist." Frederic's Mrs. Grundy is not an engine of torture who unmans as she caresses; she is a silly and sometimes bothersome woman.

The masculine quality in Frederic that many of his contemporaries emphasize in their reminiscences is one of the distinctive qualities of the artist as well as the man.[2] One cannot speak of Frederic's most important contemporaries in Amer-

[2] The insistence on his manliness which runs through contemporary descriptions of Frederic by men and women alike was inspired in part by his awesome energy and physical strength. One of the best of these accounts is by the poet Louise Imogene Guiney, who summed up Frederic as "a barbaric king." Fears of Iron Madonnas were not without grounds at the turn of the century: Miss Guiney says that her late king would have been "well worth the taming" ("Harold Frederic: A Half-Length Sketch from the Life," *Book Buyer*, XVII [1899], 602).

ican literature—Howells, James, Fuller, Norris, or Crane—as "manly" or "masculine" in quite the sense that the terms apply to him. Frederic once wrote, "I am as little [a] Puritan as another." [3] Possibly one of the reasons Frederic was so easily able to ignore the public censor and renounce "cowardly acts" in his novels is that the private censor was so liberal.

Despite his assertion to the contrary, the mysterious "agencies and influences" that Frederic became conscious of while writing *The Lawton Girl* must have been alive and stirring while he was working on *Seth's Brother's Wife* too. The murder at the conclusion of *Seth* was as cowardly in its way as the gratuitous case of pneumonia that killed off Jessica Lawton. Naked exposure to the cold winds of laughter, not a bullet through the head, was Albert's due fate. And if Annie Fairchild had had her own way and shown the independence that was hers through a good part of *Seth*, she would not have accepted Seth's belated and insulting proposal of marriage after mere token hesitation. At the very least she would have accepted only after playing Laetitia Dale to her rustic Sir Willoughby.

In speaking of his reconciliation to "the posture of spectator," Frederic called attention to one of the sources of his comedy: his ability to sit outside the action of his novels and allow events to be seen from the conflicting points of view of his characters.[4] In *Seth* and *The Lawton Girl* he relinquished authority only intermittently. In *The Damnation of Theron*

[3] From a page of notes on suicide for *The Damnation*, Frederic Papers, Library of Congress.

[4] At the time he was completing *The Damnation* Frederic was asked, "To what extent do you plan your books?" He replied, "In one sense, hardly at all. I seek only to know my people through and through. They make the story 'off their own bat' once they have been started. But you must really know them first" ("How the Popular Harold Frederic Works," *Literary Digest*, XIII [1896], 397).

Ware he remained firmly fixed in his spectator's chair throughout almost the entire novel, and the results were dazzling—as they were to be in his last novel, the sadly neglected *The Market-Place.*

As Frederic said, *The Lawton Girl* is a sequel to *Seth's Brother's Wife*, but only "a kind of sequel." Although the general setting is the same, the plots of the two works do not overlap and the main characters of *The Lawton Girl* appear only as names in *Seth*. Superficially, the four central characters of *The Lawton Girl* stand in very conventional relationship to each other. When the novel appeared, *The Nation* rather wearily typed it as another "industrious and idle apprentice" novel in which the hero "wins the race and the girl, and obtains, but nobly fails to use, the means of punishing his not at all formidable rival." [5] Reuben Tracy is the Industrious Apprentice, the Young Man on the Rise who has worked his way off the farm and through law school to become one of the up-and-coming citizens of Thessaly, New York. His rival and law partner, Horace Boyce, is the Idle Apprentice, the Young Man on the Make. He is spoiled, snobbish, lying, and weak. Even before exposure to the moral debilitations of a four-year tour of the Continent, he was a cad, for he is the father of Jessica's illegitimate son.

The two principal women of the novel seem to form an equally neat pair. Jessica Lawton is the Bad Woman. A daughter of the poorest family in town, she not only bears the stigma of her bastard but has been a prostitute as well. Kate Minster, the beauteous Good Woman, is everything that Jessica is not. She is the maidenly daughter of the richest man in town and the descendant of a prominent colonial family.

[5] LI (1890), 195.

The final disposition of this quartet is all too predictable: Horace gets his comeuppance, Kate and Reuben get each other, and Jessica, as we have seen, pays the price.

This is unpromising material to work with, but as Frederic implied later when he admitted that Jessica neither "deserved nor intended to die," *The Lawton Girl* is not an essentially conventional novel. Something of its true originality is suggested by the title, which focuses on the fallen woman rather than the virtuous Kate; Frederic's early working title, "Reuben Tracy's Partner," had similarly focused on Horace Boyce rather than Tracy.[6] The discarded title would have been the better one for the novel. Although Jessica and Kate are well-drawn, both they and Reuben (who is generally not much more than the stock hero) are of far less interest than Horace Boyce, whose characterization, as Howells said, is "masterly." [7]

"I call people rich," said Ralph Touchett in *The Portrait of a Lady*, "when they're able to meet the requirements of their imagination." Poor Ralph did not know the reaches of the American imagination in the Gilded Age as Frederic did. If he had, Ralph would have had to stretch considerably his own imagination. Horace's reach so far exceeds his grasp that he comes up empty-handed, but even had he managed to grab Kate Minster and her two-and-one-half million dollars, Horace would never have been able to satisfy the adolescent appetite of his imagination.

Horace is by no means the only character in *The Lawton Girl* who lives an elaborate fantasy life. Throughout the novel

---

[6] Paul Haines saw working notes under this title in the collection of Mrs. Eliot Keen, Frederic's daughter ("Harold Frederic" [unpub. Ph.D. diss., New York University, 1945], p. 284).

[7] *Harper's Monthly*, LXXXI (1890), 801.

Frederic juxtaposes the solid exterior world of the setting and the free-floating interior worlds of the main characters, who habitually express themselves in terms out of sentimental romantic fiction. Frederic had used this ironic device before, in his treatment of Seth and Isabel, for example, but in *The Lawton Girl* it comes closer to the brilliance it was to have in the later works.

Horace's daydreams are vividly real to him. He has only to come across some reminder of Kate Minster for his visions to become "as if by magic, all rosy-hued and definite." Once he is wed to the beautiful Kate and the beautiful Minster Iron Works, Horace will become a personage:

He might be a senator in Congress, minister to Paris, or even aspire to the towering, solitary eminence of the Presidency itself with the backing of these millions. It meant a yacht, the very dream of sea-going luxury and speed, . . . in which to loiter lazily along the topaz shores of far Cathay, to flit to and fro between spice lands and cold northern seas, the whole watery globe subject to her keel. Why, there could be a castle on the Moselle, a country house in Devonshire, a flat in Paris, a villa at Mentone, a summer island home on the St. Lawrence, a mansion in New York—all together, if he liked, or as many as pleased his whim [pp. 130–131].[8]

Passages like this, which are common in Frederic's later novels as well as *The Lawton Girl*, suggest Theodore Dreiser. Carey McWilliams thought it quite probable that Carrie Meeber owed something to Jessica Lawton, and perhaps she does, but the Dreiser novel that comes most forceably to mind when reading *The Lawton Girl* is *An American Tragedy*.[9]

[8] All page references to *The Lawton Girl* are to the first American edition (New York: Charles Scribner's Sons, 1890).

[9] "Harold Frederic: 'A Country Boy of Genius,'" *University of California Chronicle*, XXXV (Jan., 1933), 28. The strong similarities

Some of the parallels between the two works are obvious: both are set in upper New York State factory towns—Dreiser's Lycurgus could be Frederic's Thessaly a few years later; and Clyde and Horace yearn to marry rich, beautiful heiresses but manage only to seduce working girls and get them pregnant. The parallels extend further than this, however. The story of the rise and fall of Horace Boyce is a comedy, not a tragedy, but it is very distinctly an American comedy.

Like Clyde Griffiths, Horace Boyce is the victim of a hodgepodge mythology of success. Horace's revery on the possibilities of his future suggests the vulgarity of his ideals. Late in the nineteenth century, the young American's inalienable right and obligation to aspire to the Presidency became considerably enlarged. It was amended to include other

————

between the two authors have gone virtually unnoticed except for occasional brief asides like McWilliams'. Both men prepared for the writing of their novels in similar fashion, a fact attested to by the mass of extracts and clippings on subjects ranging from Methodism to plant hybridization which is to be found in the notes for *The Damnation* in the Frederic Papers, Library of Congress. Their lives are somewhat similar; both came from households in which the mother held things together, both were experienced journalists, and both had problems with women. Even in appearance Dreiser and Frederic (whose ancestry was Dutch and German) resembled each other; both were big, bearish men who combined what was sometimes the appearance of lethargy with tremendous resources of energy. Because of their blend of affectation and provincial manners, both suffered repeatedly from caricatures of themselves as loutish "country boys of genius." How familiar Dreiser was with Frederic's fiction is impossible to say. It is not likely that he could have resisted a successful *Saturday Evening Post* novel called *The Market-Place*. He once listed Frederic as one of several authors "of real literary distinction" whose work had been "most utterly and completely neglected" (letter to Edward H. Smith, Dec. 26, 1920, quoted in Robert H. Elias, ed., *The Letters of Theodore Dreiser* [Philadelphia, 1959], I, 228–229).

goals, such as villas in France and seagoing yachts.[10] Horace habitually thinks of Kate as "the daughter of the millions"; for him, as for Clyde, the glamorous beauty and the wealth of the heiress he hopes to marry are inextricably one.

Horace does not start as far down the ladder as Dreiser's hero nor even as far down as most of Frederic's other protagonists. His father, General Sylvanus Boyce, established a prosperous hardware store before going off to the Civil War to make a name for himself as Thessaly's only war hero; and Horace's mother left twenty thousand dollars for him to claim when he came of age. Horace has spent the four years preceding the opening of *The Lawton Girl* traveling and pretending to study law in Europe. His social and financial position, however, is scarcely as lofty as all this suggests.

As the novel begins, Horace is returning home from the Continent not only polished but cleaned out: he has spent all of his inheritance and arrives home the day before Thanksgiving with little to be thankful for. Walking from the station with Reuben Tracy, Horace comes upon a turkey shoot outside a ramshakle country inn of evil repute. More a snob than ever after his sojourn abroad, Horace says, "You won't find any gentlemen here." Echoing his remark, "as if in ironical

---

[10] "The turn of the century was a time when expenditure was accepted as the outward sign of Divine Grace," A. J. Liebling reminds us. "The steam yacht was the nimbus" ("The Dollars Damned Him," *New Yorker*, XXXVII [Aug. 5, 1961], 48). Although Liebling's article is on Stephen Crane and mentions Frederic only briefly, it is worth the attention of those interested in Frederic. Liebling focuses on the financial difficulties of authorship and argues that Crane's money worries were fatally aggravated by the inflated idea at the turn of the century of what a decent income was. Frederic's correspondence for the last decade of his life repeatedly refers to his frustration at being unable to sacrifice the income from his newspaper work in order to devote himself full time to his fiction.

answer," comes a strident voice through the crowd: "I'll bet five dollars that General Boyce kills his six birds in ten shots— bad cartridges barred!" (p. 45). One look at his father's alcoholic countenance, the outline of the profile "blurred and fattened," is enough to tell Horace that his father is not the first citizen of Thessaly he has always considered him to be.

Over the years since Appomattox, the sign above the hard-ware store that Vane Boyce established has changed from "Sylvanus Boyce" to "Boyce and Co." to "Boyce & Tenney" and finally—though the " & Co." has been mere formality for some time—to "S. Tenney & Co." Mr. S. Tenney—the *S* stands for Schuyler but might as well be Snopes—is a wonderful creation. "To the cursory glance," Frederic remarks, he looks "like any other of ten hundred hundreds of young Americans who are engaged in making more money than they need." Garbed in a "drab mustache," Tenney wears "neat gray clothes, of uniform pattern and strictly commercial aspect" (pp. 115–116), and his conversation is as strictly commercial as his clothes: to hear him talk is to take a course in the economic theory of the nineties.

When Tenney first comes to him with a vague deal that is little more than a plot to plunder the Minster fortune, Horace asks for more details. Tenney answers:

Broadly, what does everybody propose? To get for himself what somebody else has got. That's human nature. It's every kind of nature, down to the little chickens just hatched who start to chase the chap with the worm in his mouth before they've fairly got their tails out of the shell. . . . We are all worms, so the Bible says.

"You ought to write a book, Schuyler," is Horace's sarcastic reply, "Tenney on Dynamic Sociology" (p. 225). As Frederic notes, this is the first time Horace has called Tenney by his first name; sarcastic or not, Horace is a hooked worm. His misapplication of Lester Ward's "dynamic sociology" to describe Tenney's crude brand of Social Darwinism is surely Frederic's ironic comment on the muddled socio-economic thought of the age, an irony comparable to that implicit in Tenney's "we are all worms, so the Bible says"—a delightful blend of Darwin and the Good Book.

Other remarks of Tenney's prompt Horace to jibe at "Tenney on Faith, Justified by Works," but he listens with rapt interest. "Dishonesty is wrong," goes the spiel, "and it is foolish. It gets a man disgraced, and it gets him in jail. But commercial acumen is another thing" (p. 227). Finally settling down to the business at hand, Tenney asks:

Where do you suppose Steve Minster got his millions? Did you think he minted them? Didn't every dollar pass through some other fellow's pocket before it reached his? . . . Everybody is looking out to get rich; and when a man succeeds, it only means that somebody else has got poor. That's plain common-sense! [p. 233].

Horace quickly succumbs to "common sense," a commodity he stocks in very short supply. The offer to gain him entrée into the Minster home as family lawyer is too much for his doubts. He agrees to help Tenney and a mysterious Judge Wendover in whatever their scheme is—so long as it is honest, he feebly adds. In all this Horace is as much victim as villain. He has the catch phrases of Social Darwinism down perfectly: "If it comes to 'dog eat dog,'" he says of his new partners, "they'll find my teeth are filed down to a point quite as sharp as theirs" (p. 339). But he is most unfit to play the rugged beast in the money jungle. Like Clyde Griffiths, he is a rather helpless little animal, so much the self-deceiver that he can scarcely hope to deceive others for long.

The extraordinary nature of Horace's self-deception is revealed by the metaphors in which he thinks. Mixed in with figures of Horace the sharp-fanged is a comically incongruous strain of stock romantic images. Courting Kate, he picks up a chance reference to farthingales and immediately launches into an expansive rhapsody on the days of romance:

Perhaps they were not so altogether lovely as our fancy paints them; but, all the same, it is very sweet to have the fancy. . . . Those who possess it are rich in their own mind's right. They can always escape from the grimy and commercial conditions of this present work-a-day life. All one's finer senses can feed, for example, on a glowing account of an old-time tournament . . . as it is impossible to do on the report of a meeting of a board of directors [p. 241].[11]

Horace is playing the bantering lover's role of course, but his farewell to Kate at the end of the call is heartfelt: "I wanted so much to go away with the fancy that this was an enchanted palace, and that you were shut up alone in it waiting for—" (p. 244). The role of knight is one that comes easily to Horace's fancy. He does think of Kate as a princess in a castle, and he is determined to penetrate the "elaborate system of defenses" that the Minsters have thrown up around their "battlements" (pp. 30–31) so that he can win the daughter of millions with the "regal" bearing and the complexion of "an Oriental queen" (p. 26).

[11] Frederic had no sympathy with either *When Knighthood Was in Flower* sentimentality or with the kind of "longing medievalism" Thomas Beer finds so pronounced in Stephen Crane's poetry. Frederic's *Yellow Book* story, "The Truce of the Bishop," is typical of his medieval stories. It expresses little of the "deep nostalgia for the pagan world of cruelty, marble, pomp, and lust" which Van Wyck Brooks finds characteristic of *The Yellow Book* and *fin de siècle* writing in general (*The Confident Years* [New York, 1952], p. 263).

Even when he can no longer conceal from himself that he has joined with Wendover and Tenney to strip the Minsters clean, Horace persists in deluding himself, in playing the wolf in shining armor. At the last minute, he thinks, he will dramatically revolt against his partners, "throw himself into a virtuous attitude, and win credit and gratitude at the hands of the family by protecting them from their enemies." One course he never seriously contemplates is honesty—"the case was too complicated for mere honesty" (pp. 236–237).

On the day that Horace goes to propose to Kate, all his dreams collapse. He dresses for the event carefully: frock coat, fine tie of ribbed silk, cameo pin, fur-trimmed overcoat, glossy top hat, and fawn-colored gloves of soft suede. "He remembered that minute before the looking-glass, in the after-time, as the culmination of his upward career. It was the proudest, most perfectly contented moment of his adult life" (p. 341).

The vision of splendid success is rudely shattered soon after Horace and his father enter the Minster mansion. Waiting in the parlor, Horace hears Kate address his father in the hall: "Your son is not a good man or an honest man, and I wish never to see him again" (p. 345). While the father and son are walking home together, Horace tries to intercept a letter intended for Kate, and the General suddenly sees just how dishonest his son is: "You *are* a damn scoundrel!" he shouts. Horace's defense is self-righteous, self-pitying, and not at all convincing: all his maneuvering, he says, has been to rehabilitate a drunken father who nevertheless has pulled him down. Retribution is swift. Before he turns and strides away, the General takes a sweeping look at his elegant son and bursts "boisterously forth into a loud guffaw of contemptuous laughter" (pp. 349–350). The many nineteenth-century critics who objected, as did William Morton Payne, that Horace was "let off far too easily" for his sins cannot have heard that laughter.[12]

Whether or not something of Frederic's fallen woman went into Carrie Meeber, one can find no character in American fiction before Dreiser's great heroine with whom to compare Jessica Lawton. In one of the remarkable articles on prostitution that he wrote a few years before *The Lawton Girl*, Frederic stressed "the quieter regions of the calling which I know, [where] I never found the women other than kindly and gentle, and by no means addicted to drinking or obscene language." [13] Frederic's treatment of Jessica is distinguished by the same calm and unsensational tone. Although she has suf-

---

[12] *The Dial*, XI (Aug., 1890), 93. The conclusion of *The Lawton Girl* was not cowardly enough for many critics, for Frederic did not hand out jail sentences to Horace, Tenney, or Wendover. "How he reconciles this to his conscience," *The Nation* said, "we fail to see" (LI [Sept. 4, 1890], 195).

[13] "From a Saunterer in the Labyrinth," *Pall Mall Budget*, XXXIII (July 24, 1885), 22. This and "Musings on the Question of the Hour" (*Pall Mall Budget*, XXXIII [Aug. 13, 1885], 11-12) were part of the famous crusade which William T. Stead carried on in his *Pall Mall Gazette* and *Budget* to pass the Criminal Law Amendment Bill, aimed primarily at raising the age of consent from thirteen to sixteen. Stead's biographer says that in Frederic's articles, "a wordly-minded contributor had been allowed to give what was by way of being the Devil's point of view, and it was beyond question a very cynical and immoral disquisition, strangely out of place in the paper at such a moment" (Frederic Whyte, *The Life of W. T. Stead* [New York, 1925], I, 179). Frederic's calm discussions do indeed seem strangely out of place next to Stead's. In "The Maiden Tribute of Modern Babylon," Stead described how he publicized his cause by buying a thirteen-year-old virgin from her mother for three pounds down and two on promise. Frederic's description of Stead is admirable: a combination of "Chadband, Ignatius Loyola, Lydia Languish, and Giteau" (quoted in Whyte, *Life of Stead*, I, 114).

fered from her experience, she has not coarsened. She has been saddened, not brutalized; scarred, not hardened. Her reputation is so damaged that her passion to "live it down" in Thessaly may be impossible to realize, but it is very clear that her character has suffered no damage that cannot be repaired.

Jessica is neither the harlot of lurid realism nor the victim of the conventional maid's tragedy. When she first appears she is crying, but hers is not "a face with which one, at first glance, would readily associate tears." Frederic describes her in a passage particularly reminiscent of Dreiser's prose, from the careful description of her outfit to the smart journalese of "the managing division of the human race":

The features were regularly, almost firmly cut; and the eyes . . . had commonly a wide-awake, steady, practical look, which expressed anything rather than weakness. The effect of the countenance, as a whole, suggested an energetic, self-contained young woman, who knew her way about, who was likely to be neither cheated nor flattered out of her rights, and who distinctly belonged to the managing division of the human race. This conception of her was aided by the erect, independent carriage of her shoulders, which made her seem taller than she really was, and by the clever simplicity of her black tailor-made jacket and dress, and her round, shapely, turban-like hat [pp. 12–13].

Jessica is as self-reliant as she looks, but her plan to live with her family proves impossible. Something of the nature of the Lawton household can be guessed from the names of the five slatternly sisters poor Jess has to confront: the eldest is Melissa, then comes Lucinda, then Samantha, who seems to her mother to resemble the heroines of the serials in *The Fireside Weekly*, and finally there are the overgrown twins, Georgiana and Arabella. The mother of these five stepsisters, Frederic says, would have been happier in England; there "she would have taken to drink, and been beaten for it, and thus at least extracted from life's pilgrimage some definite sensations" (p. 77).[14] If Frederic were really a grim and bitter critical realist, one would hardly expect the Lawtons to be treated so humorously. The father of the family, Ben Lawton, was a bargeman before the canals were supplanted by the railroads. Frederic could have viewed him as a victim of technological unemployment; instead, he portrays him as a good-natured and comic ne'er-do-well.

The really odd thing about Jessica, what makes her so unconventional in her role of fallen woman, is that most of the time she is just what one exepects to find in a conventional blonde heroine. The misery of her home life and a deadly boredom drove her into Horace's arms, but Jessica remains very much as Reuben Tracy remembers her—one of the sweetest, hardest-working, best-behaved pupils he ever taught. In Frederic's fiction Jessica is not related to lush, free-mannered young women like Isabel Fairchild and Celia Madden, but to women like Annie Fairchild and Alice Ware, who combine a strain of patient endurance with a yielding weakness for men who are boyish, weak, and hypocritical.

When Jessica returns to Thessaly she thinks of Reuben and Horace as "her good and her evil genius," but her endeavor to transform her experience into melodrama does not succeed. In the scene that Frederic later singled out as one in which his characters took matters into their own hands, the scene in

---

[14] Frederic repeatedly implies parallels between the Minsters and the Lawtons. Mrs. Minster and Mrs. Lawton are stupidly alike in "the lack of definite sensation" they share, and in their custom of sleeping away as much of existence as they can. "Thanksgiving at the Minsters' " is neatly followed two chapters later by "Thanksgiving at the Lawtons'." Jessica and Kate share boredom as a major problem of their lives.

which Jessica and Horace are reconciled, Frederic's understanding of his characters proves far stronger than his obedience to convention. Jessica does not meet her seducer with recrimination but with pity and compassion; she realizes that she is not a ruined woman in the way that Horace is a ruined man, that in truth she is far more capable and strong than the man she has hitherto sentimentalized as her wicked betrayer.

Kate Minster is no more the stock Good Woman than Jessica Lawton is the Bad Woman. For one thing, Kate is sexually attractive, surprisingly more so than Jessica, the unwed mother and former prostitute. No frail blonde, Kate is a tall, forceful woman with raven hair, "softly luxuriant" olive skin, and "large, richly brown, deep-fringed eyes which looked proudly and steadily on all the world, young men included" (p. 26). With the somewhat tedious Reuben Tracy, Frederic returns to the conventional good hero he had come so close to abandoning in his portrait of Seth Fairchild. Of course the real line of development from Seth to such antiheroes as Theron Ware and Joel Thorpe is through Horace, who, if not technically the protagonist of *The Lawton Girl*, does dominate it and can hardly be called the villain in the ordinary sense of the word. In the character of Kate Minster, however, Frederic abandons the conventional heroine once and for all: Kate's portrait derives from Isabel, the bored vamp of *Seth*, rather than from the patient school-teacher Annie Fairchild.

Frederic manages with great skill to portray Kate as a passionate and spirited young woman while at the same time showing her almost entirely through the eyes of two suitors who sentimentalize her outrageously. Horace, as we have seen, turns her into a fairy tale princess, and Reuben is not much better. On two of the few occasions she and Reuben are seen together in the novel, Kate wears a gown that seems to Reuben "sanctified and symbolical . . . enshrined in his heart with incense and candles and solemn veneration" (p. 382). In a fine touch suggesting that his thoughts are far less spiritual than he thinks, Reuben dwells on the garment,

chiefly upon the large twisted silken cord which girdled the waist of that wonderful young woman, and the tassled ends of which hung against the white front of her gown like the beads of a nun. Many variant thoughts . . . rose in his mind and pleasantly excited it, but they all in turn merged vaguely into fancies circling around that glossy rope and weaving themselves into its strands [pp. 281–282].

Passages like this are common in Frederic's novels. He delights in recording the comic weakness of the American male for concealing his sexual desires by swaddling them in idealism. When one of Frederic's young men starts thinking of a woman as a Madonna, as Seth does of Isabel and Theron Ware does of Celia Madden, it is a sure sign that the young lady has charms something more than spiritual and that the young man will soon be kissing more than the hem of her gown.

It is not surprising that Kate finds Horace's flirtatious talk of knights and ladies attractive for a time, just as she appears to find Reuben's idolization even more attractive. She has a weakness for romance herself. When she becomes anxious about the tortuous financial dealings into which Horace and Wendover are leading her mother, Kate seeks Tracy's advice. His prim and lofty reminder that Horace is his law partner and that there is such a thing as a professional code of ethics is not a bit to Kate's liking. "What kind of a hero is it," she fumes, "who, when you cry for assistance, calmly says: 'Upon the lines you suggest I do not see my way'? It is high time the books about chivalry were burned, if *that is* the modern man" (pp. 285–286).

There is nothing of the Madonna or the fairy princess in Kate Minster, Reuben and Horace notwithstanding. She has inherited her father's boundless energy but has been able to find no satisfying outlet for it. Since her brother drank himself to death and her father died, Kate has had her own way in the lonely home that she shares with her mother and sister. There is a difference between having her own way and knowing which way to take, however, and Kate is bored and restless. Her family is not much company. Her sister is a sweet young girl, but she suffers from some mysterious infirmity that is probably neurasthenia. Her mother, the granddaughter of Douw and Daisy Mauverenson from *In the Valley*, is an aristocratic-looking woman who gives the appearance of unusually high intelligence and shrewdness and who suffers from an infirmity that is definitely stupidity. She too is bored, but she accepts boredom "as a natural and proper result of her condition in life, much as one accepts an uncomfortable sense of repletion after a dinner." She divides her day between naps and "the writing of long and perfectly commonplace letters to female relatives" (p. 59).

The first real introduction to the Minsters comes in a chapter describing Thanksgiving dinner in their mansion. The surroundings dampen any possibility of pleasure. Frederic's fine, detailed description of the heavy hangings, the massive furniture of dark oak and leather, and the ponderous mantel laden with bric-a-brac carries with it the very odor of smothering Victorian opulence. Frederic leaves no doubt that there is little joy or light at the Thanksgiving board in the greatest house in Thessaly.

The Minsters' isolation from life is nowhere more evident than in the distance they keep from the hundreds of workers who labor in their mill. At the conclusion of *The Lawton Girl* there is a reconciliation between capital and labor such as can be found in countless other nineteenth-century novels: the bad capitalists are routed, the misguided workers are shown the light, and the Minsters are joined once more in amity with their mill hands. Frederic's account of the Minsters' inability to find any useful function for, or even pleasure in, their millions, however, is far more convincing than the final note of the novel affirming the mutual dependence of owner and worker. A comment of Jessica's father, the poorest, most disreputable man in Thessaly, echoes far beyond that sweet note. When Ben Lawton hears that Kate is distressed to learn there is to be a lockout at the mill, he says, "She'll wear her sealskin and eat pie just the same" (p. 310).

To be fair to Kate, she does interest herself in Jessica's project to help poor factory girls. When she first hears of the plan, Kate is filled with enthusiasm, subscribes a large contribution, and begins to think of herself as an American counterpart of the wonder-working heiress in Walter Besant's *All Sorts and Conditions of Men*.[15] Her dreams quickly take form and shape in her mind "like Aladdin's palace" (p. 205), but

[15] This novel (1882) so captured the public's imagination that a "People's Palace" modeled on the one established by Besant's hero and heroine was actually built in London in 1887. An ambiguous entry in Moses Coit Tyler's diary suggests that Frederic may have accompanied Tyler on a visit to the People's Palace on May 30, 1889, after showing him the manuscript of *The Lawton Girl* (Jessica Tyler Austen, ed., *Moses Coit Tyler* [Garden City, N.Y., 1911], p. 247). The project in *The Lawton Girl* for a "Working Girls' Resting House" is a modest version of the "People's Palace."

before long she loses interest in "The Working Girls' Resting House," which she revealingly speaks of as "really a pet of mine" (p. 396).

The trouble with Kate is that she has too much ambition and energy to be content with mere pets. Frederic says of her:

As a girl she had dreamed her dreams—bold, sweepingly ambitious visions they were; but this father of whom she was so proud, this powerful father who had so manfully subdued things under his feet, was always the one who was to encompass their fulfillment. When he died, her aërial castles at a stroke tumbled into chaos. . . . Without him all was disorganized, shapeless, incomprehensible [p. 156].[16]

There is, Frederic says, "something alike grotesque and pathetic" in the record of Kate's endeavors to find something to do in the world. She has collected all sorts of thing, orchids, coins, cameos, only to turn on them "with disgust and wrath." She has taken up and abandoned music, painting, and writing short stories. She has gathered at great expense all the materials to write a definitive life of Lady Arabella Stuart, "only to discover that she did not know how to make a book, and would not want to make that kind of a book if she had known

[16] With the same reticence that leaves the reader of *Seth* wondering just what sort of politician Senator Fairchild was, Frederic never reveals whether Stephen Minster was a captain of industry or a robber baron. When Minster died, he was "mourned by a community which . . . could remember no single lapse from honesty or kindliness in his whole, unostentatious, useful career" (p. 24). Nevertheless, there is something suspicious in Kate's memory of a father who had "manfully subdued things under his feet," as there is in the fact that Minster's will did not leave a penny to charity. One hesitates to make any great point about Minster—the whole business of the will receives only a paragraph—but Frederic's treatment of him is characteristic. Even in passages of apparently straight narrative, ambiguous possibilities lie just beneath the surface.

how." [17] Kate has her dreams, her beauty, her wealth: "All the conditions for achievement were hers to command, and there was nothing to achieve" (p. 157).

Kate Minster is obviously one of those New Women who were so much the talk in the nineties. There is something in her dilemma, however, that is common to both sexes. Frederic was interested in the New Woman—Isabel Fairchild, Celia Madden, Lady Cressage, and Frances Bailey can all be classed as such—but he found that their problems were shared by the New Man as well. Later, in the career of Christian Tower, the hero of *Gloria Mundi,* he would work out with elaborate skill and interest the implications of the same question posed in his portrait of Kate: granted good will and power, what then?

The insubstantial dreams of the central characters of *The Lawton Girl* stand in vivid contrast to the solid streets and buildings of their town. When the novel opens, Jessica and Horace are arriving home after extended absences, and it is through their comparatively fresh eyes that the reader first sees Thessaly. To Jessica the town seems at moments almost unrecognizable. Four years have sufficed to transform it from little more than a village to nearly a city. The scene she beholds is a bewildering composite of decay and burgeoning prosperity. The weathered clapboard on the hotel is in even greater need of paint than it was when Jessica left, but right next door, where an uneven line of bedraggled sheds used to stand, is a new fire house; through its open door she can glimpse a modern "steamer," though it seems to her only

---

[17] Compare Frederic's statement on the composition of *In the Valley:* "I did not know how to make a book of any kind, let alone a historical book of the kind that should be the most difficult and exacting of all" (Preface to a Uniform Edition," p. viii). It is interesting to speculate that Frederic, after completing his historical novel, may have decided that he too "did not want to make that kind of book."

yesterday that the town rejoiced in the acquisition of a hand pumper.

Horace, who has been home for a flying visit a few months before, is not so surprised as offended by what he sees. He continually contrasts everything on the native scene with Europe and finds much to condemn, from the new architectural vogue of one-story, flat-topped buildings to the blackhead American sulfur matches that so offend his nose.

Thessaly is viewed directly through the eyes of the narrator as well. Observing the Minster Mills as they stand closed, Frederic looks in the grimy windows where "the huge dark forms of the motionless machines showed dimly, like fossils of extinct monsters in a museum." And he notes the way the American workingman is so bitten "with the eager habitude of labor" that even on holidays, "some time during the day finds himself close to the place where at other times he is employed" (p. 352).

The point has often been made that Frederic's residence abroad gradually sapped the native sources of his inspiration as a novelist. It seems far more likely that his concern with getting down the details of the American scene in much of his fiction was greatly stimulated by living out of the country. He saw America with a fresh eye on his real and imaginary visits home, and the uninformed interest of Englishmen who listened to his stories of New York must have suggested to him that things about American life he took for granted would be new and strange to many readers. Furthermore, he must have been particularly aware that English readers of his fiction would not understand the American background unless he described it with care.

Although Frederic finds little to admire in the raw newness and turmoil of Thessaly, he contemplates the changing scene with neither Jessica's regret nor Horace's contempt. Schuyler Tenney and others of the new breed are real Snopeses, but Frederic erects no myth of an antebellum world against which to measure the modern world. It is true that Squire Gedney and General Boyce, both older men, do have a certain generosity and chivalry, but they are also weak and drunken failures. There are, moreover, other representatives of the older generation, stupid, snobbish Mrs. Minster, for example, and Judge Wendover, Tenney's partner in crime. The judge traces his ancestry back to the Mauverensons of the Revolutionary period and maintains the dress of the old-fashioned gentleman, but the only tradition to which he really subscribes is the venerable one of grabbing everything that is not nailed down tight. Frederic is obviously neither the champion of the traditional nor the critic of the modern.

The appearance of Thessaly betrays a confusion between the ideal and the actual similar to that which afflicts the main characters of the novel. Even the farmers, who become progressively more impoverished as the town prospers, are proud of the growing town that will soon be chartered a city. Farmer and businessman alike find its drab new buildings, its smoke-grimed station, all beautiful: "Everybody was proud of Thessaly" (p. 142).

In the old days, Frederic says, Emerson used to give public lectures at the seminary on top of the hill overlooking the town. Those days are gone now, and there are hundreds of adults "in this modern Thessaly, with its factories and mills, its semi-foreign saloons, and its long streets of uniformly ugly cottage dwellings," who do not know, or care, whether the once-celebrated seminary is still open or not (p. 144). Yet one suspects that a good many of the materialistic citizens of Thessaly remain transcendentalists of a sort.

Thessaly no longer builds the sepulchers of the fathers; now she builds new firehouses. The fire engine Jessica sees is a natural fact that surely symbolizes a spiritual fact to Thessaly's uplifted eyes. The "brassy brightness" of the new fire engine casts a radiance more than material. The gleaming wagon, with its coils of hose and shining boiler, is hitched to a star. The wagon may jounce and bump a bit along the potholed, muddy streets now, but Thessaly has no doubt that soon it will soar aloft, grandly and beauteously, onward and upward.

The aspirations of the generous, well-intentioned Kate are not so very different from Horace Boyce's. Both Horace and Kate are unable to come to terms with the fact that hard cash is, after all, very hard. He assumes that money and happiness are synonymous; she, that they ought to be, that power ought to make all things possible, ought to enable one to do great and good things. Nor are Kate and Horace alone in this most unmaterialistic assumption that somehow Paradise can be regained, or at least reconstructed along the best modern lines. The same fantastic confidence that life can be spiritualized through material means is implicit in Jessica's belief that there would be no more tragedies like hers if only there were Girls' Resting Houses to provide innocent entertainment for working girls. It is implicit in Reuben Tracy, who can "never contemplate injustices, great or small, without longing to set them right" (p. 265), and who attacks the injustices of the world with the same faith in mechanical improvement that the Yankee tinkerer brought to his work shop. And it is implicit in that shiny new fire engine.

In a comic scene that stakes out ground Sinclair Lewis was to explore thirty years later, Frederic shows how Horace and the other young professional and business men of the town turn Reuben Tracy's dream of a reform club to solve social problems into a booster club.[18] Are the ideals of Horace and Reuben so very different? When the reader is allowed into the Minster dining room a second time, many months have passed since the somber Thanksgiving, and this time the reader sees the room through Reuben's eyes. Reuben has pacified the angry mill workers and sent them from the front lawn of the Minster mansion. Now he is invited into the house to take some refreshment.

The second to last chapter contains the comic resolution of the novel. It is at this point that Reuben begins to realize that he has won Kate. Henceforth his life will take him into many houses like this; he will sup at many tables like this.

The scene which opened upon Reuben's eyes was like a vista of fairyland. The dark panelled room, with its dim suggestions of gold frames and heavy curtains, and its background of palms and oleanders, contributed with the reticence of richness to the glowing splendor of the table in its centre. Here all light was concentrated—light which . . . softened the dazzling whiteness of the linen, mellowed the burnished gleam of the silver plate, reflected itself in tender, prismatic hues from the facets of the cut-glass decanters. There were flowers here . . . and fragile, painted china, and all the nameless things of luxury which can make the breaking of bread a poem.

Reuben had seen something dimly resembling this in New York once or twice at semi-public dinners. The thought that this higher marvel was in his honor intoxicated his reason. The other thought —that conceivably his future might lie all in this flower-strewn, daintily lighted path—was too heady, too full of threatened delirium, to be even entertained [pp. 451–452].

[18] *The Nation*, missing Frederic's comedy entirely but providing a little of its own, objected that "The Thessaly Citizens' Club" was "not at all what a well-conducted reform club in a novel should be" (LI [1890], 195).

Reuben, it appears, is partner to Horace Boyce in more than law practice. We cannot assume his damnation, but surely, as the language of light and intoxication suggest, he has experienced "illumination" of a most equivocal sort.

Like most of Frederic's novels, *The Lawton Girl* treats conventional materials in a highly unconventional fashion. It begins with a cast that scarcely seems to require introduction: a poor but idealistic schoolmaster become lawyer; an unscrupulous and weak-willed lawyer out to marry and defraud a wealthy heroine; a fallen woman determined to redeem herself; a beautiful heiress who wishes to devote herself to philanthropy. As the novel progresses, however, it becomes increasingly clear that it is the characters' own ideas of themselves that are conventional and sentimental. To read *The Lawton Girl* simply as a realistic rendering of small town life is to overlook the more impressive achievement: Frederic's wry and good-natured exposure of the comic contrast between the grand roles that people plan for themselves and the roles they actually play.

5 / The Damnation of
Theron Ware

A snatch of conversation preserved by Booth Tarkington from his salad days conveys the enthusiasm with which Harold Frederic was discovered in 1896:

"I'm going to take you to dinner at the Lantern Club," he said. "Irving Bacheller's the toastmaster; Steve Crane's a member and he knows Harold Frederic. Has anybody ever written a better novel than Frederic's *Damnation of Theron Ware*?"

"No, it isn't possible to write a finer novel." [1]

Frederic had never been lost, of course—his first three novels received considerable attention—but as time passed it became increasingly difficult to know where to locate him. In 1892 he had published a fourth novel, *The Return of the O'Mahony*.[2] This amazing venture into a kind of comic gothic ro-

[1] *The World Does Move* (Garden City, N.Y., 1928), pp. 21–22.

[2] New York: Robert Bonner's Sons. For an account of Frederic's deep interest in Ireland and Irish politics, see Stanton Garner, "Some Notes on Harold Frederic in Ireland," *American Literature*, XXXIX (1967), 60–74. Garner observes that *The Return*, completed the month in which Parnell died, is not the "lighthearted novel of modern Ireland" that it is usually taken to be; it "seems rather a rearguard action against despair" over Ireland's future (p. 66).

mance embodied a serious concern for the problems of Ireland in a fantastic plot revolving around a town full of vaudeville Paddies and a Yankee deserter from the battle of Petersburg, Virginia. Bad as it is, *The Return of the O'Mahony* is worth a glance, for it marks an interesting stage in the development of Frederic's thought.

In *In the Valley*, Frederic's original conception of the Revolution as a struggle between good patriots and bad Tories had been undermined by his growing conviction that men are animated not by large public motives but by small and essentially unchanging self-interests. In *Seth's Brother's Wife* and *The Lawton Girl*, although his ostensible subject remained the struggle between good and bad, his real concern was consistent and apparent: the illusions of those who think themselves the reformers of the world. Even Horace Boyce, like Theron Ware after him, can be thought of as a kind of reformer, for it is Horace's delusion that he is a triumph of self-development, an example of the worldly cultivation he promises to bring to his village when he is elected first president of the Thessaly Reform Club.

In *The Damnation of Theron Ware* and even more in the novels that follow it, Frederic continued to expose the vanity of individuals who are dazzled by their own enlightenment or by the prospect of enlightening the world. But he began to wonder whether all hopes of reform were not doomed to disappointment in the face of the essentially unchanging nature of man and the inertia of life. Even Theron Ware has moments when he begins to realize what all his "new" ideas imply. He talks to Sister Soulsby about the repelling thought that "the dead men have known more than we know, done more than we do; that there is nothing new anywhere." She brings him up short: "Never mind the dead men" (p. 181).[3] There is some sense to what she says, and certainly it is in the American grain: "history is bunk." But in *The Return of the O'Mahony* and all of the novels that follow it, the characters in Frederic's fiction are rarely able to forget the dead men for long.

Frederic's consciousness of a past that mocks man's dreams of improvement is central to *The Return*. An American named Zeke Tisdale fraudulently lays claim to an Irish estate only to find that he has acquired nothing but the responsibility for a tiny fishing village suffering from poverty, the yoke of the British, and fantastic subservience to ancient traditions. At the end of the novel the real O'Mahony shows up and promises to open coal mines and set the village on its feet, but all the efforts of the well-intentioned imposter to effect any improvements are in vain; the custom will not have it.

The pattern of the work is what the title suggests, a pattern of return. The bogus O'Mahony "returns" to the village to claim it, then leaves, then returns again. The true O'Mahony unwittingly returns to the home of his ancestors. When a British officer shows up to make trouble for Zeke, he is, inevitably, the son of a British officer who made trouble for him years before. A character named Linsky keeps returning too: left dead on an American battlefield early in the book, he returns very much alive in a chapter titled "A Face from the Winding Sheet"; "The Reinterment of Linsky" commences the twelve-year imprisonment of the man in a castle dungeon;

---

[3] All page references to *The Damnation* are to the edition edited and with an introduction by Everett Carter (John Harvard Library; Cambridge, Mass.: Harvard University Press, 1960).

and finally, in "A Bargain with the Buried Man," he returns once more. "Never mind the dead men," indeed!

Incredible webs of coincidence, ghostly moanings in castle chimneys on stormy nights, a document that comes to light after centuries of oblivion, a secret room whose discovery reveals the embalmed body of a medieval monk: the presence of such things as these has caused *The Return of the O'Mahony* to be dismissed by critics who have mistaken the romantic stage props for the drama. Frederic's use of melodramatic devices in this and some of his other fiction is very much to his purpose, however. Deeply flawed as it is, *The Return of the O'Mahony* is an imaginative portrait of a world suffering from a past that refuses to stay dead. The *cathach* that the false O'Mahony leaves behind when he goes into exile, a chest full of moldering human bones, is the proper talisman for that world.

Although it can be read only as a curiosity today, Frederic's Irish extravaganza met with a modest success when it appeared. The reading public, however, must have been surprised by the work as was virtually every one of the reviewers. William Morton Payne, a typical example, approved this novel as he had the earlier ones but found it "difficult to admit its production by the same hand." [4]

Frederic's shorter fiction of 1892 was even more bewildering. He published the realistic "My Aunt Susan," the first of his Civil War tales to appear; took a romantic excursion into the England of Richard III in "How Dickon Came by His Name"; and brought out most of the satiric sketches of contemporary London that were later collected in *Mrs. Albert Grundy: Observations in Philistia*. Frederic continued in this

[4] *The Dial*, XIV (1893), 21.

fashion for the next three years, with an early study for *The Damnation* titled "Cordelia and the Moon," several more Civil War stories (including the fine novella "The Copperhead"), and some tales about ancient Ireland.

Later, after the chic *March Hares* had followed *The Damnation* by only a few months, the reading public may have become inured to surprises from Frederic, may have been prepared, as Stephen Crane declared himself in 1898, to "conceive him doing anything." [5] When *The Damnation of Theron Ware* appeared in 1896, however, one can understand how Harold Frederic could be "discovered," even after publishing eighteen satiric sketches, over a score of short stories (and two collections of stories), one novella, and four novels. One can almost understand how it was possible for an absent-minded reporter of "Literary Chat" to announce that the European correspondent for the New York *Times* was making his debut as a novelist. [6]

"Congratulate yourselves," went a passage from Emerson that Stephen Crane once copied into his notebook, "if you have done something strange and extravagant and have broken the monotony of a decorous age." [7] Within a few months of each other in 1895–96 both Crane and Frederic had cause for self-congratulation: *The Red Badge of Courage* and *The Damnation of Theron Ware* were as strange and extravagant as anyone could wish. *The Red Badge,* the earlier of the two novels, made its original impact in England, where it exploded, Conrad recalled, "with the force of a twelve-inch shell." American remained inattentive until the echo of the detona-

[5] "Harold Frederic," *The Chap-Book,* VIII (1898), 359. "Doing anything," Crane continued, "unless it be writing a poor book."

[6] *Munsey's Magazine,* XV (1896), 378.

[7] See John Berryman, *Stephen Crane* (New York, 1950), p. 268.

tion reached New York in Frederic's booming *Times* dispatch, "Stephen Crane's Triumph."[8] Frederic's success, however, was nearly instantaneous on both sides of the Atlantic. Three months after Heinemann published *The Damnation* in England under the title *Illumination*, the novel was going into its fourth printing; at the same time Stone and Kimball in the United States could hardly keep up with the demand for copies.[9] Readers as diverse as Lady Asquith and Israel Zangwill thought it the best novel of the year; Oscar Wilde sent for a copy in jail; Prime Minister Gladstone endorsed

[8] Conrad is quoted in Robert W. Stallman, "Editor's Introduction," *Stephen Crane: Stories and Tales* (Vintage ed., New York, n.d.), p. xi. "The chief impetus for Crane's American success," Stallman writes, "was provided by British praise, and the tumultuous reception was first heralded home by Harold Frederic's London dispatch to *The New York Times* on January 26, 1896" (p. x). Alice Payne Hackett ranks *The Red Badge* seventh on her best seller list for 1896, *The Damnation* fifth (*Sixty Years of Best Sellers* [New York, 1956], p. 96).

[9] According to *The Critic*, *The Damnation of Theron Ware* was merely a provisional title, but "after the final choice of *Illumination* had been made, no one remembered, until it was too late, that the American publisher had not been informed of the decision" ("Notes," XXV, n.s. [1896], 396). *Illumination* appears as the subtitle in American editions. Advertisements in *The Chap-Book* for March, April, and May, 1898, claim that the American edition of *The Damnation* ran through 30,000 copies in less than two years. The Herbert S. Stone edition of 1900 (which has "Grosset and Dunlap" on the spine) says, "Seventy-fifth Thousand." In "Fiction Writing as a Business" Frank Norris cautioned: "Even so famous, so brilliant an author as Harold Frederic did not at first sell conspicuously. . . . Not until 'Theron Ware' . . . did Mr. Frederic reap his reward" (*Responsibilities of the Novelist* [New York, 1903], pp. 160–161). Actually, Frederic reaped only part of his reward because of the bankruptcy of his American publishers (see "Chronicle and Comment," *The Bookman* [New York], VIII [1898], 310).

it.[10] Critically, *The Damnation* was judged almost everywhere as "a literary event of very great importance," and it was obvious that Frederic had caught readers of all classes and critics alike "in a single throw of his net." [11]

Although the two novels were occasionally bracketed together in the nineties, *The Damnation* stirred up practically none of the kind of controversy waged over *The Red Badge*. It excited little contention of any kind in fact. As one might expect, what reservations there were about *The Damnation* were moral ones, but they were expressed with a mildness surprising for a literary period in which "damns were forbidden rather than rationed." [12] There were exceptions of course. *The Independent,* which had also found *In the Valley* and *The Lawton Girl* morally objectionable, lost interest in

[10] "Popular Books of 1898: Opinions of Readers," *The Academy*, LI (1897), 77–78. Rupert Hart-Davis, ed., *The Letters of Oscar Wilde* (London, 1962), p. 423, n. 1. Wilde found it "very interesting in matter." At Frederic's request, an advance copy was sent to Gladstone, whose endorsement was quoted in Heinemann's edition of the novel and in advertisements. Gladstone had been instrumental in convincing the public that *Robert Elsmere* was respectable, and he must have served Frederic similarly. Reviewers who compared Frederic's novel to Mrs. Ward's must also have helped by suggesting that despite its subject *The Damnation* was essentially moral. Nor can it have done Frederic any harm to have his novel classed with one of the all-time best sellers. Although Frederic certainly knew *Elsmere,* resemblances between it and *The Damnation* are mere details. For those details, see Robert Woodward, "Harold Frederic: A Study of His Novels, Short Stories and Plays" (unpub. Ph.D. diss., Indiana University, 1957), pp. 158–162.

[11] Harry Thurston Peck, *Cosmopolitan*, XXI (1896), 439; Arthur Waugh, "London Letter," *The Critic*, XXV, n.s. (1896), 316.

[12] Spiller, *et al.*, eds., *Literary History of the United States* (New York. 1948), II, 953.

The Damnation when "Theron Ware shrivels into a mere nymphomaniac, dancing a lust-dance around a handsome and soulless Irish girl." [13] More typical, however, were statements like that of the reviewer for the *Literary Digest*. "What good or evil may result from such psychological studies," he wrote, "we leave to the wisdom of philosophers." [14] The Reverend John Watson was simply telling God's truth when he informed an American reporter that in 1896 the greater part of the British reading public was absorbed in the scandalous career of the Reverend Theron Ware. But who would have predicted that Watson, who was better known as "Ian Maclaren," the romantic Kailyard novelist and archfoe of realism, would go on to praise *The Damnation* as "the strongest book of the year"? [15]

When skirmishing in the controversy over realism did break out, the old battle lines had shifted curiously. Critics brought Howells' name into their reviews not so much to celebrate or lament a triumph of the Dean's theories as to make comparisons at his expense. Reviewing *The Day of Their Wedding* and *A Parting and a Meeting* along with *The Damnation*, William Morton Payne belabored Howells' "weakness for queer people" and "disposition to find the salt of the earth where few would be likely to look for it" and then went on to

[13] XLVIII (1896), 770. Of the thirteen novels reviewed in this issue, *The Independent* found seven immoral or disgusting or both. The reviews suggest what novelists of the time often found themselves up against; Frances Hodgson Burnett's *A Lady of Quality*, for example, was judged "insidiously immoral."

[14] XIII (1896), 138.

[15] "Chronicle and Comment," *The Bookman* (New York), IV (1896), 196. The article noted how inexplicable it was "that the genial, sympathetic, optimistic preacher should be so strongly attracted" to a novel like Frederic's.

praise Frederic's "striking and impressive" novel, "a great and typical picture of American life." [16]

More indicative of things to come was an article by S. L. Gwynn two years later. Discussing what he took to be the most interesting American novels of the preceding few years, Gwynn judged that *The Damnation* was the strongest of the lot. Gwynn concluded:

It was not to be expected that the novel of pure analysis would go on for ever being the drawing-room production to which Mr. Howells accustomed us. Men and women naturally demand stronger meat. . . . The American novel has eschewed romance and incident, and, to excite or even to interest continuously, it must take the study of those emotions which move man and woman most profoundly.[17]

Howells' own response to *The Damnation* deserves comment. A year after the novel was published, Howells devoted about two hundred words of a long article to it. He liked it "very much," he said, and found it "of great power." One suspects from the tardiness of the notice and from his insistence that it was "a very moral book" that Howells was made uneasy by Frederic's frankness.[18] Frederic may have suspected something of the sort, for on June 16, 1898, he wrote to Howells, "You never told me whether you hated 'Illumination' as much as I feared." [19] Earlier Frederic had written of Howells to Hamlin Garland: "I always wanted to know

---

[16] *The Dial*, XX (1896), 335–336.
[17] "Novels of American Life," *Edinburgh Review*, CLXXXVII (1898), 405–406.
[18] "My Favorite Novelist and His Best Book," *Munsey's Magazine*, XVII (1897), 23.
[19] Quoted by permission of the Harvard College Library.

how Theron Ware struck him, but he never would tell me." [20]

It was not until after Frederic's death that Howells referred to *The Damnation* again. In 1899 he spoke very briefly of "the books of Mr. Harold Frederic, especially 'The Damnation of Theron Ware,' " as among the foremost of the works that gave the American novel standing in the world. The context of the remarks is revealing, for Howells listed such novels as Frederic's in argument against the "expansionists," who were protesting that "the present bounds of American fiction are not wide enough, or rather that they are too strictly patrolled by the spirit of the young girl." [21] The implication is that although Frederic had not gone too far he had traveled right to the border of the permissible. As Everett Carter observes, with the publication of *The Damnation of Theron Ware*, "the age of Howells . . . can be said to have ended." [22]

The authors of literary sensations are usually buried even deeper than literary deans. For many years after the end of his age, Howells was given a cruel kind of afterlife by those who mocked him for being an old maid, until they began to see that the old maid had been a rather noble man as well. Crane, after sleeping in near oblivion for a time and then suffering a period of resurrection as an American Chatterton, is very much alive and present today. But Harold Frederic, unless the interest of the 1960's abides, seems doomed to play the Flying Dutchman of American literature. Over the decades he has been enthusiastically sighted again and again, only to disappear

[20] May 12, 1897, quoted by permission of the University of Southern California Library.

[21] "Problems of Existence in Fiction," reprinted in Clara and Rudolph Kirk, eds., *"Criticism and Fiction" and Other Essays* (New York, 1959), p. 337.

[22] *Howells and the Age of Realism* (Philadelphia, 1954), p. 19.

into fogs of obscurity. This would be understandable if *The Damnation of Theron Ware* were merely the sensation of 1896, but it is not. Whether it is "among the four or five best novels written by an American during the nineteenth century" is perhaps idle to discuss.[23] There can be no doubt, however, that it is a work of great artistry, remarkable vitality, and enduring value.

Only recently have critics begun to look past the subject matter of *The Damnation* in order to see what the novel is really about. Obviously it is not what William Allen White called it: one of the daring books of the nineties that "had begun to carp and giggle at the old order." [24] Nor is it "the sole courageous or truthful novel ever written by an American on the subject of religion" as Thomas Beer called it.[25] And its permanent value certainly does not lie where Van Wyck Brooks' edition places it, "in the devastating perception of the age-old conflict between the moral man and the religious man." [26]

In what sense is Theron Ware damned? Everett Carter and John Henry Raleigh, the two critics who have written most perceptively about Frederic's novel, both recognize the prime importance of the question. Raleigh compares *The Damnation* to James' *Roderick Hudson:*

Theron is Roderick, the gifted but unstable young man who collapses in the face of a deeper, wider, richer culture than the one into which he had been born. . . . Both protagonists first undergo a quickening effect and then are doomed, Theron to an ignomini-

---

[23] *Ibid.,* p. 239.
[24] "Fiction of the Eighties and Nineties," in John Macy, ed., *American Writers on American Literature* (New York, 1931), p. 397.
[25] *Stephen Crane* (New York, 1924), p. 150.
[26] See the back cover of the Fawcett Premier Classics in American Realism edition of *The Damnation* (New York, 1963).

ous collapse in a New York hotel room and Roderick to suicide in the Italian Alps.[27]

Later in his essay Raleigh points out that *The Damnation* does not end with Theron's collapse but with his departure for Seattle. Theron leaves for the West "to start all over, wiser, if sadder." [28]

Rather than compare *The Damnation* to nineteenth-century works like *Roderick Hudson* and *Huckleberry Finn,* as Raleigh does, Everett Carter relates it to twentieth-century works like T. S. Eliot's. He sees in it an anticipation of "the modern tragic irony which regards man and his society as mere delusive appearances, and the cosmos as hostile and malignant." Carter's understanding of Theron's "damnation" is substantially in agreement with Raleigh's, however. He speaks of "Frederic's depiction of the fall of intellectual America from innocense into knowledge." Although the fall is specifically sexual, the strength of the novel "lies in its merging of the sexual fall with the fall from innocence to experience in other kinds of knowledge as well: religious, scientific, and esthetic." At the conclusion of the novel: "Ware turns his eyes to the future and to the West, and towards a new century, no hero, no 'angel of light,' but a man who has been told the homely, unpretty truth of the realistic, the pragmatic attitude toward life." [29]

In other words, the conclusion of *The Damnation* offers a reformed Theron, a man not damned but purged of his pretensions and romantic illusions. Certainly this is exactly what

---

[27] *"The Damnation of Theron Ware," American Literature,* XXX (1958), 220.

[28] *Ibid.,* p. 223. "Wiser, if sadder," but elsewhere in his essay Raleigh says that Theron "will in all likelihood make an ass out of himself all over again" (p. 212).

[29] Introduction to the Harvard edition of *The Damnation,* pp. xvii–xviv.

is suggested by Frederic's description of Theron as he takes one last look around him before he sets out for Seattle and a new life:

Only in the eyes themselves, as they rested briefly upon the prospect, did a substantial change [in Theron] suggest itself. They did not dwell fondly upon the picture of the lofty, spreading boughs, with their waves of sap-green leafage stirring against the blue. They did not soften and glow this time, at the thought of how wholly one felt sure of God's goodness in these wonderful new mornings of spring [pp. 353–354].

Theron, these lines appear to say, is changed and chastened, free of his illusions or, at any rate, of his transcendentalism. But what is to be made of the lines that immediately follow the description of Theron's survey of the new morning? Theron's eyes, the passage tells us,

looked instead straight through the fairest and most moving spectacle in nature's processional, and saw afar off, in conjectural vision, a formless sort of place which was Seattle. They surveyed its impalpable outlines, its undefined dimensions, with a certain cool glitter of hard-and-fast resolve. There rose before his fancy, out of the chaos of these shapeless imaginings, some faces of men, then more behind them, then a great concourse of uplifted countenances, crowded close together as far as the eye could reach. They were attentive faces all, rapt, eager, credulous to a degree. Their eyes were admiringly bent upon a common object of excited interest. They were looking at *him*; they strained their ears to miss no cadence of his voice. Involuntarily he straightened himself, stretched forth his hand with the pale, thin fingers gracefully disposed, and passed it slowly before him from side to side, in a comprehensive, stately gesture. The audience rose at him, as he dropped his hand, and filled his daydream with a mighty roar of applause, in volume like an ocean tempest, yet pitched for his hearing alone [p. 354].

No matter how heavily one underlines the "certain cool glitter of hard-and-fast resolve" in Theron's eyes, one cannot make Theron's vision pragmatic here. The Theron who smiles, shakes himself with "a delighted tremor," and turns to his companions to hint that before long he "may turn up in Washington a full-blown Senator" is the same old Theron, quite unpunctured and, it seems, well on his way to being "full-blown" already. That hand "with the pale, thin fingers gracefully disposed" should serve as a warning to the reader who thinks Theron has reformed. Earlier in the novel, at the height of his folly, the Reverend Mr. Ware "bought a small book which treated of the care of the hand and fingernails" (p. 240).

Alice Ware knows how much homely truth her husband has acquired. Picking up Theron's remark about becoming a Senator, Sister Soulsby says that Alice may someday be showing her around Washington. The following lines close the novel: " 'Oh, it isn't likely *I* would come East,' said Alice pensively. 'Most probably I'd be left to amuse myself in Seattle' " (p. 355).

Although it is a kind of Faust story, *The Damnation* is not a tragical history.[30] And, Adam-like though he is, Theron Ware does not forfeit his Paradise. Frederic's New World is a garden where men may gorge themselves on apples to their

[30] It is conceivable that Goethe's *Faust* may in some way have inspired *The Damnation*. On December 20, 1885, Frederic devoted his front page cable letter in the New York *Times* to an enthusiastic review of the première of a dramatization of *Faust, Part I*, starring Henry Irving as Mephistopheles and Ellen Terry as Margaret. Frederic apologized to his *Times* editor for giving over an entire weekly letter to a drama review (Frederic to Charles R. Miller, Dec. 21, 1885; a typescript copy of this letter made by Paul Haines is in the Frederic Papers, New York Public Library).

fill. Stomach aches may follow, and painful ones at that, but nothing more.

In *The American Adam*, R. W. B. Lewis follows the course of a classic "cultural conversation" in nineteenth-century American letters, a dialogue between "the party of the Past and the party of the Future," between "the parties of Memory and Hope."[31] In this dialogue, Frederic—who once styled himself "pretty nearly the original mugwump"[32]— wears no party label. He is not to be found with the party of the Past— seen at its worst in the puritanism of the Octavius Methodists with their allegiance to "the ways of our Fathers in Israel"— and he is not to be found with the party of the Future—heard most clearly in the boozy transcendentalism of Theron's rhapsodies on the woodland songsters in their leafy haunts, the virgin bosom of the verdant earth, and the great blue dome of the sky.

Nor, although he shares its ironic temperament, is Frederic to be found in the third party which Lewis identifies, the party of such as Nathaniel Hawthorne, characterized by "a tragic optimism: by a sense of the tragic collisions to which innocence was liable . . . and equally by an awareness of the heightened perception and humanity which suffering made possible." The image of the American Adam, Lewis writes, was "crowded with illusion . . . vulnerable in the extreme,"[33] and Frederic attacks the illusion at every vulnerable point. The debate which Lewis describes never ceased within Harold Frederic. It was between his innocent younger self and his experienced older self, and that the debate between the two

[31] (Chicago, 1955), p. 7.
[32] Robert H. Sherard, "Harold Frederic," *The Idler*, XII (1897), 537.
[33] *American Adam*, pp. 7–8, 1.

selves did not reach conclusion is borne out forcibly in *The Damnation of Theron Ware.*

For a time Frederic considered two different sets of titles for the four parts of *The Damnation:* Spring, Summer, Autumn, and Winter; People, Predilections, Passions, and Penalties (or Payments). Although he finally decided simply to number the parts, the division of the novel into the four seasons remained. The final chapter of the novel is not set in winter like the rest of the last section, however, but on a balmy spring morning. The novel travels full circle: it begins with Theron, his debts settled by a kindly friend, moving from Tyre to Octavius in the spring; it ends with Theron, his debts settled by the Soulsbys, departing for Seattle in the spring. Theron's New World does not fall; it goes around.

"The new ideas, the glimpses of luxury," one of the contemporary reviews of *The Damnation* said of Theron's experience, "act like strong drink on an unaccustomed boy." [34] The figure is apt, for Theron, who has previously sampled nothing stronger than beer, reaches his low point in the novel wandering dazedly from bar to bar until he finally has enough sense to stagger to the Soulsbys' New York apartment. He comes to them, he says, "out of hell" (p. 340). It being Brother Soulsby's professional opinion that rum rather than ruin is burning up the Reverend, he recommends a good night's sleep.

Sister Soulsby realizes that more than drink is troubling Theron, but she prescribes the same medicine her husband does: "You'll sleep this all off like a top" (p. 343). Shortly thereafter she chides her husband for taking too simple a view of the case. Some girl has made a fool of him, and decoyed him up in a balloon, and let him drop," she says. "He's been hurt bad, too."

[34] "'Illumination' and its Author," *The Bookman* (London), X (Aug., 1896), 138.

"We have all been hurt in our day and generation," responded Brother Soulsby, genially. "Don't you worry; he'll sleep that off, too. It takes longer than drink, and it doesn't begin to be so pleasant, but it can be slept off. Take my word for it, he'll be a different person by noon" [p. 348].

The different person will be pretty much the same old person, as Sister Soulsby's first close look at Theron's distraught face has already reassured her. "Under the painful surface-blur of wretchedness and fatigued debauchery, she traced reflectively the lineaments of the younger and cleanlier countenance she had seen a few months before. Nothing essential had been taken away" (p. 341). Her last look at Theron's face that night tells her the same story: as she bids Theron goodnight, "his face frankly surrendered itself to the distortions of a crying child's countenance" (p. 347).

Brother Soulsby is overly optimistic; the last paragraph of the chapter sees him off the next day to call a doctor for Theron. Soulsby's prognosis is sound, however. Theron lies ill through the winter, but he does sleep it off and mends, Sister Soulsby says, "strong as an ox." The comparison Raleigh makes between Theron Ware and Roderick Hudson is suggestive, but the contrast between them is more telling: although Theron contemplates suicide, he soon abandons the idea; Roderick does not.[35] The last chapter of *The Damnation*

[35] The notes in the Frederic Papers, Library of Congress, contain a page of observations on suicide and another page which includes the statement "Soulsby and wife at deathbed—their words finish book." Both suggest that Frederic may have considered a tragic ending for Theron, a possibility which Woodward discusses in his dissertation (pp. 154–155). In "The Ending of *The Damnation of Theron Ware*," Richard VanDerBeets argues that because Frederic considered suicide for the close of the novel Frederic cannot be considered a comic realist (*American Literature*, XXXVI [Nov., 1964], 358–359). The significant fact is that Frederic did *not* end the novel with Theron's suicide.

opens, as we have seen, with winter past and spring returned, and with Theron already planning new expansions, new balloon flights. Theron Ware's damnation is a strange one, a fall that can be "slept off."

The Damnation of Theron Ware opens at the annual Nedahma Conference of the Methodist Church, held in Tecumseh, New York. Appropriately, Tecumseh is located in Adams County. All of the business of the Conference has been attended to except the most interesting, the reading of the new pastoral appointments. As a number of critics have pointed out, Frederic's description of the crowd gathered in the brand-new church seems to imply that Methodism has seen better days. Near the front sit the old men, "bent and decrepit veterans who had known Lorenzo Dow." "The sight of these venerable Fathers in Israel," Frederic says, "was good to the eyes, conjuring up, as it did, pictures of a time when a plain and homely people had been served by a fervent and devoted clergy" (p. 4).

In so ironic a novel, talk of conjuring up pictures should perhaps serve as some kind of a warning, but the contrast between the Fathers in Israel and their successors seems straightforward. Frederic seems sincere when he notes the appearance of a decline from the old pastors, through the middle-aged, down to the youngsters who have been ordained in the last three or four days. The "modern and go-ahead" Methodism of the Tecumseh congregation, with its fine new building, its four front rows of hundred-dollar pews ("quite up to the Presbyterian highwater mark"), and its socially triumphant Ladies' Aid oyster suppers, is treated with particularly cutting irony.

No sooner has Frederic established his contrast, however, than he begins to play with it. As one reviewer noted when the novel appeared, *The Damnation* is "shiftily based on an element of relativity," [36] and the shifty element takes over quickly. Frederic turns his attention from the crowd to one individual. The Reverend Theron Ware is a broad-browed, thoughtful-eyed young man who appears exempt from the general decline through the generations. His features are "moulded into that regularity of strength which used to characterize the American Senatorial type in those far-away days of clean-shaven faces and moderate incomes before the War" (p. 8). [37] Well and good: although the fabric of Methodism may be rotting, there is a saving remnant.

But this young Theron Ware is also the preacher on whom go-ahead Tecumseh has its heart set, and his heart is set equally on Tecumseh. His handsome good looks, his stylishly-dressed wife, and above all the handsome and stylishly-dressed sermon he has preached earlier at the Conference have convinced Tecumseh that the Wares are the final adornment needed for its new church.

The shifty element shifts still farther when the Wares and Tecumseh are disappointed in their hopes. Not Theron but the Reverend Abram C. Tisdal is awarded the coveted post, and to complicate matters even more, Brother Abram not only bears the name of the Father in Israel but is one of the church veterans, "a spindling, rickety, gaunt old man" (p. 9). Theron is assigned to the tight-pursed, hard-shelled Methodists of Octavius, and the chapter ends with Alice Ware in tears while

[36] C. [Charlotte Porter], "Notes on Recent Fiction," *Poet-Lore*, VIII (Aug., 1896), 460.

[37] In the Fairchild family in *Seth*, it is the corrupt Albert who looks like his grandfather, the pre-Civil War Senator. Judge Wendover, one of the villains of *The Lawton Girl*, is described as having the appearance of the pre-war gentleman.

Theron half-heartedly reassures her that "all things work together for good." Here indeed is a snarl of possibilities for the
reader to unravel.[38] Only one thing is really clear at the time:
Sister Soulsby's advice to Theron later in the novel that the
sheep and the goats are to be separated at Judgment Day "and
not a minute sooner," must be applied by the reader from the
very start of the book.

Theron has suffered his first fall in the novel, though it may
be nothing more than a tumble from the modern pulpit of the
Tecumseh church, which his vaulting imagination had already
occupied until the Bishop's announcement brought him back
to earth. No, surely Theron has suffered no real fall. As the
second chapter opens with the Wares in their new home, he
stands outside the parsonage in the spring air of a glorious
morning. Theron suggests a long walk and a picnic lunch, but
Alice is preoccupied. She has just learned that the church
trustees do not allow milk deliveries on Sundays. "It's just
what Wendell Phillips said," she laughs. "The Puritan's idea
of hell is a place where everybody has to mind his own
business."

At the mention of the trustees (not hell) Theron's gaze
drops, and his eye wanders over his new backyard:

The garden parts had not been spaded up, but lay, a useless stretch
of muddy earth, broken only by last year's cabbage-stumps and
the general litter of dead roots and vegetation. The door of the

[38] One of Frederic's working titles for *The Damnation* may have
been "Snarl!" or "Snarl." If so, the title must have been intended to
refer to a snarl of complications, not the snarl of a beast. Theron's
life becomes snarled up with other lives, and the novel itself is a
snarl, a tangled labyrinth of ambiguities and ironies that cross each
other endlessly. Perhaps "Snarl" was also intended to imply something
of what Sister Soulsby meant when she said that "good, bad, indifferent are all braided up together in every man's nature" (p. 346).

tenantless chicken-coop hung wide open. Before it was a great heap of ashes and cinders, soaked into grimy hardness by the recent spring rains, and nearer still an ancient chopping-block, round which were scattered old weather-beaten hardwood knots which had defied the axe, parts of broken barrels and packing-boxes, and a nameless débris of tin cans, clam-shells, and general rubbish [pp. 14–15].

Perhaps Theron has fallen after all, for here he stands in a ruined garden. Or, if unfallen as yet, he is soon to be sorely tested: an ash heap appears to be his fate, and his church trustees, beside whom Job's comforters would appear companionable, are due at eleven.

But Theron looks away from the ruined garden and lifts up his eyes to the hills from whence his help cometh, or, more accurately, to the budding elms on the next street and to the blue sky above, "all radiant with light and the purification of spring." " 'What matters any one's idea of hell,' he said, in soft, grave tones, 'when we have that to look at, and listen to, and fill our lungs with?' " (p. 15). Alice, being less of a transcendentalist than Theron (or at any rate being a woman), is distracted only momentarily by the sweep of her husband's hand. Her eyes fall reflectively on the garden patch once more, and when Theron repeats his proposal for a country walk, she reminds him again of the trustees' impending visit. She returns to her dirty dishes (so much for the "purification of spring"); he to his study.

The rest of the chapter treats Theron's musing review of the years that have brought him to Octavius. The revery is so packed with irony that one wonders how *The Damnation* can ever have been taken to be a novel about the transformation of a good man into a bad man. Every weakness beneath the impressive senatorial facade is revealed as he sits and daydreams of his past, with Paley's *Evidences of Christianity* opened but unseen in his lap. His thoughts carry him back to his first charge, a poor, back-country church. He quickly reveals himself to be the climber and the snob who will later treat his Octavius flock with such contempt:

Of course, he admitted to himself, it would not be the same if he were to go back there again. He was conscious of having moved along—was it, after all, an advance?—to a point where it was unpleasant to sit at table with the unfragrant hired man, and still worse to encounter the bucolic confusion between the functions of knives and forks.

So much for his first pastorate in a truly pastoral land of fertile fields and "sleek, well-fed herds of 'milkers.'" And so much for the momentary hesitancy of "was it, after all, an advance?"

As Theron moves on to reflect upon his marriage to Alice, he betrays precisely the same attitude toward her that will later bring him to Celia Madden's feet. Indeed, out of context Theron's recollection of Alice as she first appeared to him fits Celia in almost every detail. "Though herself the daughter of a farmer," Theron recalls of the Alice he first met,

her presence on a visit within the borders of his remote country charge had seemed to make everything there a hundred times more countrified than it had ever been before. She was fresh from the refinements of a town seminary: she read books; it was known that she could play upon the piano. Her clothes, her manners, her way of speaking, the readiness of her thoughts and sprightly tongue,—not least, perhaps, the imposing current understanding as to her father's wealth,—placed her on a glorified pinnacle far away from the girls of the neighborhood [p. 17].

And finally, one learns that Theron has already undergone a period of enlightenment, not as transfiguring as the one he will later undergo, but illuminating nonetheless. Newly-wed and happier than he had ever been, he had made a great beginning with his second appointment, to a New York state village whose name might have given pause to his impetuous optimism—Tyre. In his first year there he had begun to develop previously unsuspected oratorical powers and had undergone a period of "incredible fructification and output." Frederic describes Theron during this period in a figure that recalls the countless serpent images which appear throughout the novel:

He scarcely recognized for his own the mind which now was reaching out on all sides with the arms of an octopus, exploring unsuspected mines of thought, bringing in rich treasures of deduction, assimilating, building, propounding. . . . He could not look without blinking timidity at the radiance of the path stretched out before him, leading upward to dazzling heights of greatness.

He might better have kept one eye on the ground: "At the end of this first year the Wares suddenly discovered that they were eight hundred dollars in debt" (p. 21).

Slowly and painfully the Wares came to realize what it means to fall into a hole eight hundred dollars deep. Help finally came from an unexpected source. A man who was not even a professing member of the church, another Abram—Abram Beekman—took "a fatherly sort of interest" in the Wares and set them on their feet.[39] Although Theron was strongly tempted to take his benefactor's advice and leave the ministry for the law, he remained at his post and, adding belated economy to Beekman's gift, ended his third and last year in Tyre one hundred dollars ahead.

---

[39] It will be recalled that Abram Beekman of Tyre figures importantly in *Seth.*

Even before Theron left Tyre, however, "the old dream of ultimate success and distinction," though "in a chastened form," revived. Soon, Theron was back to work on his oratory, studying:

all the principles which underlie this art, and all the tricks that adorn its superstructure. . . . He put aside . . . the thought of attracting once more the non-Methodists of Tyre, whose early enthusiasm had spread such pitfalls for his unwary feet. He practiced effects now by piecemeal, with an alert ear, and calculation in every tone. An ambition, at once embittered and tearfully solicitous, possessed him [p. 23].

For a man who has repeatedly been judged to have fallen only after coming under the influence of Dr. Ledsmar, Father Forbes, and Celia Madden, this is singular behavior. "Calculation in every tone," the study of adorning "tricks," the shifting of responsibility to the non-Methodists: Gertrude Atherton must have felt such details of Theron's biography with unusual sensitivity, for she concluded, "no character in fiction [is] so remorselessly developed. You despise the man," she said, "almost from the beginning." [40] Yet the effect is not quite what she describes: much of what Frederic reveals about Theron and what Theron reveals about himself in the early pages of the novel remains only half-perceived until later events bring it into clearer perspective. Another novelist described the effect of *The Damnation* even more precisely: "When you get to the end," Howells wrote, "although you have carried a hazy notion in your mind of the sort of man Ware was, you fully realize, for the first time, that the author has never for a moment represented him anywhere as a good or honest man." [41]

[40] "The Reader: Harold Frederic," *The Bookman* (London), XV (Nov., 1898), 37.
[41] "My Favorite Novelist," p. 24.

The pattern of *The Damnation* is not simply one of falls—for every fall there must be a new climb to new heights, a new illumination, a new spring. The disappointment of losing the ministry in up-to-date Tecumseh has again dashed Theron's hopes, but the Conference has given him more than the dismal Octavius charge. Absorbing the hymns and prayers of revivalist enthusiasm at the Conference, he has succumbed to "the high pressure of emotional excitement." Now, as he sits in his study, he wonders how he could ever have considered abandoning the ministry: "the Call sounded, resonant and imperative, in his ears" (p. 24). Theron is whole and clean once more, and a little numb when his Call is interrupted by the jangle of the doorbell announcing that the trustees have arrived.

The chapter describing the trustees' meeting has been justly admired as a broad but devastating satire.[42] Together, the aptly named Brothers Winch and Pierce insist: "We stick by the Discipline an' the ways of our fathers in Israel." (The talk of the Patriarchs plays off neatly against Alice's warning to Theron when the trustees arrive: "Don't let them jew you down a solitary cent.") In religious matters, the trustees tell

[42] Frederic's satire is not as broad as might first appear. Thomas W. Lamont's affectionate reminiscences of his upbringing by his Methodist minister father in the 1870's and 80's is filled with true stories as grotesque and funny as any in Frederic's novel (*My Boyhood in a Parsonage* [New York, 1946]). Praising the "fine realism" of *The Damnation*, Brand Whitlock expressed some reservations about the rough treatment of the Methodists. Nothing in his long and intimate association with the church, Whitlock said, had shown him anything so crude and mean. He added, however, that his Methodist minister father was reading the novel in the next room and "chuckling here and there" because "he encountered such men as those trustees in his earlier ministry" (letter to Olivia Roberts, March ?, 1897, quoted in Allan Nevins, ed., *The Letters and Journals of Brand Whitlock* [New York, 1936], I, 6).

Theron, the Discipline adds up to sermons full of "flat-footed hell," complete with the deathbeds of Paine and Voltaire (p. 29). Theron resists commenting on these "old-wife fables"; he was far from hard-shelled before he was softened up by the higher criticism. In more secular matters, Theron learns, the Discipline adds up to seven per cent on the church mortgages (held, incidentally, by the trustees), although the legal limit has been six for some time. Readers who wish to read *The Damnation* as a nineteenth-century *Elmer Gantry* need read no further than chapter 3.[43]

The irony here is far more subtle than anything Sinclair Lewis ever wrote, however. Theron stands up to the trustees when they try to stick him with the bill for repairs on the parsonage sidewalk, but he gains the point only at the expense of another: without a word of protest he agrees to tell Alice to take the flowers off her best bonnet before she next appears in church. The imagery of flowers and gardens that runs throughout the novel is nowhere used to more telling effect than here. Alice is resentful over the matter of her bonnet for awhile, and her resentment aggravates Theron's guilt in such a way that he in turn resents her and feels that he has been

[43] Mark Schorer says that Sinclair Lewis knew *The Damnation* well, but in *Elmer Gantry* "nothing came of its complex ironies. . . . One scene, with its atmosphere of complex sensuosity, may have suggested to Lewis his scene of ritualistic adultery, but nothing more" (*Sinclair Lewis* [New York, 1961], p. 481). Schorer also says that *The Damnation*—and he might have mentioned *Seth* and *The Lawton Girl* as well—"is one of the relatively few novels we can put in the background of *Main Street*" (p. 275). The reader who wishes to compare sections 2 and 3 of chapter 12 of *Gantry* with chapters 18 and 19 of *The Damnation* will see that Lewis' scene of adultery most certainly does derive from Frederic, as do other things in Lewis' novel. See Charles V. Genthe, "*The Damnation of Theron Ware* and *Elmer Gantry*," *Research Studies*, XXXII (1964), 334–343.

misunderstood and betrayed by a helpmeet who has hereto-fore been gratifyingly "the most worshipful of womankind" (p. 20). When Alice Ware sacrifices the roses from her bonnet, she loses a part of whatever paradise her marriage has been.

The Damnation of Theron Ware, then, is what its English title and American subtitle suggest, a novel of illumination. Its opening and closing chapters alike contradict the view that it is a tale of spiritual innocence falling into corruption, a study of "degeneration" (to use a favorite word of the nineties). Nothing indicates more clearly how ignorant Theron is of his true self than his disposition to view his experience in the same mistaken fashion as so many readers of *The Damnation*. The night he staggers drunk into the Soulsbys' apartment, he puts his case this way:

Six months ago I was a good man. I not only seemed to be good, to others and to myself, but I *was* good. . . . You see me here six months after. Look at me! I haven't an honest hair in my head. I'm a bad man through and through, that's what I am.

Sister Soulsby, who comes closer to expressing Frederic's viewpoint than any other character in the novel, will have none of this: "You weren't altogether good a year ago, any more than you're altogether bad now. You were some of both then; you're some of both now." And then Sister Soulsby provides a figure which neatly catches the sense in which *The Damnation of Theron Ware* describes a fall that is not a fall: "It's a see-saw with all of us, Theron Ware,—sometimes up; sometimes down" (pp. 345–346).

It is advisable to defer to Sister Soulsby's view of human nature. Seldom if ever does Frederic's irony cut with a single edge. When Celia Madden tells Theron that she is a Greek, he replies that he had always assumed her to be full-blooded Irish. Judging from the number of commentators who have thought that Frederic's portrait of Celia was unintentionally preposterous, a good many readers must have thought Theron the only character exposed to ridicule by his innocent re-mark.[44] The reader who is impatient for Judgment Day is likely to find that in throwing in his lot with what he takes to be the innocent sheep he has become the goat. Nor, to those familiar with Bohemian fashions of the nineties, is Celia out-rageously overdrawn. One would like to know what Frederic thought of Cora Crane's regular at-home costume in England: Greek sandals and "a species of blouse and skirt—'a weird kind of wrapper,' as Sanford Bennett described it—which she made herself and which was probably an adaptation to long-skirt requirements of the classical Greek chiton, with long sleeves added to lend a touch of the medieval." [45] (Photo-graphs of Sarah Bernhardt's salon in the 1890's are also in-structive.)

No sooner does Frederic invite the reader to join Theron in opposing the cant and bigotry of the Octavius Methodists than he reveals Theron's own cant and bigotry in opposing the Catholics. Once Theron comes into contact with Father Forbes, he is forced to reconsider his prejudices. He is not sure

[44] Oscar Cargill, for example, speaks of Frederic's "absurd notion of good taste, represented for us by the things with which the monied Irish hoyden, who takes Theron's fancy, surrounds herself" (*Intellec-tual America* [New York, 1941], p. 415). Of those who have written about Celia, Ralph Rogers alone discusses her for what she is, a great comic creation. "It is to Theron," he writes, "that Celia appears to be the epitome of good taste and artistic sensibility, not Frederic" ("Harold Frederic: His Development as a Comic Realist" [unpub. Ph.D. diss., Columbia University, 1961], p. 156).

[45] Lillian Gilkes, *Cora Crane* (Bloomington, Ind., 1960), p. 123.

he has ever met a Democrat before, let alone a priest. Catholicism, Irish Catholicism in particular, looms up in his imagination "like some huge, shadowy, and symbolical monument":

The foundations upon which its dark bulk reared itself were ignorance, squalor, brutality, and vice. Pigs wallowed in the mire before its base, and burrowing into this base were a myriad of narrow doors, each bearing the hateful sign of a saloon. . . . Above were sculptured rows of lowering, ape-like faces from Nast's and Keppler's cartoons. . . . [Below] glowed a spectral picture of some black-robed, tonsured men, with leering satanic masks, making a bonfire of the Bible in the public schools [p. 51].

Although this is successful when it occurs in the novel, it comes close to burlesque; the knife does not dissect—it hacks away with Menckenish abandon.[46] Read in the light of further developments, however, the passage is not so simple as it first appears. Calling on Father Forbes for the first time, Theron is baffled for a moment by the first electric doorbell he has ever encountered. "For custodians of a mediæval superstition and fanaticism," Frederic comments, "the Catholic clergy seemed very much up to date" (p. 66). Once inside, Theron finds himself in luxurious surroundings and confronted by a priest whose urbanity makes a mockery of Theron's own cultivation and of his cartoon conception of Irish Catholicism. When

---

[46] Theron's prejudices are not greatly exaggerated. Thomas Beer quotes Cardinal Gibbons of Baltimore pausing before putting a spoonful of sugar in the coffee cup of a non-Catholic visitor in 1894: "On my honour, there's not a drop of poison in the house" (*The Mauve Decade* [New York, 1926], p. 140). When Henry Seidel Canby speaks of religion in *The Age of Confidence* (New York, 1934), he says, "I leave the Roman Catholics aside, as knowing nothing of their problems" (p. 127). He did know something of their problems, however, for elsewhere in his book he recalls that when he was a boy "the fighting word was not 'liar' or 'bastard,' but 'mick'" (p. 41).

Father Forbes casually refers to "this Christ-myth of ours," Theron starts: "For the instant his mind was aflame with this vivid impression,—that he was among sinister enemies, at the mercy of criminals." Characteristically, however, he quickly recovers, and "it was as if nothing at all had happened" (p. 75).

The whole scene is not what it might at first appear to be, simply another blunt attack on Theron's prejudices. Father Forbes does not wear a satanic mask (although he does intersperse his remarks with "little purring chuckles"), but he is "making a bonfire of the Bible" nonetheless. That he uses the burning glass of the higher criticism rather than the torch of the Inquisition is irrelevant in a sense. In matters other than doorbells, the Catholic clergy seems to be very much up to date.

Grotesque as Theron's gargoyles are, carved to the pattern of yellow-press cartoons, they are more than mere fantasies. Toward the end of the novel Theron steals away from the Methodist camp meeting to another part of the grounds where the Catholics are holding their annual outing. Now quite the man of the world, Theron is not shocked to see shapely ankles and flashes of white petticoat as pretty colleens play on the park swings to the approbation of beaming priests. Nor is he horrified to find men of the cloth not only countenancing but even partaking of the beer being sold at the picnic. Instead, he marvels at what appears to be the innocence of the whole scene in contrast to the alternating gloom and orgiastic emotionalism of the Methodist revival he has fled.

Repeatedly those who have discussed the Catholic outing have made sheep of the Catholics and goats of the Methodists. Even John Henry Raleigh, who describes the witty deceptiveness of *The Damnation* so well, is deceived here and takes

Father Forbes' remarks on the Irish-American seriously. Heretofore, says the priest, the mixture of constitutional melancholia and impulsive exuberance with whiskey has proved the Irishman's undoing, "but these young men down there," he points to the beer concession, "are changing all that": "The lager-drinking Irishman in a few generations will be a new type of humanity,—the Kelt at his best. He will dominate America. He will be *the* American" (p. 248).[47] Although Theron is not sure how much of this is in jest and how much in earnest, the reader must take it as Father Forbes' joke. At the close of the chapter, Celia's brother Theodore staggers up drunk. He is running for the District Assembly and has been emptying his pockets standing the boys for drinks.[48] Now he wants Theron to "fix up the Methodists solid for me" and promises in return to come to the camp meeting that night with a twenty-dollar bill for the collection plate (p. 254). When Theron tells him he is drunk, Theodore causes an ugly

[47] Although he takes Father Forbes at face value here, Raleigh does realize that such remarks "would be nonsense and the intent of the author satiric" in most novels ("*The Damnation*," p. 219). Paul Haines, who also takes the priest too seriously, notes that in the Utica *Observer* for August 17, 1881, Frederic defended a Monsignor under attack for allowing wine and beer to be sold at a church outing ("Harold Frederic," [unpub. Ph.D. diss., New York University, 1945], p. 64). It does not follow, however, that Frederic believed in lager as a potent civilizing force. Horace Boyce, who obviously does not speak for Frederic in *The Lawton Girl*, argues that America needs light wines and beers to replace liquor (p. 113).

[48] A page titled "The Maddens" in the Frederic Papers, Library of Congress, reads: "Vicious (politics). . . . Theodore becomes great land-leaguer—looks like Robert Emmet." In his article "The Rhetoricians of Ireland," Frederic spoke of "the young men who resemble the portraits of Robert Emmet" and "crowd up like tares on every side to choke the wheat" of Irish common sense (*Fortnightly Review*, LX [1893], 713).

scene, abusing Father Forbes, offering to punch Theron in the nose, and reducing Celia to hysterical tears.

Those who, like Thomas Beer, see Frederic using the Irish "as a club on the Methodists" [49] and those who see the Irish in *The Damnation* as standing for a Jamesian idea of Europe have missed half of Frederic's subtlety, half the fun. Forbes' jesting prediction that the lager-drinking Kelt will dominate America becomes something more than a joke when Theodore enters, or at any rate it becomes a different joke. Theodore's presence adds a whole new dimension to Theron's crude fantasy of the Irish Church as sketched by Nast and Keppler —with its base "a myriad of narrow doors, each bearing the hateful sign of a saloon."

It is common in speaking of Theron Ware's illumination to say that he is exposed to the new, to the new science of Dr. Ledsmar, the new theology of Father Forbes, and the new hedonism of Celia Madden, the New Woman. It is as much to the point, however, to observe that Theron is exposed to the old. When Father Forbes subjects Abraham and the Bible to scholarly examination, Theron asks, "But this is something very new?" Forbes replies, "Bless you, no!" and cites Epicurus and Lucretius as Darwinians. "As for this eponym thing," he adds, "why Saint Augustine called attention to it fifteen hundred years ago" (p. 72). Dr. Ledsmar's one book is an anthropological history of serpent worship, and he is the foremost authority on Assyriology in the United States. Celia, when she is not playing Hypatia, wants to be a Greek pagan. "They were all there long ago," she says of the things she wants out of life, "thousands of years ago" (p. 265).

---

[49] *Mauve Decade*, p. 165. Despite his reservations, Beer felt that *The Damnation* was the sole exception to the "damned rot" of everything else written on the Irish in the nineties.

Oliver Wendell Holmes speculated that science might substitute the Rise of Man for the Fall and so cause "the utter disintegration of spiritual pessimisms." [50] As the twentieth century has appallingly shown, Dr. Holmes lacked proper confidence in the staying power of pessimisms. The new science which is so much the talk in *The Damnation* does dispense with the Fall, but it does away with the Rise of Man as well. Life becomes, as Sister Soulsby says, "a see-saw with all of us." In the novel only Theron expresses any faith in what Father Forbes terms the most "utterly baseless and empty" of all our myths, "this idea that humanity progresses" (p. 249).

To Frederic's mind evolution meant not the progress of the race but, as he puts it in *Seth's Brother's Wife*, "that process of exhaustion which we call the survival of the fittest" (p. 270). In a sense, Dr. Ledsmar suggests, ontogeny recapitulates phylogeny after birth as well as before: each man must pass through the barbarisms and blunders of all men throughout the history of the race. Undoubtedly *The Damnation* is a classic statement of beliefs and values in the latter nineteenth century, but there should be no doubt that Frederic sees the education of Theron Ware in a universal perspective. The new thought of Ledsmar and Forbes does not preach optimistically, in the manner of Shaw and Wells, on "the magnificent and well-nigh incredible conception of Change . . . gigantic, miraculous change, an overwhelming of the old in ruin and an emergence of the new." [51] Instead, it holds out to Theron that awful vision of time, of all history, that darkened the newly-opened eyes of Milton's Adam. "You see, there is nothing new," says Father Forbes to Theron: "Everything is built on the ruins of something else. Just as the material earth

[50] *Works*, III: *The Poet at the Breakfast Table* (Boston, 1891), 182.
[51] Floyd Dell, quoted in Schorer, *Sinclair Lewis*, p. 182.

is made up of countless billions of dead men's bones, so the mental world is all alive with the ghosts of dead men's thoughts and beliefs, the wraiths of dead races' faiths and imaginings" (p. 74).

When Theron decides to write a book on Abraham, he is struck by the "powerful range of possibilities in the son's revolt against the idolatry of his father" (p. 40). Later, after he has talked over the project with Father Forbes and Dr. Ledsmar, he says to Alice, "You have no idea, literally no conception, of the interesting and important problems which are raised by the mere fact of Abraham leaving the city of Ur" (p. 107). Abraham, Father Forbes tells Theron, was not an individual but a tribe, a sept, a clan, or, Frederic implies, a type. One of the many tasks to which Frederic addressed himself in preparation for the writing of *The Damnation* was the drawing up of a genealogical table listing almost one hundred of the sons of Noah. Reading the novel, one can guess what ironic lesson Frederic saw figured in those meticulously inked lines, a dark tree of bewildering and endless ramifications rooted in the ruins of man's first hopes.

The "mysterious, impersonal, Titanic forces" [52] that one perceptive reviewer of the nineties sensed beneath the realistic surface of *The Damnation* are certainly there, and the characters of the novel feel their pressure. Ledsmar's philosophy has led him to a misanthropy which is only less mild than his misogyny. He derives quite obviously from Hawthorne's violators of the human heart. When Ledsmar christens his specimen reptile "The Reverend Theron Ware," the act is a comment upon the doctor's inhumanity as well as the reverend's. Morally, it is equivalent to the gesture Theron makes

[52] *The Critic*, XXV, n.s. (1896), 310.

when, having preached a rousing sermon at the Methodist Love-Feast, he looks down upon his enthralled parishioners, lays his hand upon the pulpit Bible, and whispers to his heart, "At last! The dogs!" (p. 157). Ledsmar has come to regard people ("vertebrates," he is fond of calling them) as subjects for impersonal study, like the Chinese servant to whom he is feeding progressively larger doses of opium. A kind of Rappaccini, Dr. Ledsmar is perfectly willing to extend his experiments in plant hybridization to include the hybridization of Theron Ware. Those who wish to make Frederic a spokesman for pragmatism have not dealt adequately with the thoroughly pragmatic Dr. Ledsmar.

Father Forbes is less frightening, for he seeks his solace in urbanity. He has taught his cook to prepare French dishes, stocks a good cellar, and wears his cassock with the grace of a belle. Finding that "the most powerful forces in human nature are self-protection and inertia," he has made his adjustments: "the middle-aged man has found out that the chief wisdom in life is to bend to the pressures about him, to shut up and do as others do" (p. 249). In a novel that constantly insists, as Frederic puts it elsewhere, that sex "is the mainspring of all human activity," [53] Father Forbes' celibacy is as significant as Ledsmar's misogyny.

Of the three tempters who confront Theron, Celia Madden is the chief and the most interesting, perhaps because she appears as the tempted as well as the temptress. Despite her vow that she will never marry, a vow that we see drearily fulfilled in *The Market-Place*, she does not remove herself from life as do Ledsmar and Forbes. Nevertheless, her taste for celibate priests and married ministers is worth a glance. "The deepest

[53] "Musings on the Question of the Hour," *Pall Mall Budget,* XXXIII (Aug. 13, 1885), p. 11.

of all our instincts," she says, is "love of woman, who is at once daughter and wife and mother" (p. 266), yet Celia regards marriage and motherhood as traps to be avoided and is a very bad daughter to a very good father. She is rich, beautiful, and even talented to a degree, but Celia is one of Yeats' fine women, who eat

> A crazy salad with their meat
> Whereby the Horn of Plenty is undone.[54]

To object to Celia's absurdity is to miss the point that she is supposed to appear absurd. Her studio, decorated to complement her red hair and adorned with evidence that she dabbles in all of the seven arts, is as comic as her treatment of Theron on the night she invites him there to show him, she suggestively murmurs, "what is my very own" (p. 196). Humorous as she is, there is something sad about Celia. Between her moods of exaltation, she is struck by black depression. Beneath her comic self-dramatization, one hears genuine anguish in a plaint like this: "It seems as if all at once the world had swelled out in size a thousandfold, and that poor me had dwindled down to the meerest wee little red-headed atom—the most helpless and forlorn and lonesome of atoms at that" (p. 106).

The review that detected "more than a mere touch of the vanished hand that wrote 'The Scarlet Letter' in 'Illumination'" must have been particularly gratifying to Frederic, who once declared that his determination to write had been inspired by his "literary parentage," Erckmann-Chatrian on

[54] W. B. Yeats, "A Prayer for My Daughter," *The Collected Poems of W. B. Yeats* (New York, 1956), p. 186. Reprinted with permission of The Macmillan Company from *The Collected Poems of W. B. Yeats,* copyright 1924 by The Macmillan Company, renewed 1952 by Bertha Georgie Yeats; and with permission of A. P. Watt & Son.

one side, Nathaniel Hawthorne on the other.[55] Nowhere in Frederic's novel is Hawthorne's presence felt more fully than in the second great scene between Celia and Theron, which takes place on the afternoon she confers her ambiguous and disasterous kiss on him. Detail by detail, Frederic follows the climactic confrontation between Dimmesdale and Hester in the forest. Frederic invokes his beloved Hawthorne perversely, however; at every turn he denies and inverts what is basic in Hawthorne's fiction, the assumption that all human acts have large and lasting consequences, that the acknowledgment of sin is the prerequisite for redemption. The contrast between the English title of *The Marble Faun*, the Hawthorne novel that treats the story of the Fall most explicitly, and the English title of Frederic's novel is instructive: *Transformation* versus *Illumination*—a half-century of experience stands exposed in the shift of attitude implied in those two titles.

To Theron's befuddled mind, sitting in the forest with Celia and toying with the ribbon at her waist is an adulterous act that in itself is redemptive. As he sat there and "boldly patted and caressed" the folds of her dress, Theron tells Celia, it was "as if I were a boy again, a good, pure-minded, fond little child" (p. 266). What Theron sees as a spiritual return to innocence, however, is only reversion to what Celia rightly identifies as instinct. Or, as Frederic puts it elsewhere in the novel, Theron turns to Celia in obedience to "the universal law of nature,—the law which prompts the pallid spindling

---

[55] *The Spectator*, LXXVI (1896), 486. Frederic is quoted on his "literary parentage" in Robert Sherard, "Harold Frederic," p. 537. Frederic's early story "The Song of the Swamp-Robin" recalls Hawthorne to the point of absurdity. The heroine not only seems "a second Pearl, daughter of Hester Prynne," but also marries to become "Mrs. Hathorne" (*The Independent*, XLIII [1891], 395).

sprout of the potato in the cellar to strive feebly toward the light" (p. 191).

Hester Prynne assured the wretched women who came to her for comfort and counsel that someday "a new truth would be revealed, in order to establish the whole relation between man and woman on a surer ground of mutual happiness." [56] Many years have passed since Hawthorne's time and many more since Hester's, and once more a minister sits in the forest with the woman he loves as she lets down her hair to catch the sunlight filtering through the trees. If Theron or Celia were asked whether Hester's brighter period had come at last, they would surely reply yes. "It is the one fixed rule of my life," says Celia, "to obey my whims" (p. 260); then all was spoken indeed.

The kiss Celia confers on Theron in the forest plunges him into fantasies of life with her. Walking alone, he cannot escape the fancy that he has seen a dryad, "the wonderful form of a woman," never before seen by mortal eye, rising from the waters of "a strange hidden pool" (p. 270). Eventually, the kiss leads him to follow Celia and Father Forbes on the train to New York City. When his seat-mate calls his attention to a yacht moored on the Hudson, Theron immediately begins to dream of escape with Celia, of sailing away with her—as Hester and Dimmesdale once dreamed of sailing far from puritan shores. Frederic's ironic warning is as subtle as it was in the evocation of the Actaeon story: so intent is Theron on dreams of life on a yacht with Celia that he does not hear when his companion points out the next sight of interest, Aaron Burr's house.

In Celia's hotel room Theron learns the truth at last. The

---

[56] *The Scarlet Letter* (Modern Library ed.; New York, n.d.), p. 302.

kiss was a kiss of farewell. "We thought you were going to be a real acquisition," Celia says, but "we find that you are a bore" (p. 331). The reduction of the question of human behavior from Hawthorne's good and evil to Celia's boring and interesting is startling. Theron is denied the luxury of sailing away on a yacht, but he is not obliged to stand upon the pillory and declare his *mea culpa:* he simply sets sail for Seattle.

The Soulsbys are curiously linked to Ledsmar, Forbes, and Celia. Brother Souslby, like Ledsmar, is a kind of doctor and a botanist of sorts. Like Forbes, both of the Soulsbys see their religious function as a business of dramatics, of manipulating machinery behind the scenes. And Sister Soulsby is, like Celia, an accomplished musician particularly fond of Chopin. Like Celia also, Sister Soulsby is distinctly sexual. Her body emits, to Theron's distraction, "a delicate, significant odor, . . . something which was not a perfume, yet deserved as gracious a name" (p. 149). "I will be your doctor," Celia says the night she plays Chopin for Theron, and indeed all of them, Celia, Ledsmar, Forbes, and the Soulsbys, act as Theron's physicians, but only the Soulsbys are good doctors.

Once Celia has captured Theron, on the night that concludes with her bowing low and laughing gayly before the statue of Venus in her studio, she begins to lose interest in him. Dr. Ledsmar, the physician who no longer practices healing because it is not scientific enough, loses interest in Theron as soon as he has classified the species, as soon as he has seen Theron's lineaments in a reptile. And Father Forbes, the preacher who no longer preaches, tells Theron, when he calls for the last time at the Catholic parsonage, "I'm afraid we have nothing to tempt you very much" (p. 285), and shuts his door henceforth against the poor man.

Only the Soulsbys stick by Theron. They are neither as

genteel as Father Forbes nor as cold-blooded as Dr. Ledsmar, and Sister Soulsby could never be called what Ledsmar calls Celia, a mad ass. The Soulsbys know everything the three tempters know, but they add the comic sense to knowledge. Like many people with the gift of comic vision, the Soulsbys are outlaws, in their case literally as well as figuratively, for both of them have had brushes with the law. They are pragmatic all right, mundanely so: "You might just as well say that potatoes are unclean and unfit to eat," Sister Soulsby says when Theron questions her methods, "because manure is put into the ground they grow in" (p. 176). They are pragmatic even to the point of accepting illusion: Theron learns to his surprise that the Soulsbys are themselves converted every time they play their parts in the revivals they stage with such premeditation. But their pragmatism stops short at the idea of progress. Will Theron always be a backslider, asks Alice Ware at the close of the novel? "For mercy's sake," responds Sister Soulsby, "don't ever try to have him pretend to be anything else!" (p. 351).

There is one character in *The Damnation* who has not been mentioned so far, who is in fact never mentioned in discussions of the novel. Jeremiah Madden, Celia's father, never influences the action of *The Damnation* in any way, yet Frederic devotes over half a chapter to describing him. Of his living children, only one, Michael, is spiritually Jeremiah's. Michael is the warning angel of this Paradise Lost; it is he who talks to Theron in Eden—or at any rate in the steam heat of a conservatory crowded with tropical plants—and warns him to mend his ways before it is too late. Jeremiah is the prophet who remembers the old ways and weeps for what is past. Old Testament figures that they are, they are anachronisms in America and the modern age. Michael is on his death bed when he gives his warning to Theron, and Jeremiah is a lonely man whose chief pleasure is to smoke his clay pipe in the kitchen of his mansion.

For Father Forbes, the long perspective of history implies that man had better accept experience with good manners and equanimity; for Dr. Ledsmar, that men are things shaped by forces; for Celia, that instinct (whim) is the guiding rule; for Theron, that change is progress; for the Soulsbys, that life is a comedy. But when Jeremiah Madden looks down the corridors of the past, he sees tragedy. Born a Connemara peasant, he has fled the potato famine to the United States, and although he has become the richest man in Octavius, he is still a simple peasant. Jeremiah often visits the nearby churchyard in which his ten dead children lie, but whenever he can, he walks out into the country to a deserted and overgrown cemetery which holds the bodies of those many countrymen who crossed the seas with him only to die in the New World. In the neglected cemetery, Frederic says, the latest date on any stone is in the early fifties. To Jeremiah, "what had happened between was a meaningless vision,—as impersonal as the passing of the planets overhead. He rarely had an impulse to tears in the new cemetery, where his ten children were. He never left this weed-grown, forsaken old God's-acre dry eyed" (p. 89).

Only here in all of *The Damnation* does Frederic turn from the comedy of man the foolish to the tragedy of man the sorrowful. In *The Return of the O'Mahony* Frederic had also put aside the comic mask for a glimpse of the tragic. As the Irish heroine of *The O'Mahony* sits atop holy Mount Gabriel looking homeward, she has a strange fancy: " 'Twas that this lovely Ireland I looked down upon was beautiful with the beauty of death; that 'twas the corpse of me country I was taking a last view of" (p. 228). But in neither Kate O'Mahony nor Jeremiah Madden is Frederic's usual voice heard, the sublimely comic voice that speaks the last act of *The Damnation*.

Writing of the dénouement of *The Damnation*, where Celia tells Theron that he is a bore, John Henry Raleigh observes that Theron passes through two distinct stages in his desperation. First, his mind lapsing into the primitive, Theron's thoughts glow with what Frederic calls "that first devilish radiance ushering in Creation, of which the first-fruit was Cain." Then, when the impulse to murder Celia on the spot passes, Theron "drops into something worse," Raleigh says, "into a pre-Creation loneliness and the silence of Pascal's interstellar spaces." [57] Yet the scene does not end there, with Theron plunged alone into "the Egyptian night which lay on the face of the deep while the earth was yet without form and void. . . . alone among awful, planetary solitudes which crushed him" (p. 333). There is still one further stage in the descent, one that takes place as Theron walks down the stairs from Celia's rooms. This stage, which Raleigh does not mention, returns to the comic, yet in its way is almost more terrifying than Theron's fall into the primitive and thence to the chaos of pre-Creation. In the last lines of the chapter, when his knees begin to buckle on the stairs, Theron attributes his weakness to humiliation and a broken heart, and lets out a new cry of despair. "Then," the chapter concludes, "as he held tight to the banister and governed his descent step by step, it occurred to him that it must be the wine he had had for breakfast. Upon examination, he was not so unhappy, after all" (p. 335).

The ultimate irony in *The Damnation* is Frederic's dis-

---

[57] "*The Damnation*," p. 226.

closure that Theron's faith in his capacity for self-development ment remains undiminished and that he has learned nothing from even the last of his "illuminations." "We surmise that we have not heard the last of Ware," wrote one reviewer,[58] and the speculation is as unsettling in its way as the one that closes *The Confidence-Man*: "Something further may follow this Masquerade." That Frederic saw Theron's illusions in *The Damnation of Theron Ware* as comic, rather than tragic as Dreiser and Fitzgerald saw such illusions, detracts nothing from his achievement, one of the great achievements of American letters.

[58] *The Bookman* (New York), IV (Nov., 1896), 196.

6 / *March Hares* and *Gloria Mundi*

Harold Frederic's last three novels, *March Hares* (1896), *Gloria Mundi* (1898), and *The Market-Place* (1899), are markedly different from one another, yet they are usually grouped together because of their English settings. Although the three works were generally well received when they appeared, twentieth-century critics have had little good to say about them. To Robert Morss Lovett, they are "stereotyped and conventional"; to John Berryman, "superficial and slovenly"; and to Everett Carter, "scarcely worth mentioning." [1]

[1] Lovett, introduction to *The Damnation* (New York: Albert and Charles Boni, 1924), p. viii; Berryman, *Stephen Crane* (New York, 1950), p. 198; Carter, introduction to *The Damnation*, John Harvard Library ed., pp. ix–x. Carter's comment is the most damaging of those quoted, for the large claims he so convincingly makes for *The Damnation* are not based primarily on the importance of the novel as a piece of realism. Carter says of Frederic's last three novels: "Stephen Crane was right in looking upon them with 'a sense of desertion.'" What Crane said—and he said it before *Gloria Mundi* and *The Market-Place* were published—was this: "It is natural that since Frederic has lived so long in England his pen should turn toward English life. One does not look upon this fact with unmixed joy. It is mourn-

Harshest of all is Clarence Gohdes, who characterizes them as "apparently . . . contrived to delight shopgirls with scenes of lovely old estates." [2]

Those who have given more than a shrug of dismissal to the English novels agree on the cause of the supposed falling off: Frederic's work "lost its semblance of actuality," Van Wyck Brooks writes, "when his American memories grew dim and he began to make up romances of England." [3] Interest in Frederic's fiction was premised on his importance as a native realist; his last three novels desert the native scene and tend toward romance; therefore the English novels are presumably inferior; in fact, they must be failures. Even O'Donnell and Franchere, who in Granville Hicks's judgment "considerably exaggerate the merits of the later novels," [4] become somewhat evasive when they reach the English novels. They praise *Gloria Mundi*, for example, for presenting "a remarkable, penetrating contrast between appearance and reality," but they qualify their praise by apologetically noting that the book is "laced in a web of romance." [5]

---

ful to lose his work even for a time. It is for this reason that I have made myself disagreeable upon several occasions by my expressed views of *March Hares*. It is a worthy book, but one has a sense of desertion. We cannot afford a loss of this kind. But at any rate he has grasped English life with a precision of hand that is only equalled by the precision with which he grasped our life, and his new book will shine out for English eyes in a way with which they are not too familiar. It is a strong and striking delineation, free, bold, and straight" ("Harold Frederic," *The Chap-Book*, VIII (1898), p. 359).

[2] "The Later Nineteenth Century," in Arthur Hobson Quinn, ed., *The Literature of the American People* (New York, 1951), p. 745.

[3] Van Wyck Brooks, *The Confident Years* (New York, 1952), p. 258.

[4] "Literary Horizons: From Poe through Faulkner," *Saturday Review*, XLIV (Aug. 12, 1961), 13.

[5] *Harold Frederic* (New York, 1961), p. 161.

Calling Frederic's last three novels "English" is misleading. A statement by Lewis Mumford on the expatriate painters of the nineties applies equally well to Harold Frederic as an expatriate writer:

It is not that one requires the American painter to be specifically American in the sense that he utilizes local color, local scenery, local symbols: rather, one asks that his pictures should be a resolution or an interpretation of his total experience of life, and if he is an American that fact, along with many others, will be an inescapable element in his work.[6]

Frederic's last novels are English only in the sense that *The Marble Faun* is Italian. If it is proper to insist on the crucial importance of the American experience for such voluntary expatriates as James and Eliot, then it is equally proper to insist on that importance for Frederic, who was an expatriate not by choice but because of the requirements of his journalistic profession. Although he lived abroad for the entire period of his maturity, Frederic "combined in his work, his appearance, and his qualities of mind and temperament characteristics which seemed to his contemporaries, seem to us, in fact, curiously typical of America and Americans." [7]

The man whom Stephen Crane found still, after fourteen years in England, "a great reminiscent panorama of the Mohawk Valley," [8] the man whom Louise Imogen Guiney says spelt, ate, and dreamt American to the end of his days, cannot be thought to have lost his involvement with the American experience. Although *Gloria Mundi* has not an American scene or character in it, Miss Guiney points out,

[6] *The Brown Decades* (New York, 1931), p. 210.
[7] Lovett, introduction to *The Damnation*, p. vi.
[8] "Harold Frederic," p. 358.

"none but an American could have written it."[9] The same can be said of *March Hares* and *The Market-Place*. Frederic died at forty-two, before he could realize his plans for another novel of the American Revolution and many more stories of the Civil War.[10] Had he lived longer, however, and never returned to the American scene in his fiction, there is every reason to believe that the works would have been distinctly American.

March Hares is admittedly a slight work. Frederic himself tried to conceal his authorship of it. But *Gloria Mundi* and *The Market-Place*, although they add nothing to the reputation of the native realist, add much to the distinction of the artist. In his last three novels Frederic left the locale of the earlier work, but not the concerns. The shift from the American to the English scene did not constitute the disaster that has generally been assumed. The "English" novels develop naturally and inventively out of the preoccupations evident in *Seth's Brother's Wife* and *The Damnation of Theron Ware*. *March Hares* may be weak, but *Gloria Mundi* is excellent, and *The Market-Place* is triumphant, with the exception of *The Damnation*, the finest novel Frederic ever wrote. "Of all the younger novelists of our day, save one," *The Atlantic Monthly* wrote of Frederic at the time of his death, "he seemed to give the most virile and splendid promise."[11] The tragedy of Harold Frederic's career is not

[9] "Harold Frederic: A Half-Length Sketch from the Life," *Book Buyer*, XVII (1899), 600.

[10] For Frederic's proposed novel of the Revolution, see Chapter 3. He is quoted as planning many more Civil War stories in Robert H. Sherard, "Harold Frederic," *The Idler*, XII (1897), 536.

[11] Review of *Gloria Mundi*, LXXXIII (1899), 522. "Save one" probably refers to Stephen Crane.

that he failed to live up to his promise but that he did not live to fulfill his promise.

A few months after the appearance of *The Damnation*, Frederic published his sixth novel, under the pseudonym George Forth. *The Yellow Book* was ecstatic: "Have you seen *March Hares?*" The Yellow Dwarf (Henry Harland) wanted to make sure that his readers had, for this was none of your "Dog-literature," none of your tail-wagging productions by people like George Moore, to be adopted and petted by the Average Man. This was a Cat (Henry James was the King of the Cats), "a most spirited, lithe-limbed, and surprising Cat." *March Hares* "will mystify and irritate the Average Man," Harland predicted, "as much as it will rejoice his betters." [12]

Harland dismissed as "rank impossibility" a current newspaper report that George Forth was Frederic:

Mr. Harold Frederic has proved that he can cross Bulldogs with Newfoundlands, that he can write able, unreadable *Illuminations* in choice Americanese. He could no more flitter and flutter and coruscate, and turn somersaults in mid-air, and fall lightly on his feet, in the Cat-fashion of George Forth, than he could dance the hornpipe on the point of a needle.[13]

One must conclude that Harland was up to some mystification of his own, for the publisher of *The Yellow Book*, John Lane, was also the publisher of *March Hares*, and Harland

[12] "Dogs, Cats, Books, and the Average Man: A Letter to the Editor from 'The Yellow Dwarf,'" *Yellow Book*, X (1896), 18.

[13] "Dogs, Cats, Books," p. 21. Objections to Frederic's American English were common in English reviews. Mabel Birchenough's highly complimentary notice of *The Damnation* in the *Nineteenth Century*, for example, protested that "the terrible Yankee jargon" too often grated on English nerves (XL [1896], 769).

surely knew the secret of George Forth's identity.[14] The Yellow Dwarf's offer of a bottle of wine to the first person who could tell him the name of the two, or even three or four, authors who had collaborated on *March Hares* must have been intended to throw readers off the scent of the novel's true authorship.

Perverse as Harland's (or Lane's) game was, it does seem almost impossible that Frederic could have written two such different novels as *The Damnation* and *March Hares*. Had Frederic's secret been better kept, it seems unlikely that many would ever have guessed it, but it "was let out very quickly, against his will." [15] Despite his fears that the reputation of *The Damnation* would suffer if his authorship of the slighter *March Hares* were known, nothing of the sort occurred. *The Damnation* continued to boom, and *March Hares* sold briskly.

[14] Lane had published *Mrs. Albert Grundy* earlier in 1896 and "The Truce of the Bishop" in the October, 1895, *Yellow Book*. Katherine Mix offers no source for her story of a quarrel in which "the brawny" Frederic "was said to have put over one or two arguments with such telling effect that Lane took to his bed" (*A Study in Yellow* [Lawrence, Kans., 1960], p. 40). Gertrude Atherton also reports the rumor of a fist fight over money, but she says nothing about Frederic sending Lane to his bed. In 1898, Frederic mentioned to Miss Atherton his "deep disinclination to put an added penny into John Lane's pocket" (letter of July 10, quoted in Atherton, *Adventures of a Novelist* [London, 1932], pp. 304–305).

[15] " 'Illumination' and its Author," *The Bookman* (London), X (1896), 138. The discovery that a virtuoso like Frederic was trying to conceal his authorship appears to have made some people suspicious. When the unsigned manuscript of Ellen Glasgow's *The Descendant* arrived at Harper's, the reader there identified it as Frederic's (Frederick P. McDowell, *Ellen Glasgow and the Ironic Art of Fiction* [Madison, Wis., 1960], p. 17). Among those who disliked Frank Harris, the rumor persisted that all of his stories were written by Frederic (Grant Richards, *Memories of a Misspent Youth* [London, 1932], p. 240).

Under Frederic's own name by then, the book was still in print a year later in England and also in the United States, where, according to Frederic's obituary in the New York *Tribune*, it enjoyed a real vogue.[16] The critics were kindly disposed. Although "one does not like to name *March Hares* in the same breath with *Illumination*," said *The Academy*, Frederic's book could be welcomed for what it was, a light-hearted "holiday effort." [17] Most of the other reviewers treated the book with similar tolerance and moderate approval.

In their critical biography of Frederic, O'Donnell and Franchere briefly discuss *March Hares* as a pleasant "exercise for the left hand," and no critic in the twentieth century has ever tried to make out more of a case for it.[18] As a period piece it can still be read with a certain pleasure. Frederic's pseudonym suggests the spirit in which much of the novel was written: Victorianism is dead; long live George IV and a

[16] Oct. 20, 1898, p. 7.

[17] William Wallace, *The Academy*, L (1896), 143.

[18] *Harold Frederic*, p. 118. The notes in the Frederic Papers, Library of Congress, indicate that this novel, unlike the others, was written quickly. Frederic wrote the major part, roughly 45,000 words, between the end of August and November 19, 1895, a rate of more than 550 words a day from the pen of a man already heavily burdened with journalistic assignments. Reminiscences of Frederic repeatedly express wonder at his prodigious energy and powers of concentration. When an interviewer asked him how he managed to get so much work done and yet have time for leisure, Frederic replied, "System, my boy, system. I have working hours and I have playing hours. When I am at work, I shut myself up and nobody sees me; when I play, I am en [*sic*] evidence" ("Harold Frederic: Author of Theron Ware," *Current Literature*, XX [July, 1896], 14). Play, one might add, included loving attention to the children of both his households, an active club life, a passion for fishing and antiquarianism, and hobbies—horticulture, photography, sketching, stamp collecting, and bookbinding.

return to freer, happier days! Through many of its pages, *March Hares* is a self-consciously gay novel of the gay nineties, the whimsical sort of thing that made James M. Barrie, Clyde Fitch, and the Richard Harding Davis of the Van Bibber stories so popular. Indeed, the reviewer who innocently recommended Fitch's *The Smart Set* (1897) as "excessively up to date" could have been speaking of *March Hares*. Like *The Smart Set*, Frederic's novel is a kind of hornbook of the nineties for those aspiring to learn "what wit and frivolity are" and "how to attain just that little touch of audacious vulgarity which is nowadays the 'cachet' of fashion." [19] It is unpretentious and often charming, but Harold Frederic's reputation would be none the weaker if George Forth had retained title to the novel indefinitely.

March Hares is, however, a far more interesting novel than has been recognized. Perhaps because it was written with the left hand, as Frederic's other novels were not, it reveals in almost blunt terms some of his deeper preoccupations. *The Yellow Book* called the novel "*opéra-bouffe* masquerading as legitimate drama," [20] but one wonders whether it is not, in fact, legitimate drama masquerading as *opéra-bouffe*. The situation at the beginning is hardly what the reviews of a gay and light-hearted novel lead one to expect. The hero, appropriately named Mosscrop, stands on Westminster Bridge at seven in the morning. He has been out all night drinking and, it is implied later in the novel, whoring as well. Standing there in the cold morning light, David Mosscrop is a miserable figure:

[19] The review, from the Chicago *Times-Herald*, is quoted in an advertisement for *The Smart Set* placed by H. S. Stone and Co. in the *Chap-Book*, VIII (1898), 223.

[20] "Dogs, Cats, Books," p. 18.

His thoughts were a burden to him, and his head ached viciously. This was no new experience of a morning, worse luck; he had grown accustomed to these evil opening hours of depression and nausea. The fact that it was his birthday, however, gave uncomfortable point to his reflections. He had actually crossed the threshold of the thirties, and he came into the presence of this new lustrum worse than empty-handed. . . . He stared down at the slowly-moving flood, and asked himself angrily why a man of thirty who had learned nothing worth learning, achieved nothing worth the doing; who didn't even know enough to keep sober over-night, should not be thrown like garbage into the river [pp. 1–2].[21]

Watching the crowd of people crossing the Thames on their way to work, Mosscrop muses on the mystery of London's economy, the mystery "of all its millions playing dumbly, uninstructedly, almost like automata, their appointed parts in the strange machinery" (p. 5). Out of the mass of worn, sleepy faces, Mosscrop finds himself gazing at a particular face and suddenly realizes that it belongs to a young woman he has seen many times working in the reading room of the British Museum.

He starts a conversation with her and soon learns that despite her fashionable appearance she is out of work, has no resources, and has been locked out of her room that morning for back rent. When he chides her for keeping as her last possession a stylish but impractical dress, she tries to explain, and he suddenly realizes what she is trying to tell him. All else having failed, she has resolved to go on the streets. "What else

<hr />

[21] All page references to *March Hares* are to the first American edition (New York: D. Appleton and Co., 1896).

could I do?" she cries. "Nothing but throw myself into the river. And that I *won't* do" (p. 42). Mosscrop is ashamed of his own thoughts of suicide and is all the more intrigued by this sad young woman with the improbable name of Vestalia Peaussier (really Skinner, it develops). He takes her off to a magnificent breakfast, and after some two hundred and fifty pages of trivial complications, Mosscrop and Vestalia are married.

The legend in Kate Lyon's family that *March Hares* was inspired by Frederic's first meeting with Kate is plausible.[22] Mosscrop bears a striking resemblance to Frederic. In several of his Civil War stories Frederic left pictures of himself in the small boys who see and sometimes relate the events of those stories, and, as has long been recognized, Frederic must have put a good deal of himself as a naive young man into his portraits of Seth Fairchild, Horace Boyce, Reuben Tracy, and Theron Ware. But, although one catches echoes of his mature voice in Father Forbes and Dr. Ledsmar, not until *March Hares* did the author reveal very much of the worldly, "grown-up" Frederic whom Frank Harris remembered as "one of the most extraordinary and fascinating personalities of our time." [23]

Like the mature Frederic, Mosscrop is a burly and strong-featured man who combines a knack for making crushing remarks with a habit of impulsive generosity. Again like Frederic, he is a gourmet and expert on wine, a *bon vivant* who knows both the dives of the back streets and the best

---

[22] See O'Donnell and Franchere, *Harold Frederic*, p. 118.
[23] "Harold Frederic: Ad Memoriam," *Saturday Review*, LXXXVI (1898), 527.

restaurants in London.[24] Although Frederic's education was largely informal and Mosscrop is university trained, both author and character share an encyclopedic knowledge of any topic that happens to come up. And, above all, one sees, or rather hears, Frederic in Mosscrop's positive torrent of lively talk. With Mosscrop, as nowhere else in Frederic's fiction, one gets some sense of the vast fund of wit, epigram, learning, and anecdote that made Frederic famous as a conversationalist in an era that is celebrated for its brilliant talk.

Only once before had Frederic come so close to portraying his older, his successful self. In a story published in 1888, "The Editor and the School Ma'am," he had drawn a hero who looks very much like Frederic at the time he was editor of the Albany *Evening Journal*.[25] Alexander Waring is very young for his lofty position as editor of an established and influential newspaper, so young that people find pretexts to drop by his office so that they can see for themselves whether reports of his tender years are true, just as people used to stop by Frederic's office in Albany to see whether a boy in his twenties was really sitting in Thurlow Weed's chair.[26]

[24] At the meetings of the Ghouls, an eating club which met monthly at a restaurant in High Holborn, no matter who was chairman for the month, Frederic ordered the food and wines, with the same delight in his gourmet's knowledge that Mosscrop shows at the lavish meals which are consumed in *March Hares* (Arthur Warren, "Harold Frederic: The Reminiscences of a Colleague," New York *Times*, Oct. 25, 1898, p. 19). Frederic's anonymous articles on prostitution for *The Pall Mall Budget* imply a first-hand acquaintance with the bordellos of London.

[25] New York *Times*, Sept. 9, 1888, p. 14. The story is in part a dramatization of Howells' famous remarks on "the smiling aspects of life" and the unsuitability of Dostoevskian realism to the American scene; see "The Editor's Study," *Harper's*, LXXIII (1886), 641–642.

[26] See Charles R. Sherlock, "The Harold Frederic I Knew," *Saturday Evening Post*, CLXXI (1899), 616.

Alexander Waring does not feel young, however; he feels terribly old. Like David Mosscrop on his thirtieth birthday, Waring is oppressed by the sense that for all intents and purposes his life might as well be over.

There are indications that Frederic had these feelings even before he reached thirty. In a letter written in 1883, Frederic speaks in a mood hardly to be expected in a young man who nine months before had been called to Albany and an extraordinarily early success:

Death and disease up above made me a leader-writer, then an editor. At last I am here, in a place which my wildest vision of the "Sebastian" epoch scarcely reached, and there are ashes inside the apple. I am four years older; I know better than they are worth knowing a host of eminent political humbugs and sharpers; I get five or six times as much money; I do not eat or sleep as well and drink better; I am unhappy. . . . Surely it is all vanity and emptiness.

Then Frederic says something that points to one of the true sources of his power as a novelist: "I have treated you with this introspective analysis, because I have come to take a quite impersonal interest in studying myself. . . ." [27]

The note of bitterness is rare (though by no means unique),

[27] Frederic to Benjamin Paul Blood, May 9, 1883, quoted by permission of the Harvard College Library. "The 'Sebastian' epoch" refers to Frederic's story "Brother Sebastian's Friendship," published in the Utica *Observer*, Sept. 6, 1879, p. 2. Ironically, considering the tone of Frederic's letter, Blood was the author of *Optimism: The Lesson of the Ages* (1860). Part of the great interest of the letter to Blood is that it reveals Frederic already dreaming "of the day when I can command a living by honest work in good humane literature" very early in his journalistic career and at a time when he had published no fiction outside of six stories in the Utica *Observer* and the Albany *Evening Journal*.

for Frederic was Johnsonian not only in his conversation and physical presence but also, with far greater success than Johnson, in his exercise of sheer will power to dispel depression.[28] When he was in his early thirties Frederic wrote to a younger man offering advice in which one hears both Frederic's disenchantments and his efforts to maintain good spirits:

Enthusiasm dies early enough, my dear fellow, and gets frostbitten, water-soaked, mildewed, worm-eaten, quickly enough, without taking off its wrappings and exposing it to all the chance draughts which think themselves winds. And enthusiasm is so good a thing that all the wisdom in our outfit should be used to guard it from misuse.[29]

Even if it were certain that *March Hares* was inspired by Frederic's first meeting with Kate Lyon, obviously one would have no right to assert that Frederic, his marriage a failure and the apples of success turned to ashes, exposed his own mood in every detail of Mosscrop's unhappiness. Kate Lyon may have been Frederic's "true companion, his real wife," as George Gissing said, may have been the woman who "saved him and enabled him to do admirable things," but it does not follow that she saved him from the brink of suicide as Vestalia saves Mosscrop.[30]

[28] The reports Frederic made on the cholera epidemic which swept Italy and France in 1884 reveal that he believed ill-health, like depression, might be combatted with will: "Courage and hope are of the greatest importance to him [the cholera patient]. If he can keep from yielding to despair, the chances in his favor are trebled" (New York *Times*, July 27, 1884).

[29] Letter to an unnamed American poet living in London, 1889 or 1890, quoted in Guiney, "A Half-Length Sketch," p. 603.

[30] Letter to John Stokes, 1898 or 1899, quoted in Lillian Gilkes, *Cora Crane* (Bloomington, Ind., 1960), p. 168. Gissing's own sorry experiments with common-law marriage, one assumes, disposed him to particular sympathy for Kate and his friend Frederic. Although

It seems clear, however, that many of the thoughts that burden the hero of *March Hares* weighed on Frederic as well. Partly because of his meteoric rise in a profession he found to be a "vile and hollow fool rink," [31] partly because of whatever was melancholiac in his temperament, and partly, perhaps, because of his response to the mood of *fin de siècle*, Frederic appears to have felt the past a heavy load to bear at times. At one point in *March Hares*, Mosscrop asks Vestalia whether she remembers Henley's lines:

> The smell of ships (that earnest of romance),
> A sense of space and water, and thereby
> A lamplit bridge ouching the troubled sky,
> And look, O look! a tangle of silvery gleams
> And dusky lights, our River and all his dreams,
> His dreams of a dead past that cannot die! [p. 89] [32]

Miss Gilkes identifies Frederic's friend Julia Frankau, who published under the name Frank Danby, as "Frank Danby Frankau, an agnostic old gentleman," she offers an accurate and ample account of the scandal which followed Frederic's death. At the same time the details of Frederic's private life were being dragged into the open at Kate's trial for murder, two rival appeals for funds to support his children were addressed to the public, one for Mrs. Frederic's children, the other, organized by Cora Crane, for Kate Lyon's children. Before the dust settled, countless clergymen, members of Parliament, journalists, publishers, artists, and writers were debating whether Frederic's illegitimate offspring had any right to charity. See *Cora Crane*, pp. 164–172, and the entries indexed under Kate Frederic plus the entries on pp. 210–211 in Robert W. Stallman and Lillian Gilkes, eds., *Stephen Crane: Letters*, (New York, 1960). See also C. W. E. Bigsby, "The 'Christian Science Case,'" *American Literary Realism*, No. 2 (Spring, 1968), pp. 77–83.

[31] Letter to Benjamin Paul Blood, May 9, 1883, quoted by permission of the Harvard College Library.

[32] Frederic quotes Henley's lines, from the *Andante con moto* section of the very popular "London Voluntaries," as they appear in their first publication, in *The Song of the Sword and Other Verses*

These are the only lines of poetry that Frederic, who generally disliked poetry, ever quoted in any of his works.[33] If they had some special meaning for him, as seems likely, it cannot have been the meaning Henley intended. Rather than affirming the hopeful continuity of life to Mosscrop, they suggest the human incapacity ever to be done once and for all with past error and folly.

Despite a disregard for convention shocking even to the liberated nineties, and despite the modernity that Vestalia and Mosscrop claim (Vestalia calls herself a New Woman) they are bound to the past by their very professions. He is a professor of history; she, a compiler of genealogies. *March Hares* opens approximately where *The Damnation* closes. Mosscrop gazes into the garbage-strewn Thames with much the same sense of personal waste and disgust that must have driven Theron Ware to the East River on the night he thought of committing suicide on the Brooklyn Bridge. Mosscrop is much closer to jumping than Theron was, however, for he has long lived with the sense of the past that Theron encountered for the first time in the remarks of Father Forbes and Dr. Ledsmar. "Never mind the dead men" is Sister Soulsby's ad-

---

(1892). In subsequent editions, "ouching" (*i.e.*, adorning as with brooches) appears as "touching," and the last line of the passage is altered to "His dreams that never save in our deaths can die." Henley and Frederic were well enough acquainted for the poet to invite Frederic to his home (John Connell, *W. E. Henley* [London, 1949], p. 245).

[33] "I cannot, with here and there a modern exception," Frederic said, "even read poetry. . . . I have never written two lines of poetry in my life, . . . and I never will" (quoted in Robert H. Sherard, "Harold Frederic," p. 540). Actually, Frederic did write some lines of bardic Irish verse for *The Return of the O'Mahony* and "The Wooing of Teige." Frederic is known to have published only one poem, "The Opium-Eater" (Utica *Observer*, Jan. 19, 1879, p. 6).

vice to Theron. But, Frederic asks in *March Hares,* how does one forget them? What if the past will not die?

Mosscrop's dilemma is implicit not only in Theron's experiences but in those of the protagonists of the other works as well. The young men and women of Frederic's earlier novels struggle and strive to attain the sophistication and knowledge that Mosscrop has attained at thirty. Even at eighteen, Mosscrop jokes, "Confucius, John Knox, and Lord Bacon rolled in one would have been frightened of me" (p. 57). Application, intelligence, and opportunity have taken him through the years of schooling that characters like Seth Fairchild lacked, until he now holds the most highly-endowed chair his university has to offer.

All his intelligence, all his learning, however, have left Mosscrop in a position as absurd as any the country boy heroes ever fell into. Thanks to the hobbyhorse of the man who endowed his university and his chair, he is doomed to lecturing on the crackpot thesis that the Culdees of ancient Scotland were the Chaldeans of the Bible. Mosscrop lectures on the Culdees three weeks a year to half-empty classrooms and has nothing more to do. When Vestalia asks him how he earns his living, he answers bitterly and honestly: "I am an habitual criminal by profession" (p. 48).

Even when *March Hares* does speak in the light-hearted tones that the reviewers heard to the exclusion of all else, sadness is not far away. The pleasant description of the first day Mosscrop and Vestalia spend together, for example, includes a somber backdrop of ruined temples, fragments of classical statuary, and ancient sarcophagi in the British Museum. Love finally does save Mosscrop, as love saves Alexander Waring in "The Editor and the School Ma'am." At the conclusion of that story, Waring abandons the Russian novels on which he has been feeding his gloom. Commenting on the suitability of Gogol's realism for the American scene, he gives his office boy the money for a new overcoat; and casting aside his copy of *Dead Souls*, he says in the closing line, "let them go to their own funeral. I like to feel that I am alive." Even here there is a note of qualification: "I like to feel." So also in *March Hares* one senses a shadow of doubt beneath the high spirits of its brighter passages and right through to the conventional happy ending.

Vestalia and Mosscrop take shelter in each other's arms, resolving to "wipe the slate clean, and begin all over again quite fresh" (p. 38), but Frederic does not seem certain that their resolution can be kept. To start over again as Theron Ware intended to do at the conclusion of *The Damnation* may be possible for a Theron Ware, but how does a Mosscrop, or a Forbes or a Ledsmar, start over? Although one can caution against the misuse of precious enthusiasm "with all the wisdom in our outfit," what if one has already misused enthusiasm?

"It isn't like real life at all," Vestalia says of the love she and Mosscrop share, and he elaborates upon the remark:

I take my stand upon that definition. We have deliberately repudiated what are described as the realities of life. We discard them, cut them dead, decline to have anything whatever to do with them. We declare that it is fairyland that we are living in, and that we refuse to come out of it to the end of our days [p. 257].

The problem of the past, of the dead men, was not to be solved by fiat, however. Frederic's next novel, *Gloria Mundi*, begins with the fairytale story of a poor orphan who discovers that he is heir to a fabulous title and fortune, but the novel is no retreat into Mosscrop's fairyland. It is the saddest novel Frederic ever wrote, a somber assessment of just how heavy a weight the past can be.

Taken as a whole, the reviews of *Gloria Mundi* (1898) were the least favorable any book of Frederic's ever received. Although almost everyone had something good to say about it, the critics were dissatisfied. One suspects, moreover, that they would have expressed even more dissatisfaction if they had not been writing about a recently dead author whose other works they admired. The London *Bookman*, after paying high praise to Frederic's work in general, went on to warn its readers that *Gloria Mundi* "does not represent very completely the power or the attitude toward life of the gifted and respected author."[34] William Morton Payne placed the blame for the presumed failure of the work where it has lain ever since, on Frederic's lack of understanding of the English scene.[35]

Not all of the reviews were adverse by any means. The London *Daily Chronicle* spoke of "a triumph of characteriza-

---

[34] XV (1898), 83. *Gloria Mundi* was published in the United States and England in December, 1898, shortly after Frederic's death on October 19. Despite the mixed reviews, the novel sold fairly well. For some months after its publication it appeared sporadically on the best seller lists of the London *Bookman*. The year after its original American publication by Herbert S. Stone, *Gloria Mundi* was issued in a paperback edition by the International Book and Publishing Company of New York, and in 1913, Heinemann reissued the novel in paperback under the title *Pomps and Vanities*.

[35] *The Dial*, XXV (1898), 459. In his review of *The Market-Place*, Payne referred again to *Gloria Mundi*: "a failure precisely because its author had gained only a superficial knowledge of the society which he sought to depict" (*The Dial*, XXVII [1899], 21). Significantly, English reviewers did not object as did the American Payne to Frederic's understanding of the English scene. *The Athenaeum* protested that Frederic was too much of an outsider to good society to differentiate between types of English gentlewomen, but praised his men and found the book "distinctly European" (CXII [1898], 637).

tion rare indeed in fiction, even in such fiction as is given us by our greatest." [36] Frederic's thought had "clarified wonderfully" between *The Damnation* and *Gloria Mundi*, said the *Atlantic Monthly:* "We were confident that the clearing would go on; that *Gloria Mundi* also would prove but a provisional effort, making one stage more in an indefinite development." [37] *The Athenaeum* was equally laudatory: "The world lost a great novelist when Harold Frederic died. His 'Gloria Mundi' will be pronounced by some inferior to his 'Illumination.' Inferior, perhaps, though we do not think so." [38]

Reading the reviews, good, bad, and mixed, written in the nineties and the remarks that have been made about *Gloria Mundi* in the twentieth century, one gets the impression that the novel has never been understood. Despite the title, which should have served as some kind of a guide, Frederic's ironic intentions have been almost completely ignored. One reviewer went so far as to object that "there is hardly enough gloria mundi" in the book.[39] Some of the confusion arose over the Utopian system that one of the characters in the novel propounds at elaborate length. *The Dial* confessed that it could not decide whether Frederic was for or against the system, while *The Spectator* was pretty sure that he was for it.[40] The

[36] Quoted in Heinemann's advertisement in *The Academy*, LV (1898), 312.

[37] LXXXIII (1899), 522.

[38] CXII (1898), 637.

[39] *The Bookman* (London), XV (1898), 83.

[40] William Morton Payne, *The Dial*, XXV (1898), 459; *The Spectator*, LXXXI (1898), 655. Arthur Hobson Quinn also mistakenly assumes that Frederic approved of the system in *Gloria Mundi*. According to Quinn, Frederic "represented the strength and weakness of the English patrician system and the materialistic basis of its social structure . . . as a contrast to the truer democracy of the Middle Ages" (*American Fiction* [New York, 1936], p. 452).

truth of the matter, as O'Donnell and Franchere point out, is that everything said about reform in *Gloria Mundi* leads to the conclusion that "if Frederic had once been attracted to the Utopian dreams of Morris and Ruskin, or to those of Bellamy and Howells, he now rejects them totally." [41]

The confusion was about more than the system, however. Because *Gloria Mundi* has some witty things to say about lords and ladies, the reviewers appear to have assumed that it was a light-hearted romance. They compared it repeatedly to *March Hares*, a novel whose implications had escaped them entirely. Even O'Donnell and Franchere, who have so many fine things to say about *Gloria Mundi*, miss the pervasively somber tone of the novel. They find it written "with such eminent good humor that one almost thinks that the author took neither himself nor his subject seriously." [42]

Evidence of how good Frederic's humor was at the time he wrote *Gloria Mundi* is to be found in the pages and pages of elaborate notes for the novel in the Library of Congress. One set opens, "Custom is the ultimate law," and another, titled "England," speaks of a "land without sunsets" peopled by a race "subtle, planning, intriguing to [a] degree," a middle class in awe of titles, an upper class of "many vicious, stupid people." And the lower class: "The Smiths went on the Crusades as well as the Nevills. . . . There was the same vanity, selfishness, ferocity of the male in all of them—and *is*." Still another set of notes, listed under "The Sex Passion," speaks of man's readiness to steal, murder, or commit suicide for passion and remarks on the "filthy meanness, cruelty, egotism of 'confessions' of faults to the loved one."

Still more remarkable are the twenty or so lists of words that Frederic copied out from entries in Roget's *Thesaurus*.

[41] *Harold Frederic*, pp. 127–128.
[42] *Ibid.*, p. 121.

A few of the lists suggest good spirits: one is from the entry under *Pleasure*, and six others—very short lists—are from such entries as *Greenness* and *Energy*. The remaining lists bespeak a far different mood, however. There are lists drawn from Roget's entries under *Grey*, *Brown*, and *Roughness*, and from *Adversity*, *Hopelessness*, *Inexcitability*, and *Transientness* (which concludes with "*sic transit, gloria mundi*"). The longest list by far, a dreary recital of fifty-eight words from *Pain*, ranges from "unfortunate, unhappy, unblest," to "wretched, miserable, woebegone." Copying out words from *Vegetable*, Frederic chose "creepers" and "lichens" but left "blossom" and "bud"; he took "squall, storm," and "tempest" from *Wind* but left "zephyr." Just why Frederic troubled to make up these lists is not clear,[43] but *Gloria Mundi* fulfills what his elaborate preparations imply: long regarded as an essentially frivolous exercise in escape literature (Van Wyck Brooks classed it with *Little Lord Fauntleroy*),[44] *Gloria Mundi* is a work painful in its disenchantments.

[43] There are no such word lists for the other novels in the Frederic Papers. Although many of the words from the lists appear in the completed novel, they are of the common sort. Frederic was not the kind of writer to work up purple passages of description, and when he did go in for "fine writing" his intentions were usually ironic. According to Robert Barr, it was Frederic's custom to take adjectives out of his prose, not put them in. Frederic would have a typescript prepared from his corrected longhand manuscript, says Barr, and then have a reader underline all of the adjectives in the typescript in blue. "The novelist could thus see at a glance in his final revisions how heavily he had drawn on the adjectival resources of the language" ("Harold Frederic, The Author of the Market-Place," *Saturday Evening Post*, CLXXI [1898], 397).

[44] *Confident Years*, p. 258. Frederic may well have had such novels as the immensely popular *Little Lord Fauntleroy* in mind, but *Gloria Mundi* is a frontal attack on the sentimental assumptions of novels like Frances Hodgson Burnett's. Her little lord enjoys the wealth he

One of the things that may have deceived readers about Frederic's true accomplishment in *Gloria Mundi* is that it harks back to many of the conventions of the mid-Victorian novel. The work is complete with hard-riding lords out of Trollope, idealistic Jews who recall *Daniel Deronda* and the novels of Disraeli, scenes of a London that is specifically related to *Little Dorrit*, and a family tree that is almost a parody of the Victorian last chapter—more than twenty characters are related by blood or marriage. For his hero, Frederic went to that old standby, the lost heir; for one of his heroines he went to Dickens and came up with a Lady Edith Cressage who has been sold into a fashionable and disasterous marriage by her parents, as Edith Dombey wos sold by her mother and Major Bagstock.

Although the many echoes of the mid-Victorian may have persuaded some readers that Frederic, until then always the most up-to-date of authors, had regressed, *Gloria Mundi* is in the best sense a novel of its moment. Frederic began it in 1897, the year of Victoria's Diamond Jubilee, an occasion that may have set him to wondering just what "modern" meant. The celebration of the Jubilee, Osbert Burdett recalled, "had a vague suggestion of make-believe, for what were we celebrating if not Victoria's victory over Time?" [45]

Gloria Mundi opens in the late nineties. At an age nearly as great as that of his century, Christian Torr, the oldest peer in England, head of the oldest family in England, still prevails

---

falls heir to and converts his crusty grandfather to the pleasures of rethatching cottage roofs and sending soup to the sick; Frederic's little lord quickly finds that his grandfather is no such pushover.

[45] *The Beardsley Period* (London, 1925), p. 84. Burdett says a good many people began to wonder "what title would be chosen for the occasion ten years ahead when the seventieth year of Queen Victoria's reign would undoubtedly be solemnized."

over time. This veritable Victoria of a Duke is ill, however, at death's door in fact:

But he has the strength and will of a giant, and though he is half paralyzed, half blind, half everything, still he has his weight against the door, and no one knows how long he can hold it closed [p. 38].[46]

The Duke, like Victoria and her century, cannot last forever. Inevitably, the door of death must swing open, but what other doors will open then? What future will lie open to the living when the obstructions blocking the way are gone?

An heir presumptive—who is as worthless as the Duke—stands impatiently by to inherit and perpetuate. If he does succeed, the future will bring no change. The Duke's brother Julius and Julius' son Emanuel, however, intend to see that change does come. Under the moral influence of Julius' late wife and Emanuel's mother, a Jew who carried the blood of Spinoza in her veins and the millions of a Dutch colonial fortune in her dowry, they feel profoundly obligated to do good with the power of the Torrs. Hoping to break the immemorial family tradition of selfish irresponsibility, "the Jews" (as the father and son are called although they have not embraced Judaism) have gained control of the Duke's property by buying up his debts with their Dutch fortune. Now all they need is a Duke who will fall in with their plans. So it is that the Jews have summoned a grandson of Lord Torr from poverty and obscurity, and young Christian Tower, as he calls himself, arrives to claim the title that will rightfully be his.

---

[46] All page references to *Gloria Mundi* are to the first American edition (Chicago: Herbert S. Stone, 1898). The novel appeared originally as a serial in *Cosmopolitan*, running from XIV (Jan., 1898) through XVI (Nov., 1898).

There is something of the fairy tale in this story of a giant dying in his castle and of a penniless orphan who finds family and fortune through the efforts of an uncle with a beard as big and white as Santa's. And Frederic makes it all the more like a fairy tale by freely producing astonishing coincidences. The devices of the fairy tale, however, are exploited to make the point that life is not really what it is in storybooks, that even if a man finds that a ducal coronet has descended on his head from nowhere he still remains subject to all the limitations of being human. The novel begins more or less at the point where fairy stories conclude—"they lived happily ever after"—and it is poor Christian's lot to discover that the ever after may be very long and not so very happy.

From the start, Christian's hopes are frustrated. He thinks that his fortune will make him free, but the Jews quickly make it clear that he is to be the slave of the Utopian system they have devised. He thinks that now he will find something substantial to replace his blurred childhood memories of his father, but he soon learns that his father left England under a cloud of disgrace and is not mentioned in mixed company to this day. As heir to the oldest family in England, Christian must "belong," yet he seems conspicuously out of place. His father was a family scandal; his tutelage was under the Catholic Brothers of Toulon and his Masonic-Garibaldist-Socialist brother; his sponsors are the Jews, who intone the needs of the future in terms of the feudal past; and his blood is the bluest in England. Even his accent is a mix-up: the English he has learned in France sounds American to all the Englishmen he meets. In short, the forces and counterforces of his past are both too strong to evade and too contradictory to provide a tradition within which he might live comfortably. He is a hero for a new age.

Before the novel ends, the old Duke finally dies. Christian not only inherits his grandfather's estate, cleared of debts by the Jews, but finds that he is to be the Jews' heir as well. He has come into possession of "a small kingdom—a little nation." Jamesian vistas of possibility lie open before him. He is free to live in accordance with the family "philosophy": "There is nothing on earth that we want to do that we don't do—and there's nothing we don't want to do that any mortal power can make us do" (p. 174). The question is, what does Christian want to do?

Since their legendary conversion by Saint David in the sixth century, the Torrs have borne great names—David, Anselm, Ambrose, Augustine, and Christian—but they have never borne responsibility. Their power began and grew with Caermere, the family stronghold, built to defend a pass and enlarged over the centuries "single to the idea of blocking the path that Caermere overhung" (p. 46). Like their castle, the Torrs are an obstruction; like their lord, a half-paralyzed giant who holds his broad back rigid even against death, the Torrs are a breed that manifests its vitality only as inertia. Against this inertia move the Jews. Through their own exertions, but even more through Christian's when they have made a new kind of Torr out of him, they hope to justify the power that the family has enjoyed for over thirteen hundred years. It is appropriate that Emanuel should experiment with hybrid plants. If he and his father can cross the Hebraic dedication they derive from Spinoza with the feudal authority of the Torrs, perhaps they will breed a philosopher-duke true to their hopes.

Emanuel has always been a visionary. His Oxford classmates predicted great things from him in the seventies, in the days when Disraeli's remarkable individuality was a part of England's current history, and when the English imagination, in part from the stimulus of this fact, dwelt upon the possibilities of a new Semitic wave of inspiration and ethical impetus. The dreams, the aspirations, the mysterious "perhaps" of Daniel Deronda were in men's minds . . . [p. 178].

After leaving Oxford, Emanuel proceeded to develop his elaborately medieval "System." The System, expounded at tedious length to the detriment of the novel, is little more than a blend of Disraeli's Young England and William Morris' Nowhere. Put in so many words, Frederic says, it boils down to "our immemorial platitudes" on the necessity for mercy, justice, loyalty, and cheerfulness (p. 218).

The Jews want to justify their power, but they have no intention of giving up a bit of it. Although they speak expansively of the bright future they are building, they look directly back to the Dark Ages for all the forms and ideals of their System. So do all Utopian planners, Frederic implies. To Christian, the talk of the Jews sounds pretty much like what he has heard from his Socialist half-brother. The Jews are horrified by the ideas of Socialism, and a Socialist in the novel is equally horrified by their ideas, but to Frederic all programs of reform leave one just where one begins—with a hierarchy of power.[47] The situation is comic: in the name of progress the Jews are trying to convert the Torrs of this world back to a dream of medieval Christianity; and the Torrs—Christians,

[47] "Granted the premise of government by dreams," Frederic said, there are other dreams he preferred to the "amorphous Utopia" of the Socialists (*The Young Emperor* [New York, 1891], pp. 197–198). Some of Frederic's newspaper reports show a high regard for the good work done by the Christian Socialists among the London poor.

Anselms, Augustines—have unconcernedly carried medievalism, brutal and real, right up to the threshold of the twentieth century.

Although the System has its difficulties, it does function. Two thousand workers live reasonably contentedly and industriously under lavish paternalism on the fifteen square miles of the Jews' estate. If Christian will bring the nearly twenty thousand dependents of the ducal estates into the System, Emanuel's dream will be realized. Yet the System is little more than a dream. Its final significance is neatly summed up in a *Fortnightly Review* article that Emanuel gives Christian to read: If the System has accomplished nothing else, the article says, it has "gathered for the instruction and delight of the intelligent observer almost a complete collection of examples of early English domestic architecture of the humbler sort" (p. 223).

Before Christian can even consider the System, however, he must see for himself the family tradition that it is designed to thwart. Christian's first meeting with his dying grandfather is superbly described. The Duke lies on a terrace off his sickroom in one of the Caermere turrets. Climbing the narrow stairs, Christian is puzzled by the teasingly familiar smell that mingles with odors of medicine and musty rooms. The puzzle is solved when he finds that the kennel has been moved up into the tower so that the hounds can be with the master who remembers them better than he does his own children. As Christian comes onto the terrace, one of the hounds is thrusting her muzzle against the hand at her side:

This hand was what Christian saw first of his grandfather—an immense limp hand, with thick fingers twisted and misshapen, and skin of an almost greenish pallor. The dog's nose, thrust under it, moved this inert hand about, and the young man felt himself thrill unpleasantly, for some reason, at the spectacle [p. 148].

Little wonder that Christian is disturbed: he feels the weight of this dead hand of the past.

Christian thinks his grandfather unconscious of his presence, but the Duke finally acknowledges the grandson he has never seen. The Duke blesses his heir with a succinct piece of advice: when dealing with farmers who build fences to protect their land, "a kick in the stomach first and reasons afterward. That's the only way this country can be hunted" (p. 155). The Duke is one of Frederic's great achievements. A brute with a face "as devoid of significance . . . as if it had been in a coffin" (p. 150), a giant who lives on and on amid the vile odors of the apothecary and the kennel, he is an awesome and unforgettable image of what Father Forbes calls the most powerful of all forces—inertia.

As a brilliant set piece, Christian's meeting with the Duke merits comparison with the first meeting between Coningsby and his grandfather, Lord Monmouth. Indeed, Frederic's novel repeatedly suggests Disraeli. *Gloria Mundi* has its prehistorically ancient family, its fabulously wealthy Jews with fabulous plans (that duplicate in part those of *Sybil*), its witty conversations between epigrammatic young ladies and gentlemen, and its hero facing the problem of what to do with the world before him. The parallels between Frederic's novel and Disraeli's, however, point up the divergencies. Bearing "The World's Mine Oyster" on bright banners, Disraeli's heroes set forth to restore past glories;[48] Frederic's hero stands still under his drooping "*Gloria Mundi*."

[48] The epigraph to *Vivian Grey* (1827) is "Why then, the world's mine oyster / Which I with sword will open."

"By George! do they do that still?" someone asks when the will that leaves the Glastonbury estates to Christian is read before the assembled family. "I know they did in Trollope and George Eliot—but I thought it had gone out" (p. 472). The remark is suggestive of the dilemma that faces Christian: he lives bound by the wills of the willful past. Disraeli's "New Generation" of 1844 is moribund by the time of *Gloria Mundi*, and Frederic's youngsters do not feel very new: "By the almanac I am four-and-twenty," says one of them, ". . . but by my own feelings, I seem to have been left over from the reign of William the Fourth" (p. 453). *Coningsby* concludes with the hope that young English men and women will "restore the happiness of their country by believing in their own energies, and daring to be great." [49] Frederic's hero cannot believe and will not take the dare.

Neither the Torr use of power, the enjoyment of power *qua* power, nor the Jews' System, however, is what Christian wants. Other responses to the responsibilities of power occur to him. Shocked by the parade of prostitutes he sees at a theater promenade, he is seized by the desire to help his fallen sisters. [50] But a knowing young man warns him that "every

[49] The Bradenham Edition; New York, 1926, VIII, 503.

[50] The theater is the Empire Music Hall, on Leicester Square, and was the site of Winston Churchill's first public speech. It seems that in 1894 a Mrs. Ormiston Chant and her Purity League had closed the bar at the Empire. Churchill, feeling that the closure was "contrary to the best traditions of British freedom," formed an "Entertainment Protection League" in protest. One evening after a mob ripped down the canvas barricade covering the bar, Churchill climbed up on the debris and, thoughts of the storming of the Bastille in his mind, delivered his maiden address, an appeal to the crowd to resist tyranny to the end. It was one of Churchill's finer hours, but his claim that the Empire was innocent of "the prude's" charges is false. It was as Frederic paints it, a notorious whore-market. (Winston S. Churchill, *A Roving Commission* [New York, 1930], pp. 50–58.)

young fellow worth his salt that I have ever known, or that anybody's ever known, has swelled himself out with precisely these same reform sentiments" (p. 308). And as an object lesson he describes Slingsby Chetwynd, who got keen on settlement work: "He went down to stop a whole week—at Shoreditch or Houndsditch or the Isle of Dogs, or somewhere like that—and a woman smashed his hat in, and he fell into a cellar—and he was jolly glad to get back again the same night" (pp. 298–299).[51]

Futher possibilities suggest themselves. Christian wonders whether he should not enlist in the Greco-Turkish War: "In an obscure way, he comprehended that good people in Western Europe always sympathized with the Christian as against the Moslem" (p. 441). More seriously, he dallies with the idea of marrying Lady Cressage. The death of her brutish husband, one of Christian's cousins, has cheated her of the title and fortune for which she bartered her power as the most beautiful woman in England. Perhaps Christian can devote himself to salvaging her listless and unhappy life. Or perhaps, he thinks, he should throw aside the whole question of responsibility and live a life of pleasure on the Continent.

At his grandfather's funeral, Christian does find a sense of purpose, but it is short-lived. He is momentarily awed by the thousands of people who come out to see the funeral procession, by the two hundred horsemen of the cortege that follows the casket on its way to the last rites. Little realizing that the real question of the hour is "would the new Duke set the Hunt on its legs again?" Christian feels only respect in the countless

---

[51] The humor of a Chetwynd doing settlement work among fallen women may have gained something from the fact that *Chetwynd vs. Chetwynd* was one of the most scandalous and widely reported divorce cases in nineteenth-century England (see Cyril Pearl, *The Girl with the Swansdown Seat* [New York, 1958], pp. 202–203).

eyes turned his way (p. 489). As he walks down the aisle of the cathedral, *his* cathedral now, he is overwhelmed by the armorial bearings blazoned on every wall, cut into the very stones he treads. He catches the significance of the clerkly pun of *taurus* on *torr* graven into some of the ancient hatchments. Perhaps power is its own end. Christian listens to the funeral service:

> " 'He shall have put down all rule, and all authority, and power.' "
> It was the old parson who was reading now. " 'For He must reign, till He hath put all enemies under His feet.' "
> Yes, even in this Protestant religion to which he had passively become committed, force was the real ideal! [p. 496].

But slight, shy Christian, "the uncased antennae of his self-consciousness . . . extended in all directions, as if to solicit injury" (p. 24), is not the heir to live by the example of the "dull, unintelligent, sinister, half-barbarous" power of Grandfather Torr (p. 496). Christian has not inherited the power; it has inherited him.

Still another alternative appears in Frances Bailey, a New Woman, a typewriter girl trying to break into journalism, who promises to send Christian instructive books on economics. Frances abhors the anti-feminine bias of Emanuel's System and is quick to point out that what the Jews are trying to do is use Dutch money sweated out of an East Indian colonial empire to justify the possession of an English estate that was sweated out of feudal serfs. But she is remarkably susceptible to systems herself. Waiting in her office, Christian glances at the books that line her shelves:

"Economics of Socialism," "Capitalist Production," "The Ethics of Socialism," "Toward [sic] Democracy,"—so the titles ran that first met his eye. . . . The legend on a thin red book, "Civilization: Its Cause and Cure," whimsically caught his attention. He put his hand to the key in the bookcase door to get out the volume; then, hesitating, yawned, and looked over the shelves once more. There was nothing else—and really he desired to read nothing [pp. 371–372].[52]

Christian has come to woo Frances Bailey, and "at last, by some curious and devious chance, he had stumbled upon the thing that was genuinely worth doing" (p. 372). At the novel's end Frances will give up her feminist independence to marry Christian, and Christian will devote himself to little else but Frances. They will live out their lives in Caermere, which he already knows for "a grave, a mausoleum, a place of skulls and dead men's bones" (p. 297). Christian is free of the Jews. They now ask nothing more of him than that he produce an heir, for ill-health has forced the childless Emanuel to abandon the System. Christian promises a lavish donation to the hunt.

Thus Frederic answers the questions he puts to the century about to be born. What will men do with their power? In their wars, the Christians will continue to side against the Moslems. Their programs will rest on the same old platitudes. The Caermeres will remain. The New Women will settle down as did their mothers,[53] and heirs will devote themselves to producing heirs. At one point in the novel Christian buys

---

[52] There actually was such a book (1889), written by Edward Carpenter, who is clearly the "E.C." repeatedly referred to in the notes for *Gloria Mundi*. Carpenter, who also wrote *Towards Democracy*, is best remembered for his work on Whitman but was also a student of Thoreau and Oriental quietism, a vegetarian teetotaler, a socialist, a sexologist, a maker of sandals, and a reformer of prisons and just about everything else.

[53] The first entry in the column of notes for *Gloria Mundi* titled "The New Woman" is "Hens who won't sit."

baked potatoes from a street vendor to feed some dozen of the London poor.[54] It is unlikely that he will do much more. *Sic transit.*

Gloria Mundi is a romance, but it is certainly not the light-hearted romance it has been taken to be. As his name suggests, it matters very little that Christian is an Englishman raised in France rather than an American raised in New York. The Cinderella story, Van Wyck Brooks points out, has always been a favorite with Americans,[55] and Christian's story, like most of the stories Frederic tells, is a variation on it. Frederic's young men and women are always deciding that the glass slipper fits, that they are born to something wonderful. Christian is called from obscurity to wealth and position; Seth leaves the farm for the city of his ambitious dreams; Reuben Tracy, armed with a law degree and a secondhand set of Carlyle, intends to right the wrongs of the world; Kate Minster and Celia Madden are convinced that their wealth and beauty must mark them for notable achievements; and Horace Boyce, looking in his dressing room mirror, swells with pride at the well-tailored vision of imminent success. Whether their dream is the generous hope of public reform or the selfish egotism that mistakes self-cultivation for salvation, they are all true believers in the millennium.

The lesson that Christian learns is implicit in Frederic's earlier works. A remark of Abe Beekman's in *Seth's Brother's*

---

[54] The implications of the scene where Christian ministers to the hungry are bitter. A policeman appears and calls the poor wretches to their handout by beating on the pavement with his nightstick. Then, as Christian and his companion stand by, the bobby keeps order among the small crowd of beggars, composed of all different nationalities. "It's like the Concert of Europe," is the sad joke of Christian's companion (p. 352).

[55] *Confident Years,* p. 586.

Wife might serve as an epigraph for *Gloria Mundi:* "Reform spurts don't winter well. They never last till spring" (p. 274). And Christian's problem is clearly ennunciated in Frederic's comment on Kate Minster in *The Lawton Girl:* "All the conditions for achievement were hers to command, and there was nothing to achieve" (p. 157). Zeke Tisdale, the American hero of *The Return of the O'Mahony*, learned what Christian learned, that his good intentions were no match for inertia. Zeke tried to transform a little Irish fishing village into a modern "go-ahead operation" but soon found out that dead tradition had a great deal of life left in it. "This havin' dead men slung at you from mornin' to night, day in an' day out, rain or shine," he complains, "would have busted up Job himself" (p. 84). Before *The Return of the O'Mahony* is over, Zeke becomes what he only claimed to be at first, the real chief of the clan, and in becoming the O'Mahony, he becomes a living fossil from the medieval past.

One can trace the theme of *Gloria Mundi* even farther back, back to a story Frederic wrote when he was only nineteen and was still very much under the influence of Erckmann-Chatrian. One of the characters in "The Story of Peter Zarl" is a benevolent Alsatian Count who fills in his castle moat, turns his forest into farms for his tenants, and tries to destroy the feudal order of things.[56] The peasants grow to love Count Reual, but they never lose their "lingering mistrust" of his radical innovations. Some of the peasants move off, but to the end of the Count's life those who remain resist doggedly "any and all attempts having for their object their being independent of Reualstein." Even in his teens, Frederic felt that the past

---

[56] The manuscript for the unpublished "Peter Zarl," which bears Frederic's inscription "completed copy May 12, '76," is in the Frederic Papers, Library of Congress.

does not die easily. Writing of the heroes of Frederic's American novels, Carey McWilliams spoke of the untrained and uneducated young man who "suddenly finds himself an heir to the culture, lore, and wisdom of the ages." [57] Although for some reason McWilliams was not able to see it, the description obviously fits Christian Tower as well as Seth Fairchild or Theron Ware. All of Frederic's heroes might be said to be "lost heirs," and the dilemma they face when they come into their inheritance is cruel.

On the one hand, the heir can react like Theron. "He lacked even the impulse to turn round and inspect the cocoon from which he had emerged. Let the past bury the past. He had no vestige of interest in it" (p. 210). But such egotism as this, which smugly confuses process with progress, seldom goes unpunished, and even if it does, it is contemptible. To Frederic the naiveté that is damning is that which looks upon its own former innocence and on the innocence of others without sympathy. On the other hand, if one learns the lesson of history, one is unlikely ever to stir far from his chair. Although humility is a safeguard against the excesses of egotistical enthusiasm, it is uncomfortably allied to paralyzing self-distrust in Frederic's thinking.

Christian comes to an understanding of life that the protagonists of the other novels never attain, but his discovery is implicit in all of the novels. "We learn only one thing from all the numberless millions who have gone before us," Christian says at the end of *Gloria Mundi*, "that man is less important than he thinks he is" (p. 571).

[57] "Harold Frederic: 'A Country Boy of Genius,'" *University of California Chronicle*, XXXV (Jan., 1933), 30.

7 / The Market-Place

When it appeared, *Gloria Mundi* seemed a little flat and tired to some critics, a little anticlimactic for the last novel of a career as brilliant as Frederic's. There was yet another posthumous novel, however, a work that showed beyond question that Frederic had not burned himself out with *The Damnation*. When *The Market-Place* was published, in 1899, not everyone liked it, but no one could deny its vitality. *The Dial* found it "unquestionably both strong and interesting," and *The Nation* said, "the leaves of the book turn as by electric cyclone." [1] J. E. Hodder Williams, writing in the London *Bookman*, was particularly enthusiastic:

"The Market-Place" is a great piece of work, incomparably the best novel of the year, a literary legacy that will be remembered, almost an heirloom. . . . It throbs with the hum of life. . . . "The Market-Place" has been described as an immoral book—immoral because a barefaced scoundrel holds the reader's admiration. We admit that we identified ourselves with few heroes of fiction as

---

[1] William Morton Payne, *The Dial*, XXVII (1899), 21; *The Nation*, LXIX (1899), 95.

with Thorpe. . . . We admit our admiration for a swindler. But against this you must set the whole atmosphere of the book, which seems to us healthy and moral.[2]

Not all readers were able to detect anything healthy and moral in the air surrounding Frederic's unscrupulous protagonist. *Literature*, in fact, protested that "the atmosphere of the story is brutally sordid," and *The Spectator*, after calling it "a very brilliant piece of work" and conceding that "it may be true to life," warned its readers that the late Mr. Frederic's novel was "essentially immoral."[3]

It is easy to see why many found *The Market-Place* dangerous. If Oscar Wilde's Miss Prism was right and fiction means that the good end happily and the bad unhappily, then Frederic's novel is not what fiction should be. Some critics had been unhappy when the swindlers of *The Lawton Girl* were permitted to escape prison sentences, and some had protested that Father Forbes, Dr. Ledsmar, and Celia Madden had not been chastened properly for their parts in Theron Ware's downfall.[4] Whatever comfort such critics may have found in

[2] XVI (1899), 136. When Williams' review appeared a month later in the New York edition of *The Bookman*, it was cut by two-thirds, partially rewritten, and lacked a by-line. The opening sentence of the passage quoted above was changed to "*The Market-Place* is a fine piece of work, one of the best novels of the year, a literary legacy which will be remembered almost as an heirloom" (X [1899], 91). One suspects that the New York editors were unwilling to laud as "incomparably the best novel of the year" a work under attack as immoral. At any rate, the New York version of the review deleted every word Williams had written on the question of whether Frederic's novel was guilty as charged.

[3] *Literature*, No. 27, n.s., p. 17, quoted in Grant C. Knight, *The Critical Period in American Literature* [Chapel Hill, N.C., 1951], p. 152; *The Spectator*, LXXXIII (1899), 129.

[4] For such criticism of *The Lawton Girl*, see Chapter 4, n. 12. The *Atlantic Monthly* objected that the three "plotters" of Theron's downfall escaped scot-free (LXXVIII [1896], 272).

the very chastened Celia who reappears in *The Market-Place* must have been more than offset by the spectacle of Joel Thorpe, a swindler in the grand manner who sails triumphantly through life without a twinge of conscience or cause for regret. Even readers who approved of the novel found something disturbing in the idea that a man might smile and smile and be a villain—and finally burst out laughing with the sheer fun of it all. Henry Holland, the Canon of St. Paul's, hoped that there were not really such people as Thorpe in the world but was afraid there were. Holland was so unstrung by the time he finished *The Market-Place* that he fled to Fanny Burney's *Evelina* "as an antidote." [5]

It is apparent why some reviews warned of immorality, but it is difficult to understand why others concluded that Frederic had tied a moral to the end of his story. Noting that ordinarily "the ethics of such a story are supposed to demand that the speculator shall be exposed and come to grief," William Morton Payne thought that he saw a less conventional moral: "riches, however acquired, are a doubtful good to the man without the inner resources to make possible their enjoyment." [6] The *Saturday Review*, which did not seem to care whether or not a fictional character was moral so long as he was real, objected to what it thought was a belated attempt to redeem the hero by giving him a desire to help the London poor. [7] The New York *Tribune*, on the other hand, apparently indifferent as to whether a character was real so long as he was moral, reassured its readers that they could read Frederic's

[5] H. S. H. [Henry S. Holland] to Mrs. Mary Drew, n.d., quoted in Lisle March-Phillipps and Bertram Christian, eds., *Some Hawarden Letters* (New York, 1918), p. 252. Mrs. Drew was Gladstone's daughter.

[6] *The Dial*, XXVII (1899), 21.

[7] LXXXVIII (1899), 108.

story with safety because its hero "finds out that to be happy he must also do some good to his fellow men." [8] The inability of the *Tribune's* critic to make a clear distinction between doing good to people and doing good for them was shared by all those who so misread the novel as to take Thorpe's plans to become a philanthropist as evidence of a last-minute change of heart.[9]

The charge of immorality did Frederic's novel no harm that one can see. Although the editors of the staid monthlies refused the serial rights to it because it seemed "cynical," the recently refurbished *Saturday Evening Post* had no such qualms and was happy to bring the novel to its rapidly growing body of readers.[10] Neither the editors nor the readers of the *Post* seem to have found anything incongruous in seeing Frederic's story of rampant financial corruption in a magazine

[8] *Illustrated Supplement,* May 14, 1899, p. 14.

[9] Many novelists at the turn of the century were prompt "in pronouncing a verdict of guilty against American business and businessmen" but proved all too willing "to accept sentimental confessions or romantic atonements or deathbed repentances" (Henry Steele Commager, *The American Mind* [New Haven, 1950], p. 258).

[10] Thomas Beer, *The Mauve Decade* (New York, 1926), p. 224. *The Market-Place* ran in *The Post* from December 17, 1898, through June 3, 1899. When Cyrus Curtis bought the ailing magazine in 1897, he immediately began building a popular, nationwide circulation, but the real expansion did not begin until George Horace Lorimer became editor in March, 1899. The success of Frederic's serial caught the attention of Lorimer, and he immediately began trying to interest authors in writing such fiction for *The Post,* which ran Frank Norris' *The Pit* in 1902 (John Tebbel, *George Horace Lorimer and "The Saturday Evening Post"* [Garden City, N.Y., 1948], p. 27). In 1924, Lorimer told Clarence Barron, the financial editor, publisher, and journalist, that he thought *The Market-Place* "the best business novel ever written" (Barron, *They Told Barron* [New York, 1930], p. 319).

that habitually regarded the millionaire as the finest flower of American life. Week after week the installments of *The Market-Place* ran next to a series of photographic essays on the happy homes of the virtuous rich—"American Kings and their Kingdoms"—and inspirational articles by kings like Philip Armour on "Success in Business: Practical Tales by Practical Men." Whether because of serialization in the *Post*, the high praise of some reviewers, or the intriguing notices that warned of its immorality, *The Market-Place* was a success, one of the best sellers of 1899.[11]

Some of the appeal of Frederic's novel must also be attributed to its subject: chicanery in high finance. Although muckraking did not become a national pastime until Ida Tarbell's articles on the Standard Oil Company began to appear in *McClure's* in 1903, fictional and nonfictional works of exposure were already coming into fashion in the late nineties.[12] Charles Dudley Warner's *A Little Journey in the*

[11] Alice Payne Hackett lists the novel tenth on her list of the ten American best sellers for 1899 (*Sixty Years of Best Sellers* [New York, 1956], p. 99). See also the booksellers' reports in the London editions of *The Bookman* for July through December, 1899.

[12] Although the muckraker did not begin to receive nationwide attention until the early twentieth century, as Richard Hofstadter says, "the practice of exposure was not an invention of the muckraking era" and dozens of books published in the last three decades of the nineteenth century could be designated muckraking novels (*The Age of Reform* [New York, 1959], pp. 185–186). Announcing the forthcoming publication of *The Market-Place* in its pages, the *Saturday Evening Post* capitalized on a recent scandal, saying that the novel, "though written before the famous Hooley disclosures, seems almost prophetic" (CLXX [1898], 383). One wonders whether Frederic knew Ernest Terah Hooley, who was involved with the Dunlop Rubber Company and was eventually sent to prison for his "promotions." Frederic's friend Frank Harris claims close association with the swindler in *My Life and Loves*.

World and Will Payne's *The Money Captain* appeared in 1898; Warner's *That Fortune* and Margaret Sherwood Pollock's *Henry Worthing, Idealist* in 1899; Robert Grant's *Unleavened Bread* and Robert Herrick's *Web of Life* in 1900; and David Graham Phillip's *The Great God Success* and Frank Norris' *The Octopus* in 1901.[13] Nor was the vogue of economic novels limited to the United States. A few months after he published *The Market-Place*, William Heinemann brought out an English novel titled *Mammon and Co.*[14]

Frederic's interest in the world of business did not develop simply in response to literary fashion. Shortly after *The Rise of Silas Lapham* appeared in 1885, he had written Howells an enthusiastic letter of praise. The English, Frederic said, "were not able to understand as well as I do, I think, how much more there is in the story—to realize that it means the scrutiny of a master turned for the first time upon what is the most distinctive phase of American folk life. . . ."[15] Frederic's own inter-

---

[13] For an extensive list of such novels, see the bibliography in Walter F. Taylor's *The Economic Novel in America* (Chapel Hill, N.C., 1942). One difficulty in talking about the economic novel is that so many novels—*Middlemarch* and *Moll Flanders*, to take two examples—can be classified as such. *Unleavened Bread*, for instance, does have a great deal to say about money and is often cited as a typical economic novel of its period, but surely the work is primarily interesting as a study of the destructive power of the American woman.

[14] Heinemann, who published Frederic's *New Exodus* and six volumes of his fiction, also published Gertrude Atherton, Edward Bellamy, James McNeill Whistler, Henry James, and Stephen Crane. In the nineties he was "very possibly the outstanding specialist of new American books of a literary sort" in England (Clarence Gohdes, *American Literature in Nineteenth-Century England* [New York, 1944], p. 36).

[15] Frederic to Howells, May 5, 1885, quoted by permission of the Harvard College Library.

est in that "most distinctive phase" had already been evident in *Seth's Brother's Wife* and was to be clearer still in *The Lawton Girl*. The concern is evident in most of his fiction, in fact: one of the episodes in *Mrs. Albert Grundy* treats the rise and fall and rise again of the Grundy fortunes in response to the stock market, and a Standard Oil millionaire named Laban Skinner (the name suggests the portrait) figures in *March Hares*. Whether he is defining the economic interests that split Whig from Tory in the American Revolution or is setting down the precise terms of Seth Fairchild's and Theron Ware's salaries, Frederic shows a continuing awareness that the dollar, if not almighty, is very powerful.

One of the surprising things about Frederic's fiction is that it so seldom betrays his deep disgust with getting and spending in the Gilded Age. A note of bitterness escapes occasionally in *In the Valley* when Douw complains that New York has forgotten the promise of its history in the scramble to make money, and one hears Frederic's indignation once or twice in Reuben Tracy's comments on "the economic and social evils underlying the system of trusts" and "the sentiment back of it that rich men might do what they liked in America." [16] But these occasions are rare. Frederic almost never allowed his personal disgust with predatory society to interfere in his fiction with his inquiry into the failings and shortcomings of the individual. There is nothing in his fiction, for example, as bitter as this passage from a letter to Cleveland:

The public tendency since the war, in business, in politics, in social life, has rotted and infected almost every condition of our existence. Moral sensibility has been blunted, the keen edge of honor

[16] *The Lawton Girl*, p. 380.

turned, the standards of justice clogged, the ardor of patriotism chilled, the confiding ignorance of the half-educated tampered with, the ambitions of good men perverted. . . .[17]

All of the control that one perceives in the earlier fiction, however, does not prepare one for the degree to which Frederic sustains the pretense of moral neutrality throughout *The Market-Place*. One does not expect a sermon, a tract, or an exposé meant to shock; one does not expect either the outrage that makes *The Jungle* so powerful or the baffled appeal to conscience that makes *A Hazard of New Fortunes* so poignant; but one does expect some direct criticism. Frederic had always been primarily interested in those who deceive themselves rather than in those who deceive others; in the reformers Seth Fairchild and Richard Ansdell rather than in the target of reform Albert Fairchild; in the idealistic Reuben Tracy and Kate Minster and in the hapless victim of his own ambitions Horace Boyce rather than in the swindlers Tenney and Wendover. Yet there had always been irony to spare for everybody. If the main concern in *The Damnation of Theron Ware* was with Theron's weak and petty hypocrisies born of self-delusion, the practiced and conscious hypocrisies of Brothers Winch and Pierce were not overlooked.

Knowing Frederic's earlier work, one opens *The Market-Place* with no expectation that Thorpe need fail in business or be carried off to jail, but one does anticipate that sooner or

[17] Nov. 8, 1884, from the original in the New York State Library, Albany. Frederic quickly discovered that Europe offered the same spectacle of greed and rapacity as the United States. A month after his arrival in London he was cabling home a vivid account of English slums and indifferent landlords (New York *Times*, July 13, 1884, p. 1). Frederic's reporting shows a persistent concern for the oppressed, whether London slum dwellers, American farmers, Irish peasants, or Russian Jews.

later the tycoon with the Midas touch will wake to find that he has grown ass's ears. One waits in vain. The shafts of irony are never loosed; the moment when one can laugh at the collapse of the millionaire's pretensions never comes. To be sure, the novel does end with laughter. In the last paragraph, Thorpe has just decided what new worlds to conquer. As he walks into his living room, one of his guests, Celia Madden, is speaking of him: "I shall always insist . . . that crime was his true vocation" (p. 401).[18] Thorpe laughs hardest of all—and laughs last.

Thorpe has been truer to his vocation than even the skeptical Celia dreams. When *The Market-Place* opens, he is found at the point of achieving the success he has lusted after for the greater part of his life. A group of financiers has sold short on the worthless rubber stocks that Thorpe has been promoting, but he has turned ruin to triumph. He has cornered his own market, and the men out to crush him will now have to buy, at whatever price he names, the stocks they have contracted to deliver to his dummy purchasers.

Cornering the bears is the least of Thorpe's crimes, for he does not even own the worthless rubber plantations in which he has sold stock. He has already sold the property to a gullible adventurer in South America and has used the proceeds to float his stock company in London. To Thorpe's mind, it makes little difference whether the tract of inaccessible jungle really belongs to him or to the hapless Tavender. "If there wasn't any such property in existence," he explains, "it would be just the same" (p. 37). These are rubber stocks in more than one sense.

When Tavender inconveniently shows up in London as

[18]All page references to *The Market-Place* are to the first American edition (New York: Frederick A. Stokes, 1899).

Thorpe is about to close his deal, the tycoon hardly blinks an eye. He repurchases his rubber plantations—an act of charity that really warms his heart—and sends poor Tavender out of the country. Thorpe's agent succeeds so well in keeping the old man out of sight that Tavender is dead of alcoholism within a fortnight. Although Thorpe cannot be held directly responsible for Tavender's death, he comes very close to cold-blooded murder when Tavender's brother-in-law shows up as head gardener on Thorpe's estate. Thorpe thinks that there is at least a chance that the gardener knows too much, and the chance does not seem worth taking. The tycoon is resourceful as ever: he will strangle the gardener and leave the body to be found in a greenhouse full of lethal pesticide gas.

Then some objections to the plan rose up before him: they dealt almost exclusively with the social nuisance the thing would entail. There was to be a house-party, with that Duke and Duchess in it, of whom his wife talked so much, and it would be a miserable kind of bore to have a suffocated gardener forced upon them as a principal topic of conversation. Of course, too, it would more or less throw the whole household into confusion [pp. 380–381].

No, Thorpe decides, he must think of his wife's feelings. Far more terrifying that his casual stroll to the brink of homicide is the warm glow of virtue he derives from letting husbandly tenderness interfere with the course of business. Far more terrifying than the berserker rages of blood lust that seize the natural men of capitalism in the works of Jack London is Thorpe's "softening, radiant consciousness of how much this meant to him" when he decides, out of sentimental protective-ness for his wife, to spare the gardener and save the house party.

The detachment with which Frederic views Thorpe is so

great that *The Market-Place* is unique among the many economic novels produced at the turn of the century. To find a fit companion for Thorpe, one must go forward more than a decade to Frank Algernon Cowperwood. Frederic's attitude toward Thorpe is similar to Dreiser's toward Cowperwood in *The Financier* (1912) and the greater part of *The Titan* (1914): the genus financier is an appropriate subject for impartial study, and the reader can be left to draw his own moral, if he wishes, from the spectacle of a man who elevates desire into the principle of existence.

Even in the brilliant portrait of Cowperwood, however, one feels an inconsistency that Frederic, virtually alone of the novelists who have studied the tycoon, is refreshingly free of. Fictional millionaires like Cowperwood, for all the insistence on their naked rapacity, are typically clothed in what seem strait jackets of self-control. The title of Dreiser's third volume in his "Trilogy of Desire," *The Stoic*, points to the inconsistency in the conception of Cowperwood and many of the financiers of fiction. Dreiser's own imagination is excited by the splendor of Cowperwood's possessions, but Cowperwood himself seems indifferent to them. He builds palaces, accumulates art treasures, and seduces women like the modern Renaissance prince he is supposed to be, but his habitual dark suits of conservative cut give him away. "Dreiser's desire to exalt his hero," F. O. Matthiessen says, "has in a sense raised him above the level of being affected by success or defeat." [19] Like too many of literature's natural men of finance, Cowperwood seems unnatural in his chilly dispassion.

The intention here is not to disparage Dreiser's achievement but to show how Frederic escapes the convention of the mil-

---

[19] *Theodore Dreiser* (New York, 1951), p. 148.

lionaire that can be detected in Cowperwood and traced at least as far back as the Merdle of Dickens and the Melmott of Trollope—the convention of representing the financier as the joyless slave of his own enterprises. Although the financiers of the fiction written around the turn of the century are supposed to be wolves and tigers, the recurrent image is either that of the machine or the spider, a creature of solitary concealment who is proverbially patient and cold-blooded. These tycoons have the coolness of the Machiavel but not enough of the flamboyant exuberance. One misses the riotous pleasure in improvisation that makes opportunists like Shakespeare's Richard III antically gay at times. For men who are supposed to live in a moral accord with the pleasure principle, these tycoons simply do not have enough fun.

"Unemotional," "dispassionate," and "secret" are the words that Robert Grant uses to introduce the magnate Horace Elton in *Unleavened Bread*, and the same kind of adjectives cluster about most fictional financiers. The language seems strangely out of place with talk of robber barons, bears and bulls, dog eating dog, crashes, and panics. The typical portraits may do well enough for puritan millionaires like John D. Rockefeller, but it is difficult to find any which suggest the buccaneering spirits of a Jay Gould or a Pierpont Morgan. One suspects that neither of these men would have taken the drunken blow of an Irish ward boss as calmly as Will Payne's *Money Captain* does. Were the cartoonists completely wrong? Were there never smiling tycoons who smoked huge cigars and wore vests covered with dollar signs over their paunches?

In one of his notes for *Gloria Mundi* Frederic wrote:

Business! Business! . . . You can read in histories, memoirs, state papers, every conceivable detail of how such a war was waged, such a revolution created; everything in political and social history can be investigated. But in financial history, the great capitalists who [are the] true rulers of [the] world work in impenetrable mystery.[20]

The odd thing about Frederic's attempt to penetrate the impenetrable mystery is that the hero of *The Market-Place* is no mystery at all. The abundance of Thorpe's vitality remains ultimately inexplicable; but the man is simple, almost a child in his emotions.

Thorpe develops less from the shrewd and worldly Albert Fairchilds, Schuyler Tenneys, and Dr. Ledsmars, than the naive young men—the Seth Fairchilds, Horace Boyces, and Theron Wares. The same cheerful egotism, the same utter failure to feel any humility before history which brought these young men to disaster, makes Thorpe a disaster to others. *The Damnation of Theron Ware* concluded with Theron, the epitome of American innocence, defeated but promising to "start over" and succeed the next time. He returns, in a manner of speaking, in Joel Thorpe. It comes as no surprise that Thorpe, though born and educated in England, is considered by those he meets "an American, to all intents and purposes" (p. 10).[21]

---

[20] Frederic Papers, Library of Congress. In 1894 Lafcadio Hearn wrote, "Fancy a good romance about Wall Street—so written that the public could understand it!" (Hearn to Elwood Hendrick, Sept., 1894, quoted in Elizabeth Bisland, *Life and Letters of Lafcadio Hearn* [Boston, 1906], II, 182). A quarter of a century later so many novelists had penetrated Frederic's impenetrable mystery and written Hearn's romances of finance that F. Scott Fitzgerald's Amory Blaine protested, "I wish American novelists would give up trying to make business romantically interesting" (*This Side of Paradise* [New York, 1920], p. 234).

[21] Thorpe has spent a number of years in the United States before the action of the novel. "Marvelous country for assimilation that

Most of the time there is real charm to Thorpe. His optimism, bumptious self-confidence, and cheerful honesty about his own dishonesty are winning. One cannot help sympathizing with Thorpe's reflection that all his forty years of hardship and struggle were worth it, if only for the "one privilege now of being able to appreciate to the uttermost the touch of double-silk underwear" (p. 45). But there are moments when the overgrown boy becomes a bully of threatening possibilities. Holding up his clenched fist for the admiration of his sister, Thorpe waxes philosophical:

"That's the kind of hand . . . that breaks the Jew in the long run, if there's only enough grit behind it. I used to watch those Jews' hands. . . . Their fingers are never still; they twist round and keep stirring like a lobster's feelers. But there ain't any real strength in 'em. . . . It's their hellish industry and activity that gives them such a pull, and makes most people afraid of them. But when a hand like that takes them by the throat"—he held up his right hand as he spoke, with the thick uncouth fingers and massive thumb arched menacingly in a powerful muscular tension —"When *that* tightens round their neck, and they feel that the grip means business—my God! what good are they?" [pp. 205–206].

This violent anti-Semitism, which is so pronounced that Thorpe's squeeze on the market is taken to be a *Judenhetze*, offers a clue to what Frederic sees represented in his tycoon. In 1892, Frederic had published *The New Exodus: A Study of Israel in Russia,* which attempted to explain the conditions and events that had returned Russian Jewry at the close of the nineteenth century to the suffering of the Middle Ages.

___

America is!" says Lord Plowden to Thorpe. "You remember what I told you—it's put such a mark on you that I should never have believed you were English" (p. 65).

Analyzing the "carnival of brute force" that he had seen unleashed against the innocent Jews, he had written:

> Whenever men engage in an unhealthy and un-natural competition, those with the worst and most dangerous qualities rise to the top, trampling the weaker and softer ones underfoot. We have something like that in Wall Street... [p. 32].[22]

And in describing the Russian character, Frederic had in effect described Thorpe:

> The temptation continually arises to find parallels for all things Russian in the fantasies and queer aberrations of childhood. The Slavic brain is nothing if not juvenile. It is invincibly optimistic; it rushes headlong into enthusiastic beliefs founded upon the merest hearsay or imagining; it invents lies and excuses with incredible swiftness and an entire disregard for probabilities, or for cause and effect; it has no conception of responsibility, of duty, or of any other abstract virtue. Withal, it is kindly and ferocious by turn . . . childlike always [pp. 13–14].

When Frederic visited Russia in 1891, the frank relapse into medieval brutality that he witnessed there had seemed something local, a "strange and monstrous excrescence upon the history of our century" (p. 3). He had felt that "the engulfing return wave of barbarism" would go so far and no farther (p. 2). Judging from *The Market-Place*, the passing years left him less and less confident that the tide would recede before it engulfed the entire civilized world. The references in the novel to China, Mexico, France, Italy, Holland, the United

----

[22] All page references to *The New Exodus* are to the first English edition (London: William Heinemann, 1892). The implications of Frederic's remarks are worth noting: what to so many of his contemporaries is a natural struggle for the survival of the fittest is to him "an unhealthy and unnatural competition."

States, Argentina, Africa, and dozens of other places suggest that Thorpe represents a spirit in the world that moves beyond the confines of London.

How far Thorpe will go, or as Celia Madden puts the question, "How will he use his power?" (p. 184), is the real issue of the book. The suspense over whether or not Thorpe will be able to pull off his *coup* is only secondary, for he is fully confident of victory from the start:

His triumph was so sweeping and comprehensive as to be somewhat shapeless to the view. He had a sense of fascinated pain when he tried to define to himself what its limits would probably be. Vistas of unchecked, expanding conquest stretched away in every direction [p. 1].

As the novel ends, it is abundantly clear that for Joel Thorpe there is no satisfactory limit to conquest.

The uses of power that momentarily caught the interest of Christian Tower have no appeal for Thorpe. The days when one could profitably invest one's energies in causes seem gone. Lord Plowden, one of Thorpe's dummy directors, knows the lesson only too well. Plowden's father, a general who fought in the Crimea, left a legacy of little more than stocks in such ventures as the Confederate States of America and Kossuth's Hungarian Republic.

Not that Thorpe is mean with his money, far from it; he often hands out money with lavish generosity. But to be generous to dependents who never contradict and who know how to express gratitude is no uncommon quality. What is uncommon in Thorpe is "something which stands quite apart from standards of morals or ethics or the ordinary emotions. . . . The kind of organization in which, within a second, without any warning or reason, a passing whim may have worked itself up into an imperative law" (p. 269). When he capriciously turns on an associate whom he has befriended earlier with equal caprice, Thorpe examines his behavior: "Why had he done this? He asked himself the question in varying forms, over his brandy and soda, but no convincing answer came. He had done it because he had felt like doing it. It was impossible to trace motives further than that" (p. 258). The whole question of motives behind the exercise of power, in fact, goes by the board with Thorpe. In him, nothing intrudes between wish and act.

Describing his tycoon's appearance, Frederic almost describes himself. A big, bearish man, Thorpe is engagingly frank in conversation, a brash, boastful boy full of enthusiasm and animation. When Thorpe is concentrating, however, his face becomes curiously immobile and he appears dull and lethargic.[23] At these moments, his lackluster gaze contains the image of "a hundred thousand dead men" (p. 183). In another novelist, one would pass off the business of the dead men in the eyes as a momentary lapse into melodramatic nonsense, but "the dead men," as we have seen, figure in many of Frederic's works.

Repeatedly Frederic uses the term "the dead men" to describe the past that the living carry within themselves whether they are aware of it or not. Henley's "dreams of a dead past that will not die" haunt all men and frustrate their dreams of self-improvement, reform, and progress. The dead men exist,

[23] Louise Imogen Guiney comments on the strange combination of virile strength and frank boyishness in Frederic, and she notes that, for all the energy and flow of talk, Frederic's face—the face "of one who is afraid of nothing"—was "somewhat immobile" ("Harold Frederic: A Half-Length Sketch from the Life," *Book Buyer*, XVII [1899], 601). Miss Guiney's characterization of Frederic as "a barbaric king" does very well for Joel Thorpe too (p. 604).

in a sense, in the collective unconscious of the race. "There is really nothing new under the sun," Father Forbes says to Theron Ware:

> Though there seem to have been the most tremendous changes in races and civilizations and religions, stretching over many thousands of years, yet nothing is in fact altered very much. Where religions are concerned, the human race are still very like savages in a dangerous wood in the dark, telling one another ghost stories around a campfire [p. 247].[24]

The dead whom Thorpe's wife and Celia Madden see in his eyes represent not only the savagery that he is capable of but also the savagery that humanity is capable of. Although Thorpe is a barbarian, the lords and ladies who at first appear to provide such a contrast to him are really what Veblen would call "advanced barbarians." [25] Before the novel is over,

[24] Dr. Ledsmar makes a similar point when he observes that boys "traverse in their younger years all the stages of the childhood of the race. They have terrifying dreams of awful monsters and giant animals of which they have never so much as heard in their waking hours; they pass through the lust for digging caves, building fires, sleeping out in the woods, hunting with bows and arrows,—all remote ancestral impulses; they play games with stones, marbles, and so on at regular stated periods of the year which they instinctively know, just as they were played in the Bronze Age, and heaven only knows how much earlier" (pp. 224–225).

[25] Grant C. Knight calls Thorpe's story "an unplanned fictionalization of *The Theory of the Leisure Class*" (*Critical Period*, p. 152). Although *The Market-Place*, particularly in its description of Lord Plowden's estate, is anticipatory of Veblen's book (1899), *Gloria Mundi* is even more strikingly so. Throughout *Gloria Mundi* Frederic insists that the power of the Torrs is manifest not in what they produce (they produce nothing) but in what they consume. Unused rooms, libraries of unread books, untilled fields, unharvested forests, and unemployed sons are the visible sign of the Torrs' power. Christian's first real glimpse of what he is to inherit comes when he strolls

General Kervick (a gentleman with the nose, forehead, mouth, and chin "of a soldier grown old in the contemplation of portraits of the Duke of Wellington") offers Thorpe his daughter, and Lord Plowden delicately hints that his sister, the Honorable Winifred, is Thorpe's if he will have her. "I don't want toadies about me," Thorpe explains to Lord Plowden, "but I do want people who feel bound to me, and are as keen about me and my feelings and interests as they are about their own." And Plowden replies, "It is delightfully feudal" (p. 306). Thorpe may be only a king of the rubber market, but lords and ladies, ministers and generals, are quick to recognize the legitimacy of his claim to fealty.

The paradox of Thorpe is that he is both the newest of men and the oldest.[26] Once the "golden consummation" of wealth has come, he is rejuvenated. (So intent is Frederic on rejuvenating Thorpe that he absent-mindedly makes his hero forty at the beginning of the novel and thirty-five later.) Thorpe arrives for a weekend at a country house with a completely new wardrobe, still done up in the tradesmen's packages. When he shaves off the beard he has worn for years, "even his face was new" (p. 43). Yet as the dead men in his gaze imply, he is also the oldest of men. He is an aggressively innocent Adam who numbers all creation as his.

---

around the grounds of Caermere and comes upon a group of beaters heaping up the dozens of pheasants which his cousins have spent the morning slaughtering.

[26] In *The New Exodus*, Frederic makes much of the paradox that Russia, although it is ancient in its barbarism, is also "a new world— so new as to tread upon the heels of the hindermost things in old worlds." The Russian landscape presented a "weird likeness" to "the more backward agricultural regions of the United States," and Frederic could not rid himself of the thought that Russia "was a kind of America in which the early civilized settlers had been overwhelmed and absorbed by the aborigines" (p. 36).

The power that enables Thorpe to dominate the Exchange enables him to dominate women as well. He meets and wins Lady Cressage, the same beautiful young woman Christian Tower flirted with in *Gloria Mundi*. Although her patrician composure keeps him at bay for the first months of their marriage, Thorpe eventually comes to understand that Lady Cressage has married him because she wants him to master her as he masters everything else. "Happiness through terror" is her own phrase for the exhilaration that brings her to life when she is with Thorpe (p. 273).

Long before he has come to understand his relationship with his wife, Thorpe has begun to sense a connection between his pecuniary instinct and his libido. Talking to Celia Madden, he realizes that he has not seen her before in "so much low-necked dress," and his subsequent revery links financial and sexual success in a fashion anticipatory of Theodore Dreiser:

Thorpe noted the somewhat luxuriant curves of these splendid shoulders, and the creamy whiteness of the skin, upon which, round the full throat, a chain of diamonds lay as upon satin. . . . The deep fire-gleam in her broad plaits of hair gave a wonderful brilliancy to this colouring of brow and throat and bosom. He marvelled at himself for discovering only now that she also was beautiful—and then thrilled with pride at the thought that henceforth his life might be passed altogether among beautiful women, radiant in gems and costly fabrics, who would smile upon him at his command [pp. 260–261].

The question of the New Woman is raised in *The Market-Place* as it was in *Gloria Mundi*, and it is settled in the same way, by marriage. "Marriage, a home, children," says Celia Madden, "these are great things to a woman. We can say that she pays the price of bondage for them—but to know what that signifies, we must ask what her freedom has been worth to her." Lady Cressage's reply is her acceptance of Thorpe: "Yes. . . . What have I done with my freedom that has been worth while?" (p. 190).

Celia is a woman of far greater vitality and wealth than Edith and is not yet ready for "bondage," but she is far from happy in her own freedom. Her spirit is chastened by the memories of the pain she caused others back in the United States, and she has long since decided that "the free woman is a fraud—a myth." "I used to have the most wonderful visions of what independence would mean," she says. "I thought that when I was absolutely my own master, with my money and my courage and my free mind, I would do things to astonish all mankind. But really the most I achieve is the occasional mild surprise of a German waiter" (p. 187). Celia has, in fact, already lived through the experiences that the modern women of *Main Street* will later undergo. Two decades in the future, Carol Kennicott reads of Celia's freedom in *The Damnation of Theron Ware*.[27] One wonders whether she ever reads of Celia's regrets in *The Market-Place*.

[27] Sinclair Lewis, *Main Street* (New York, 1920), p. 66. Quoting a letter to Lewis in which F. Scott Fitzgerald writes "to say that *Main Street* has displaced *Theron Ware* in my favor as the best American novel," Mark Schorer expresses surprise that Fitzgerald should have so admired Frederic's "treatment of village life" (*Sinclair Lewis* [New York, 1961], p. 275). One guesses that what Fitzgerald found in *The Damnation* was a treatment not of village life but of a young man captivated by dreams of worldly success and beauty. *This Side of Paradise* not only mentions *The Damnation* but is filled with echoes of the work. Fitzgerald included "Theron Ware, Fredericks" [*sic*], in the "Substitute List of Good Novels" he drew up for Sheilah Graham when he was supervising her education (Sheilah Graham, *College of One* [New York, 1968], p. 208). Edmund Wilson thinks he may have given Fitzgerald *The Damnation* to read when they were at Princeton together (personal interview with Edmund Wilson, Aug. 5, 1967).

After Thorpe finally marries and secures his fortune, Frederic asks the question that is crucial to both *Gloria Mundi* and *The Market-Place*, asks a question that twentieth-century American literature was to pose repeatedly: after success, what? Thorpe quickly realizes his dream of becoming an English country gentleman. His Hertfordshire estate is suitably rural, his cottagers suitably humble, and his manor house foundations suitably Tudor. But, as Tocqueville sardonically remarks, "a man cannot gradually enlarge his mind as he does his house." [28]

For a time Thorpe almost convinces himself that he loves it all. Yawning at the landscape that opens out before his windows, he is reassured: "Its inertia, when one came to comprehend it, was undeniably magnificent, and long ago he had perceived within himself the growth of an answering repose, a responsive lethargy, which in its full development was also going to be very fine" (p. 327). On the same day he decides that he had better take a little trip to liven himself up. "Rich men who live among democratic nations," to quote Tocqueville again, "are more apt to become enervated than debauched." [29] Lady Cressage is equally bored. She tries to keep busy in her greenhouses and quietly mourns the fact that her pirate has transformed himself into an alderman.

The revelation comes sudden and clear to Thorpe:

What gross trick had the fates played on him? He had achieved power—and where was that power? What had he done with it? What *could* he do with it? He had an excess of wealth, it was true, but in what way could it command an excess of enjoyment? The very phrase was a paradox, as he dimly perceived. There existed only a narrow margin of advantage in favor of the rich

[28] *Democracy in America* (New York, 1945), II, 245.
[29] *Ibid.*, p. 132.

man. . . . So it ran indefinitely—this thin selvedge of advantage which money could buy—with deprivation on the one side, and surfeit on the other. Candidly, was it not true that more happiness lay in winning the way out of deprivation, than in inventing safeguards against satiety? The poor man succeeding in making himself rich—at numerous stages of the operation there might be made a moral snap-shot of the truly happy man. But not after he had reached the top. Then disintegration began at once [pp. 341–342].

Once he recognizes his problem, Thorpe loses no time in checking his disintegration, in forming new plans. Return to the market is out of the question. "I kill every pheasant I fire at" has been his boast, but one cannot find satisfaction in shooting the same sort of bird over and over again (p. 127). A walk through the slums of London, where he is surprised to find himself taking an almost esthetic pleasure in the picturesqueness of poverty, and a talk with his sister, who thinks that he should do some good with his money, determine Thorpe's new course. He will become a philanthropist. In the vast misery of the London poor, Thorpe has found a project worthy of his prodigious energies.

Just as some of the reviews of *The Market-Place* said, Thorpe discovers that he must do some good to others in order to be happy, but the critics who took Thorpe's resolution at face value were as mistaken as those who overlooked it entirely. As in the earlier novels, Frederic was using convention for his own ironic purpose. In making his tycoon reform, Frederic was making his final comment on reform. Thorpe feels neither compassion nor shame when he views the misery of the poor. What he feels is opportunity:

His old dormant, formless lust for power stirred again in his pulses. What other phase of power carried with it such rewards, such gratitudes, such humble subservience on all sides as far as the eye could reach—as that exercised by the intelligently munificent philanthropist? [p. 383].

When his wife asks him what his new plans are, Thorpe is ready with his answer: "Rule England!" (p. 386).

Although there is no reason to believe that Frederic had a pair of novels in mind when he began *Gloria Mundi*, he must have been aware by the time he finished it that he still had a great deal more to say about the uses of power and the possibilities of social reform. Unlike as the two novels at first appear to be, *Gloria Mundi* and *The Market-Place* are companion pieces, connected not only by the several characters they share but by their themes as well. Together the two works form a kind of dialogue. In *Gloria Mundi* Frederic's viewpoint is that of an older man, a man who has outlived the enthusiasms of his youth and for whom the glory of this world has passed away. In *The Market-Place*, insofar as Thorpe's viewpoint controls the narrative, the world is seen through youthful eyes, delighting in the vigorous exercise of vulgar, vain, amoral energy.

The Market-Place actually concludes with a dialogue between the protagonists of the two novels. In the final chapter Thorpe entertains the Duke and Duchess of Glastonbury, for Christian Tower and his wife Frances are old friends of Lady Cressage. After dinner Thorpe and Christian retire to the study to talk about Thorpe's plans. Yes, Christian says, he does know something about philanthropy; since he became Duke, he and his wife have tried to do something for London working girls. Christian, who assumes that Thorpe's motives are altruistic, offers little encouragement. The last of the family lands are now his, but the people who live on them show no sign of having been regenerated by the great "System." Christian's bitter comment on the ungrateful tenants, who failed so completely to be transformed by Emanuel into Utopians, is brilliantly revealing of the egotism that can underlie benevolence: "I cannot bear those people. I have sometimes the feeling that if it were feasible I should like to oppress them in some way—to hurt them" (p. 393). Thorpe brushes away Christian's objections. Through philanthropy he will win the backing of the London poor, and with that backing he will rule England. This man "with the visage of a dictator" has no program, no ideology, beyond that. What does it matter? He will be kept happy.[30]

Gloria Mundi follows hapless Christian Tower through to the numbing conclusion that man's dreams and hopes are impossible of fulfillment, are doomed to failure because of the brute resistance that life offers to any meaningful sort of change. *The Market-Place,* on the other hand, presents a hero possessed of an energy that men of self-distrustful conscience like Christian can scarcely conceive of. The supremely confident Thorpe seems a force in himself. He is an awesome embodiment of that raw vitality which Henry Adams found almost oppressive in Theodore Roosevelt: "the singular primitive quality that belongs to ultimate matter—the power that medieval theology assigned to God—... pure act." [31]

Against *Gloria Mundi* and its evocation of Ecclesiastes—its

[30] For a reading of *The Market-Place* markedly different from the one offered here, see Larzer Ziff, *The American 1890s* (New York, 1966), pp. 216–217. Ziff sees Thorpe as Frederic's model for the new age, "the technocrat [who] must be given power." In "Philanthropy in Frederic's *The Market-Place,*" Clayton Eichelberger correctly observes that "the picture of Thorpe, philanthropist, is equally as negative as the picture of Thorpe, buccaneer" (*American Quarterly,* XX [Spring, 1968], 115).

[31] *The Education of Henry Adams* (Boston, 1927), p. 441.

sense of history as repetition—stands *The Market-Place* and its dynamic financier. Is Christian right when he protests to Thorpe that whether one leaves the world alone or not "it goes round just the same" (p. 393)? Or is Thorpe right in his faith in his own vitality? He reminds Christian that there was a Thorpe among the judges who condemned Charles I; Christian counters by reminding Thorpe of the Restoration.

In *Gloria Mundi* and *The Market-Place* Frederic writes out of an acute sense of his historical moment. To what extent, he asks, will the age about to die determine the future? To what extent will the age about to be born depart from the past? Standing at the end of the nineteenth century, Frederic looks back upon nearly one hundred years of power garnered in the name of progress, and, turning to the century ahead, he asks just what that power implies.

8 / The Coming Man

Harold Frederic's brief career as a novelist corresponds exactly to the period that Henry Steele Commager identifies as the "watershed" of American history. "With the decade of the nineties—or roughly from the mid-eighties to the Spanish War—the new America came in as on flood tide." [1] The England of Frederic's residence during those years offered no refuge. "A sense of vagueness, of incoherence and indirection, grows on us," G. M. Young writes in *Victorian England: Portrait of an Age*, "as we watch the eighties struggling for a foothold in the swirl and wreckage of new ideas and old beliefs." [2] To some, Shaw for example, the more treacherous the currents, the more exhilarating the challenge to steer. And to others (particularly in America) the period seemed placid. Henry Seidel Canby memorialized the nineties as "the last era in the United States when there was a pause, and everyone, at least in my town, knew what it meant to be an American." [3] If numbers of Americans really had answered

[1] *The American Mind* (New Haven, 1950), p. 44.
[2] Second ed. (New York, 1953), p. 165.
[3] *The Age of Confidence* (New York, 1934), p. 24.

Crèvecoeur's famous question—"What then is the American?"—it must have been because so many were asking the question.

Certainly there was cause for anxiety in an age that saw its defects criticized by the Utopian standards of *Looking Backward* and *A Traveler from Altruria* or revealed by *How the Other Half Lives*, an age that opened with the Haymarket Riot and moved on to the Homestead, Pullman, and American Railway Union strikes, that experienced an unprecedented depression, that saw the Populist Party and Coxey's army on the march. Yet the confidence that such writers as Canby and Van Wyck Brooks speak of did exist.[4] One is struck, however, by how self-conscious and vulnerable that confidence often seems. There is something uneasy in an age that so often proclaimed its assurance with such assertiveness. Closing with the Spanish-American War, the watershed years produced a representative man in the Rough Rider, aggressively manly, dressed with rakish theatricality, and surrounded by war correspondents. The gay nineties, for all their undoubted gaiety, were as unstable in their way as the yellow nineties in England, which produced among their representative men Oscar Wilde, the embodiment at once of a sublimely confident poise and a tragic precariousness of balance.

Born in 1856, Frederic was young enough to be free of the memory of antebellum America that haunted Howells and Twain; in his mid-thirties when the nineties began, he was old

---

[4] Ellen Moers says of Brooks' *The Confident Years, 1885–1915*, "in spite of its title, [it] conveyed confusion rather than confidence" ("Shook-up Generation," *New York Review of Books*, VIII [May 18, 1967], 26). Miss Moers' review of several books on American literature in the nineties admirably sums up the general failure to understand this complex period.

enough to be fully aware of just how much was new and different in the modern world then being born. With the exceptions of Stephen Crane and Frank Norris, no American novelist belongs so thoroughly and exclusively to the years of the watershed as does Frederic, and in the works of no other American novelist does one so fully sense what it was like to be alive in those turbulent years.

It was Frederic's special gift to be able to share emotionally in the zest and enthusiasm of the confident years and yet to perceive clearly how insubstantial the basis for optimism was. By means of comic balance he was able to leave a record that does justice to both the enchantments and disenchantments of his age. His rapid rise in the world, and his youth, energy, and courage made him an insider, a participant in the hopeful dreams of his age, yet other experiences and qualities developed in him a detachment from the times. Although it was Frederic's ambition to be free to devote himself fully to his fiction, one cannot regret the career in journalism that gave him so remarkable an education, so broad an experience of life in upstate New York, of back-room politics in Albany, of Bohemian London—that sent him traveling to Dublin, Paris, Berlin, and as far as Moscow. Nor need one regret Frederic's enforced absence from his homeland as a separation from his native subject, for he remained in his fiction, as in his cable letters to the New York *Times*, "*our* special correspondent." And, remaining throughout his London years thoroughly American, he gained from residence abroad a perspective on the American experience and on himself as instructive as the perspective he derived from his deep conviction that the past sits in judgment on the present.

In his obituary tribute to his friend's memory, Frank Harris catches the essential facts of Frederic's life as well as anyone ever has. Harris describes "a long-legged gawky lad . . . full of unripe political enthusiasms and half-baked beliefs in regenerated men and a possible millennium." The boy soon decided that the millennium was not at hand, for he learned early that men are swayed, finally, "by self-interests and petty vanities." "The general truth not only did not ensavage or envenom him, it called out in him a deep tolerance and kindliness." Frederic met his awakening with laughter instead of tears, and as Harris says, "Laughter hastens growth." [5]

"Full of unripe poltical enthusiasms and half-baked beliefs in regenerated men and a possible millennium": the description fits most of the central characters in Frederic's fiction perfectly. To make a critical realist of Frederic, one must attribute to him the very enthusiasms and beliefs he criticized as unripe and half-baked. "In about every other novel I pick up nowadays," wrote a reviewer in 1891, "the hero or heroine has undertaken the regeneration of society." [6] One often feels that Frederic's heroes and heroines must have read too many such volumes at an impressionable age. Isabel Fairchild is not the only character in Frederic's fiction who can be said to "talk like a book." Kate Minster dreams of becoming a benefactress like the heroine of *All Sorts and Conditions of Men;* the political reformers of *Seth's Brother's Wife,* as Albert Fairchild comments in the novel, are right out of Francis Marion Crawford's *An American Politician;* and in *Gloria Mundi* Frances Bailey's bookcase includes a slender volume entitled *Civilization: Its Cause and Cure.*

Whatever the cause of civilization, Frederic thought it unlikely that the cure would be effected by creatures as fallible as men. When his novels are described in general terms, they

---

[5] "Harold Frederic: Ad Memoriam," *Saturday Review,* LXXXVI (1898), 527.

[6] "In the Library," *Book Buyer,* VIII (1891), 107.

sound tiresomely conventional. *Seth's Brother's Wife* can be described as the tale of a young idealist who escapes from the farm, becomes a crusading newspaper editor, and finally wins the virtuous blond while seeing his reform candidate sweep into office despite the machinations of corrupt politicians. But such a summary ignores Frederic's characteristically ironic treatment of stock materials, ignores Seth's entanglement with his brother's wife, which comes to crisis at the very time Seth denounces his brother and impulsively proposes to Annie, ignores the role of Beekman the machine boss in securing the election of Ansdell the reformer, and ignores the final irony of the novel—the announcement that Ansdell is dividing his time in Washington between reforming the Republic and courting the irrepressible Isabel.

The same comic manipulation of conventional materials can be seen in the other works—in *The Lawton Girl,* for example, which concludes with the hero who has routed the pirates of high finance entering the Minster mansion and scarcely daring to wonder whether henceforth his life will be spent amid such opulence. Or it can be seen in *Gloria Mundi,* which showers fortune upon an idealistic orphan boy only to teach him how intractable the world is. And, of course, it can be seen in *The Damnation of Theron Ware,* which takes the basic situation of a *Robert Elsmere* or *John Ward, Preacher* and proceeds to show a young minister who sheds his religious faith with as little regret as a snake shedding its skin.

In an age when too many novelists presented characters who were, as Arnold Bennett said of the cast in one of Marie Corelli's extravaganzas, "sharply divided into two groups—the sheep and the goats,"[7] Frederic followed the advice of

---

[7] *Fame and Fiction: An Inquiry into Certain Popularities* (New York, 1901), p. 86.

Sister Soulsby and left the division for Judgment Day. With her, he believed that "as long as human life lasts, good, bad, indifferent are all braided up together in every man's nature, and every woman's too. . . . It's a see-saw with all of us . . . sometimes up; sometimes down" (p. 346).

There was another see-saw that interested Frederic, "the Great See-Saw" he called it in his notes for *The Damnation*: "Epicurean vs. Stoic—Greek vs. Jew— . . . Cromwell vs. Charles II." "See Arnold also," he added.[8] Frequently one does seem to see the classifications of *Culture and Anarchy* illustrated in Frederic's work, in *Observations in Philistia*, for example, and especially in *Gloria Mundi*, with its "Jews," its aristocratic Barbarians, and its hero—an alien in Arnold's terms as in all others.[9] The irony of the title *Illumination*, moreover, might almost be in illustration of the admonition that Arnold quotes repeatedly in *Culture and Anarchy*: "Take care that your light be not darkness." Frederic's "Greek vs. Jew" is not really worked out in particularly Arnoldian fashion, however. "The great see-saw" is essentially the opposition of past and present, age and youth, innocence and experience, liberalism and conservatism.

The Jews, Frederic wrote in *The New Exodus*, "watched the dawn of history with calm meditative eyes," watched "Chaldea, Assyria, Babylon, Media, Egypt, Phoenicia, Greece, Carthage rise, flourish, and fall," as they watched still later empires rise, flourish, and fall (p. 55). Frederic's Jew has seen enough to be safe from the enthusiasms of the young. He will

[8] Notes for *The Damnation*, Frederic Papers, Library of Congress.
[9] Echoes of Arnold in *Gloria Mundi* and *The Market-Place* have been noted by Kenneth E. Silverman in his unpublished Columbia University Master's essay, "Harold Frederic: His Themes, Techniques, and Place in American Literature" (1958), pp. 84–85.

neither follow the irresponsible course of Celia Madden nor succumb to the adolescent egotism of Theron Ware, who wants so much to be a "Greek pagan" like Celia. Unfortunately, the Jew is often reduced to inertia by his consciousness of the past; he is too likely to become, in the popular sense of the word, a stoic. If he does dream, as do the "Jews" in *Gloria Mundi*, his dream is all too likely to be reactionary and puritanical, to hark back to a tightly ordered past, and it is likely to end, as does the great System of Emmanuel Torr, in disillusion and resignation.

The Greek on the other end of the see-saw is really more romantic than classical. The plea in *Culture and Anarchy* for a Hellenistic faith in the possibility of personal perfection was answered in the last decade or so of the nineteenth century by "pagans" who conceived of personal development in terms considerably less rigorous than Arnold's. Frederic's Greek spirit is the active spirit of the New World, disdainful of history (though often charmed by the beauty and picturesqueness of the past), either unsophisticated or naively "advanced," youthfully and optimistically forward-looking. It is, presumably, the spirit that stirred in the young Harold Frederic who strode around Utica dressed in a Kossuth hat and a garibaldi shirt.

Greek versus Jew: Frederic understood it as a see-saw, a constantly shifting relationship between extremes in human nature. In his book on William II of Germany, *The Young Emperor*, Frederic wrote of the Kaiser:

One sees a constant struggle between two Williams. . . . Such conflicts and clashings between two hostile inner selves have a part in the personal history of each of us. Only we are not under the searching glare of illumination which beats upon a prince, and the records and results of these internal warrings are of interest to ourselves alone.[10]

"Of interest to ourselves alone," unless of course one happens to be a novelist. Out of the tensions of his own character Harold Frederic wrote a series of remarkable novels. He did not have to go to Arnold to find his metaphor of Greek versus Jew: he found it readymade in the countryside of his upbringing with its Uticas, Syracuses, and Ithacas, and its sons named after the children of Israel. Conscious of the conflict in life and in himself—"I have come to take a quite impersonal interest in studying myself" [11]—he was far enough removed from his own enthusiasms to view his characters from the distance of his disenchantments, yet he was never so far removed that he lost the power to communicate the rapture which sees life as a field of opportunity.

In his essay "La Jeune France" Frederic wrote of the French romantics with obvious sympathy:

They leavened the world with republican notions of liberty, fraternity, and equality. They familiarized the race with the great idea—the brotherhood of humanity. They were the pioneers of a new world. . . . Standing on the threshold of this new sphere, they were dazzled by its wonderful contrasts of light and shade, its sumptuous coloring, its sensuous luxuriance of form, its appalling heights and depths, its amazing infinity of possibilities.

Sympathetic though he was, however, Frederic saw the weakness of "La Jeune France" as he saw the weakness of all the young: "They rushed into extravagances, like Ponce de Leon and De Soto of old." [12]

[10] (New York, 1891), p. 107–108.
[11] See Frederic's letter of May 9, 1883, to Benjamin Paul Blood, quoted in Chapter 6.
[12] *Appleton's Journal*, XI, n.s. (1881), 562. This article reveals Fred-

The dreams of triumphant self-development or visions of sweeping reform that possess Frederic's enthusiasts are absurd, and so he treats them. "The Observer in Philistia," the *persona* for Frederic who narrates *Mrs. Albert Grundy*, muses on the peculiar test that London's Strand offers to humanity:

Whole legions of our friends, decent and deeply reputable people, fall altogether out of the picture, so to speak, on this ancient yet robust thoroughfare. They do very well indeed . . . where they are at home. . . . But to encounter them in the Strand is to be shocked by the blank incongruity of things. . . . They offend your perceptions by revealing limitations and shortcomings which might otherwise have been hidden to the end of time. You see suddenly that they are not such good fellows after all. Their spiritual complexions are made up for the dim light which pervades the outskirts of the four-mile radius—and go to pieces in the jocund radiance of the Strand [pp. 133–134].

In each of his novels Harold Frederic provides a Strand for his characters to walk upon. His young men and women, usually decent enough at first glance, are thrown into unfamiliar surroundings and expose their flaws and weaknesses. Under the glare of illumination, in the "jocund radiance," their spiritual complections simply go to pieces.

Although he is sometimes offended by the pretensions of man, Frederic has in abundance the tolerance and the kindliness that Harris and many others ascribed to him. It has been said that Frederic was "the most forgiving of men," [13] and

---

eric to have a surprising knowledge of French literary history. Although expressing reservations about the excesses of romanticism, it reveals a strong admiration for the historical romance and is notable for its unwillingness to oppose romance and realism.

[13] Robert W. Stallman and Lillian Gilkes, eds., *Stephen Crane: Letters,* (New York, 1960), p. 173.

he proved forgiving in his fiction as well as his life. He seldom allows his characters to blunder into complete and ruinous catastrophe, almost as though he cannot bear to see them punished too harshly for what are, after all, follies born of naiveté. Like Sister Soulsby scrutinizing Theron Ware's face under the lamplight to see what goodness yet remained under the "surface-blur" of debauchery, Frederic does not permit his interest in the flaws that show under the light of exposure to destroy his generous sympathy. "Dear, crude, asinine, illusioned Americans": the line is Dreiser's, but Frederic would have appreciated it.

"Self-development," said Grant Allen speaking both to and for the nineties,

is the aim for all—an aim which will make us all the stronger, and saner, and wiser, and better. . . . To be educated, to be emancipated, to be free, to be beautiful—these are the ends towards which one should strive, and by attaining which all are happier in themselves and more useful to others.[14]

To Frederic, Allen's New Hedonism appeared built into American life. A note for *The Damnation* reads: "Socrates—happiness first object of life—Thomas Jefferson—(American idea—Dec. Ind.—quite pagan)." [15]

"I set myself out on this ground which I suppose to be self-evident," Jefferson once wrote, " *'that the earth belongs in usufruct to the living'*; that the dead have neither power nor rights over it." [16] If Jefferson's assumption was self-evident, then perhaps the millennium could be reached. Frederic's

---

[14] "The New Hedonism," *Fortnightly Review*, LV, n.s. (1894), 380.
[15] Frederic Papers, Library of Congress.
[16] Quoted in R. W. B. Lewis, *The American Adam* (Chicago, 1955), p. 16.

young men and women do not need to be told "never mind the dead men"; they do not need Hamlin Garland to preach to them of crumbling idols and to tell them that "youth should be free from the dominion of the dead." [17] They know they are free, for they have declared their independence, proclaimed their emancipation, and set out on the high road of progress. They speak in the accents Frederic mimicked in one of his notes for *Gloria Mundi:* "We have put the world, the mere terrestrial ball, well under our feet. We have measured and photographed it. . . . Roentgen Rays show us the bones in my lady's hand—that dear hand! The thought of the skull under her face could frighten Byron. Not us." [18] Frederic had traveled the high road himself, but somewhere along the way he had paused, looked over his shoulder, and begun to wonder just how far he had come and just where he was headed.

The novels of Harold Frederic have a breadth that clearly goes beyond what the epithet "pioneer realist" suggests. Although much of his fiction was set in the same small area of upper New York State, his concerns were far from regional. He often returned to the hills and valleys of his home, but he always looked beyond them. His reputation must rest most heavily on *The Damnation of Theron Ware*, a work whose greatness has yet to be fully appreciated, despite the current revival of interest. As long as it is commonly thought to be what Van Wyck Brooks' edition proclaims it, a classic of realism "which exposes the cultural barrenness of the small town," [19] the novel will probably never attract the kind of reader who would most appreciate its fine and subtle ironies,

[17] *Crumbling Idols* (Chicago, 1894), p. viii.
[18] Notes titled "Progress," Frederic Papers, Library of Congress.
[19] *The Damnation* (New York, 1962), back cover.

its complex and original treatment of the most American of themes—the ambiguous relationship between innocence and experience.

The other novels deserve wider attention too. Not all of them, to be sure, not *In the Valley*, *The Return of the O'Mahony*, and *March Hares*. But the remaining works have in rewarding measure the artistry and intelligence which distinguish *The Damnation*. From *Seth's Brother's Wife* through *The Market-Place* they tell a story worth telling, a paradoxical tale of an innocence that discovers itself endowed with new ideas, new opportunities, new powers, only to discover itself as still innocent, still limited, still banal.

"Illumination," said The *Edinburgh Review* in 1898, "seems to be working over the whole continent of America very much as it worked in the respective instances of Mr. Ware and Miss Madden." [20] In choosing "illumination" as his theme, Frederic found material worthy of the largest talent. Inheritors of the ages, his heroes and heroines, in their giddy emancipations, their strident vitality, and their rude awakenings to the deflations of success or failure alike, are New Men and New Women indeed. And, living in a world which cannot escape the past and will not respect it, they reveal a dilemma all too modern. When Harold Frederic graduated from the Utica Advanced Academy in 1871, the role he played in the commencement "Colloquy and Recitation" was that of "The Coming Man." [21] He was well cast.

[20] S. L. Gwynn, "Novels of American Life," CLXXXVII (1898), 407.

[21] Utica *Morning Herald*, July 7, 1871, p. 2.

Selected Bibliography

BY HAROLD FREDERIC

UNPUBLISHED SOURCES

The Papers of Harold Frederic in The Library of Congress include uncatalogued materials as follows: autograph, typescript, and proof copies of some of Frederic's fiction and nonfiction; notes and outlines for published and unpublished fiction and nonfiction; notes, outlines, and uncompleted manuscripts for several plays; letters; financial records; appointment diaries; and an assortment of newspaper clippings, pamphlets, periodicals, and memorabilia. A full description of these papers is given in the appendix to Robert H. Woodward, "Harold Frederic: A Study of His Novels, Short Stories, and Plays" (unpub. Ph.D. diss., Indiana University, 1957), pp. 265–292.

The Harold Frederic Papers in the Manuscript Division of the New York Public Library, an uncatalogued collection, consists of an extensive file of copies made by Paul Haines of letters by, to, and concerning Frederic. The heart of the collection is made up of typescripts of numerous letters from Frederic to his New York *Times* editor, Charles R. Miller, the originals of which have been lost.

The letters below are listed according to recipient:

Blood, Benjamin Paul. May 9, 1883, Albany. Houghton Library, Harvard University.

Cleveland, Grover. Nov. 8, 1884, London. William Gorham Rice Papers, New York State Library.

———. Mar. 24, Sept. 4, 1885 (two letters), Feb. 8, Nov. 11, 1887, Dec. 8, 1888, Nov. 13, 1889, London. Grover Cleveland Papers, Library of Congress.

Conkling, Mrs. Roscoe. Sept. 11, 1890, London. Roscoe Conkling Papers, Library of Congress.

Crane, Stephen. Undated, Kenley. Stephen Crane Collection, Butler Library, Columbia University.

Crane, Mrs. Stephen. Feb. 8, 1898, Kenley. Stephen Crane Collection, Butler Library, Columbia University.

Garland, Hamlin. Dec. 30, 1891, London; May 12, 1897, Kenley. Hamlin Garland Collection, University of Southern California.

Gilder, Richard Watson. May 29, 1896, Kenley. Century Collection, New York Public Library.

Guiney, Louise Imogen. Jan. 30, 1890, London. Century Collection, New York Public Library.

Howe, John. May 11, 1892, London. Berg Collection, New York Public Library.

Howells, William Dean. May 5, 1885, London; Dec. 11, 1890, New York City; June 16, 1898, Kenley. William Dean Howells Papers, Houghton Library, Harvard University.

Lamont, Daniel S. Feb. 26, Oct. 22, Dec. 18, 1885, April 24, April 29, 1886, July 27, 1887, Jan. 25, 1888, London; June, 1888, Utica; Dec. 25, 1888, London. Grover Cleveland Papers, Library of Congress.

———. March 21, March 30, April 2, Aug. 6, 1893, March 4, 1894, London. Daniel Lamont Papers, Library of Congress.

Moulton, Louise Chandler. Undated, London. Louise Chandler Moulton Papers, Library of Congress.

Oppenheim, Ernest L. Oct. 12, 1889, London. Miscellaneous Papers, New York Public Library.

Tyler, Moses Coit. Oct. 21, 1885, Nov. 1, 1887, Oct. 16, 1894, London. Moses Coit Tyler Papers, Cornell University.

PUBLISHED SOURCES

Nonfiction

Frederick worked for the following newspapers in the periods indicated: the Utica *Observer*, Dec., 1875–Aug., 1882; the Albany *Evening Journal*, Sept., 1882–March, 1884; the New York *Times*, June, 1884–Oct., 1898. Only those articles written outside of the line of regular newspaper work and quoted or referred to in the text are included here. A bibliography of Frederic's nonfiction exclusive of regular newspaper work is given in Robert H. Woodward, "Harold Frederic: A Bibliography," *Studies in Bibliography*, XIII (1960), 250 and 252:

"From a Saunterer in the Labyrinth." *Pall Mall Budget*, XXXII (July 24, 1885), 22.

"La Jeune France." *Appleton's Journal*, XI, N.S. (1881), 555–562.

"The Mohawk Valley during the Revolution." *Harper's New Monthly Magazine*, LV (1877), 171–183.

"Musings on the Question of the Hour." By A Saunterer in the Labyrinth. *Pall Mall Budget*, XXXIII (Aug. 13, 1885), 11–12.

The New Exodus: A Study of Israel in Russia. London: William Heinemann, 1892.

"On Historical Novels, Past and Present." *The Bookman* (New York), VIII (1898), 330–333.

"The Rhetoricians of Ireland." By X. *Fortnightly Review*, LX (1893), 713–727.

The Young Emperor, William II of Germany: A Study in Character Development on a Throne. New York: G. P. Putnam's, 1891.

Fiction

I have listed the editions I used. For periodical publication and other editions, see Robert H. Woodward, "Harold Frederic: A Bibliography," *Studies in Bibliography*, XIII (1960), 247–251.

This is supplemented by Robert H. Woodward and Stanton Garner, "Frederic's Short Fiction: A Checklist," *American Literary Realism*, No. 2 (Spring, 1968), pp. 73–76.

"Barbette's Christmas." Utica *Observer*, Dec. 23, 1876, p. 2.

"The Blakelys of Poplar Place: A Legend of the Mohawk." Utica *Observer*, June 30, 1877, p. 2.

"Brother Angelan." *Harper's New Monthly Magazine*, LXXIII (1886), 517–528.

"Brother Sebastian's Friendship." Utica *Observer*, Sept. 6, 1879, p.2.

"The Connoisseur." *Saturday Review*, LXXXII (Special Christmas Number, 1896), 18–21.

"Cordelia and the Moon." *The First Book of the Author's Club: Liber Scriptorum*. New York: Authors Club, 1893. Pp. 241–252.

The Damnation of Theron Ware; or, Illumination. Ed. Everett Carter. Cambridge, Mass.: Harvard University Press, 1960.

The Deserter and Other Stories: A Book of the Two Wars. Boston: Lothrop, 1898. (Contains "The Deserter," "A Day in the Wilderness," "How Dickon Came by His Name," and "Where Avon into Severn Flows.")

"The Editor and the School Ma'am." New York *Times*, Sept. 9, 1888, p. 14.

"A Fortunate Confidence." By "Edgar." Utica *Observer*, Nov. 18, 1876, p. 2.

Gloria Mundi. Chicago: Herbert S. Stone, 1898.

"In the Shadow of Gabriel: A.D. 1550." *New York Ledger*, LI (Dec. 21, 1895), 12–13.

In the Sixties. Uniform ed. New York: Charles Scribner's, 1897. (Contains "Preface to a Uniform Edition," "The Copperhead," "Marsena," "The War Widow," "The Eve of the Fourth," and "My Aunt Susan.")

In the Valley. New York: Charles Scribner's, 1890.

"The Jew's Christmas." Albany *Evening Journal*, Dec. 23, 1882, p. 4.

The Lawton Girl. New York: Charles Scribner's, 1890.

March Hares. By "George Forth." New York: D. Appleton, 1896.

The Market-Place. New York: Frederick A. Stokes, 1899.

"The Martyrdom of Maev." *New York Ledger*, XLVI (March 22, 1890), 1–3; (March 29), 1–3.

Mrs. Albert Grundy: Observations in Philistia. London: John Lane, 1896.

"The Path of Murtogh." *The Idler*, VII (1895), 455–479.

The Return of the O'Mahony. New York: Robert Bonner's, 1892.

Seth's Brother's Wife: A Study of Life in the Greater New York. New York: Charles Scribner's, 1887.

"The Song of the Swamp-Robin." *The Independent*, XLIII (1891), 394–395; 430–432.

"The Truce of the Bishop." *Yellow Book*, VII (1895), 84–111.

"The Two Rochards." By "Edgar." Utica *Observer*, Sept. 30, 1876, p. 2; Oct. 7, 1876, p. 2.

"The Wooing of Teige." *Pall Mall Magazine*, X (1896), 418–426.

ABOUT FREDERIC

The indispensable guide to material about Frederic's life and work is "Harold Frederic (1856–1898): A Critical Bibliography of Secondary Comment," *American Literary Realism, 1870–1910*, No. 2 (Spring, 1968), pp. 1–70. Prepared by the editors of *American Literary Realism (ALR)*, this annotated bibliography lists 221 items under "Books" and 280 items under "Periodicals." Another useful article in the second number of *ALR* is C. W. E. Bigsby's "The 'Christian Science Case,' " pp. 77–83, which includes an extensive list of British newspaper reports and editorials on the death of Frederic and on the subsequent inquest and court proceedings.

The listing of reviews under "Periodicals" is augmented in the same issue of *ALR* by Robert H. Woodward, "Frederic's Collection of Reviews: Supplement to the Checklist of Contemporary Reviews of Frederic's Writings," pp. 84–89. This supplement, which is not annotated, consists almost entirely of reviews of *Seth's Brother's Wife* and *The Lawton Girl.*

I do not duplicate here the listing of contemporary reviews cited in *ALR*, but include all other contemporary reviews.

I have also included a number of items which mention Frederic but were not given in the *ALR* bibliographies. (The notation *ALR* follows all entries below that are annotated in the *ALR* "Critical Bibliography.")

CONTEMPORARY REVIEWS

I have read the reviews of Frederic's works listed in the *ALR* "Critical Bibliography" for the following periodicals: *Academy, Athenaeum, Atlantic, Book Buyer, Bookman* (London), *Bookman* (New York), Boston *Evening Transcript*, Brooklyn *Daily Eagle, Catholic World, Cosmopolitan, Critic, Dial, Edinburgh Review, Harper's Monthly, Independent, Life, Literary Digest, Literary News, Literary World, Munsey's Magazine, Nation*, New York *Daily Tribune*, New York *Times*, New York *Tribune Illustrated Supplement, Nineteenth Century, Overland Monthly, Poet-Lore, Review of Reviews, Saturday Evening Post, Saturday Review, Spectator,* and *Yellow Book.*

Other reviews of Frederic's work are listed below.

The Damnation of Theron Ware; or, Illumination
"American Fiction." *The Athenaeum,* No. 3569 (March 21, 1896), p. 378.
"Droch" [Robert Bridges]. "Life's Tips to Summer Reading." *Life,* XXVII (1896), 442.
Hutton, Lawrence. "Literary Notes." *Harper's Weekly,* XCIII (Sept., 1896), Supplement, 3–4.
Zangwill, Israel. "Mr. Frederic's Illumination." *The Critic,* XXVI, n.s. (1896), 156.

The Deserter and Other Stories

"Books and Authors," *The Outlook*, LX (1898), 427.

Gloria Mundi

"Books Readable and Charming." *Book Buyer*, XVIII (1899), 62.
"Notes on New Books." *Illustrated London News* (New York), XXIII (1898), 962.
"The Season's Books." *The Outlook*, LX (1898), 877.

The Market-Place

"Books of the Week." *The Outlook*, LXII (1899), 314.
"Notes on Books." *Illustrated London News* (New York), XXV (1899), 184.

Mrs. Albert Grundy: Observations in Philistia

"Books of Varied Interest." *Book Buyer*, XIII (1896), 475.

Tales of Our Coast (includes "The Path of Murtagh") "Fiction." *Saturday Review*, LXXXII (1896), 453.

ESSAYS AND ARTICLES

Allen, Grant. "The New Hedonism." *Fortnightly Review*, LV, N.S. (1894), 377–392.
Atherton, Gertrude. "The American Novel in England." *The Bookman* (New York), XXX (1910), 633–640 (*ALR*).
——. "The Reader: Harold Frederic." *The Bookman* (London), XV (1898), 37 (*ALR*).
Barr, Robert. "Harold Frederic, the Author of the Market-Place." *Saturday Evening Post*, CLXXI (1898), 396–397 (*ALR*).
Brooks, Van Wyck. Introduction to *The Damnation of Theron Ware*. Premier Classics of American Realism Series. New York: Fawcett, 1962 (*ALR*).
Carter, Everett. Introduction to *The Damnation of Theron Ware*. The John Harvard Library. Cambridge, Mass.: Harvard University Press, 1960 (*ALR*).

"Chronicle and Comment." *The Bookman* (New York), III (1896), 200; III (1896), 383–384 (*ALR*); IV (1896), 196–197 (*ALR*); VIII (1898), 284–311 (*ALR*); IX (1899), 12–13; XVII (1903), 442–447 (*ALR*).

Crane, Stephen. "Harold Frederic." *The Chap-Book*, VIII (1898), 358–359 (*ALR*).

Eichelberger, Clayton L. "Philanthropy in Frederic's *The Market-Place*." *American Quarterly*, XX (1968), 111–116.

Falk, Robert P. "The Rise of Realism, 1871–1891." In Harry Hayden Clark, ed., *Transitions in American Literary History*. Durham, N.C.: Duke University Press, 1953, pp. 381–442 (*ALR*).

[Frankau, Julia]. "Some Recollections of Harold Frederic." *Saturday Review*, LXXXVI (1898), 571–572 (*ALR*).

The Frederic Herald. Vol. I, No. 1 (April, 1967), through Vol. II, No. 1 (April, 1968) (*ALR*).

Garner, Stanton B. "More Notes on Harold Frederic in Ireland." *American Literature*, XXXIX (1968), 560–561.

———. "Some Notes on Harold Frederic in Ireland." *American Literature*, XXXIX (1967), 60–74 (*ALR*).

Genthe, Charles V. "*The Damnation of Theron Ware* and *Elmer Gantry*." *Research Studies* (Washington State University), XXXII (1964), 334–343 (*ALR*).

Gohdes, Clarence. "The Later Nineteenth Century." In Arthur Hobson Quinn, ed., *The Literature of the American People: An Historical and Critical Survey*. New York: Appleton-Century-Crofts, 1951, pp. 569–809 (*ALR*).

Guiney, Louise Imogen. "Harold Frederic: A Half-Length Sketch from the Life." *Book Buyer*, XVII (1899), 600–604 (*ALR*).

Gwynn, S. [Stephen] W. "Novels of American Life." *Edinburgh Review*, CLXXXVII (1898), 396–406 (*ALR*).

"Harold Frederic." *The Criterion*, XVIII (1898), 26–27 (*ALR*).

"Harold Frederic" [obituary]. New York *Times*, Oct. 20, 1898, p. 7 (*ALR*).

"Harold Frederic" [obituary editorial]. Utica *Observer*, Oct. 20, 1898, p. 4 (*ALR*).

"Harold Frederic: Author of Theron Ware." *Current Literature*, XX (July, 1896), 14 *(ALR)*.

"Harold Frederic Died in London." Utica *Observer*, Oct. 19, 1898, p. 6.

"Harold Frederic Received by the Local Irish League." Utica *Observer*, June 10, 1886, p. 3.

"Harold Frederic's Last Story." *Saturday Evening Post*, CLXXI (1898), 383.

Harris, Frank. "Harold Frederic: Ad Memoriam." *Saturday Review*, LXXXVI (1898), 526–528 *(ALR)*.

"How the Popular Harold Frederic Works." *Literary Digest*, XIII (1896), 397 *(ALR)*.

Howells, William Dean. "My Favorite Novelist and His Best Book." *Munsey's Magazine*, XVII (1897), 18–25 *(ALR)*.

"Illumination and Its Author." *The Bookman* (London), X (1896), 136–138 *(ALR)*.

Kantor, J. R. K. "*The Damnation of Theron Ware* and *John Ward, Preacher.*" *The Serif*, III (March, 1966), 16–21 *(ALR)*.

Lovett, Robert Morss. Introduction to *The Damnation of Theron Ware*. New York: Albert and Charles Boni, 1924 *(ALR)*.

McWilliams, Carey. "Harold Frederic: 'A Country Boy of Genius.'" *University of California Chronicle*, XXXV (Jan., 1933), 21–34 *(ALR)*.

May, H. S. "London Letter." *The Bookman* (New York), III (1896), 250.

"Notes." *The Critic*, XXV, n.s. (1896), 396 *(ALR)*.

O'Donnell, Thomas F. Editor's foreword to *Harold Frederic's Stories of York State*. Syracuse, N.Y.: Syracuse University Press, 1966 *(ALR)*.

——. "Frederic in the Mohawk Valley." *Occasional Papers from Utica College*. Utica, N.Y.: Utica College, 1968.

——. "Harold Frederic (1856–1898)." *American Literary Realism, 1870–1910*, No. 1 (Fall, 1967), pp. 39–44 *(ALR)*.

——. "Harold Frederic: Utica's Forgotten Wonder Boy." *North Country Life*, VIII (Spring, 1954), 6–11 *(ALR)*.

"Our Utican in London." Utica *Observer*, Dec. 31, 1886, p. 8.

Peck, Harry Thurston. "Then and Now." *The Bookman* (New York), XXX (1910), 586–602 (*ALR*).

Raleigh, John Henry. "*The Damnation of Theron Ware.*" *American Literature*, XXX (1958), 210–227 (*ALR*).

Ravitz, Abe C. "Harold Frederic's Venerable Copperhead." *New York History*, XLI (1960), 35–48 (*ALR*).

Rideing, William H. "Stories of a Famous London Drawing Room." *McClure's*, XXXIII (1909), 388–398 (*ALR*).

Sherard, Robert H. "Harold Frederic." *The Idler*, XII (1897), 531–540 (*ALR*).

Sherlock, Charles R. "The Harold Frederic I Knew." *Saturday Evening Post*, CLXI (1899), 616 (*ALR*).

[Shorter, Clement King] C. K. S. "A Literary Letter." *Illustrated London News* (London), CXXIII (1898), 234; (1898), 308; (1898), 382.

———. " 'The Sketch' Regrets the Loss to London of Mr. Harold Frederic, the Well-known American Author and Novelist." *The Sketch*, XXIV (Oct. 26, 1898), 4 (*ALR*).

"Some Recollections of Harold Frederic." *Saturday Review*, LXXXVI (1898), 571–572 (*ALR*).

Stallman, Robert Wooster. Editor's introduction to *Stephen Crane: Stories and Tales*. New York: Alfred A. Knopf, n.d.

VanDerBeets, Richard. "The Ending of *The Damnation of Theron Ware.*" *American Literature*, XXXVI (1964), 358–359 (*ALR*).

———. "Harold Frederic and Comic Realism: The 'Drama Proper' of *Seth's Brother's Wife.*" *American Literature*, XXXIX (1968), 553–560.

Walcutt, Charles Child. "Harold Frederic and American Naturalism." *American Literature*, XI (1939), 11–22 (*ALR*).

Warren, Arthur. "Harold Frederic: The Reminiscences of a Colleague." New York *Times*, Oct. 23, 1898, p. 19 (*ALR*).

Waugh, Arthur. "London Letter." *The Critic*, XXV, N.S. (1896), 316–317.

Wilson, Edmund. Introduction to *Harold Frederic's Stories of York State*, ed. Thomas F. O'Donnell. Syracuse, N.Y.: Syracuse University Press, 1966 (*ALR*).

Woodward, Robert H. "Harold Frederic: A Bibliography." *Studies in Bibliography*, XIII (1960), 247–257 (*ALR*).

——. "The Political Background of Harold Frederic's Novel *Seth's Brother's Wife*." *New York History*, XLIII (1962), 239–248 (*ALR*).

——. "Some Sources for Harold Frederic's *The Damnation of Theron Ware*." *American Literature*, XXXIII (1961), 46–51 (*ALR*).

BOOKS

Åhnebrink, Lars. *The Beginnings of Naturalism in American Fiction, 1891–1903*. Cambridge, Mass.: Harvard University Press, 1950 (*ALR*).

Atherton, Gertrude. *Adventures of a Novelist*. London: Jonathan Cape, 1932 (*ALR*).

Austen, Jessica Tyler, ed. *Moses Coit Tyler: Selections from His Letters and Diaries*. Garden City, N.Y.: Doubleday Page, 1911 (*ALR*).

Beer, Thomas. *The Mauve Decade: American Life at the End of the Nineteenth Century*. New York: Alfred A. Knopf, 1926 (*ALR*).

——. *Stephen Crane: A Study in American Letters*. New York: Alfred A. Knopf, 1924 (*ALR*).

Berryman, John. *Stephen Crane*. American Men of Letters Series. New York: William Sloane, 1950 (*ALR*).

Berthoff, Warner. *The Ferment of Realism: American Literature 1884–1919*. New York: The Fress Press, 1965 (*ALR*).

Blumenfeld, Ralph David. *In the Days of Bicycles and Bustles*. [New York]: Brewer and Warren, 1930 (*ALR*).

Bond, F. [Frank] Fraser. *Mr. Miller of "The Times": The Story of an Editor*. New York: Charles Scribner's, 1931 (*ALR*).

Brooks, Van Wyck. *The Confident Years: 1885–1915.* New York: E. P. Dutton, 1952 *(ALR).*

Burgin, George B. *Some More Memoirs.* London: Hutchinson, 1925 *(ALR).*

Burlingame, Roger. *Of Making Many Books: A Hundred Years of Reading, Writing, and Publishing.* New York: Charles Scribner's, 1946 *(ALR).*

Cady, Edwin H. *The Realist at War: The Mature Years, 1885–1920, of William Dean Howells.* Syracuse, N.Y.: Syracuse University Press, 1958 *(ALR).*

——. *The Road to Realism: The Early Years, 1837–1885, of William Dean Howells.* Syracuse, N.Y.: Syracuse University Press, 1956.

Canby, Henry Seidel. *The Age of Confidence: Life in the Nineties.* New York: Farrar and Rinehart, 1934.

Cargill, Oscar. *Intellectual America: Ideas on the March.* New York: Macmillan, 1941 *(ALR).*

Carter, Everett. *Howells and the Age of Realism.* Philadelphia: J. B. Lippincott, 1954 *(ALR).*

Commager, Henry Steele. *The American Mind: An Interpretation of American Thought and Character Since the 1880's.* New Haven: Yale University Press, 1950 *(ALR).*

Davies, Horton. *A Mirror of the Ministry in Modern Novels.* New York: Oxford University Press, 1959 *(ALR).*

Davis, Elmer. *History of the New York Times, 1851–1921.* New York: New York Times, 1921 *(ALR).*

Durant, Samuel W. *History of Oneida County, New York.* Philadelphia: Everts and Fariss, 1878.

Gilkes, Lillian. *Cora Crane: A Biography of Mrs. Stephen Crane.* Bloomington: Indiana University Press, 1960 *(ALR).*

Gohdes, Clarence. *American Literature in Nineteenth-Century England.* New York: Columbia University Press, 1944 *(ALR).*

Greene, Nelson, ed. *History of the Mohawk Valley.* Vol. IV: *Biography.* Chicago: S. J. Clarke, 1925 *(ALR).*

Haines, Paul. "Harold Frederic." Unpub. Ph.D. diss., New York University, 1945 (*ALR*).

Harris, Frank. *My Life and Loves.* New York: Grove Press, 1963 (*ALR*).

Herron, Ima Honaker. *The Small Town in American Literature.* Durham, N.C.: Duke University Press, 1939 (*ALR*).

Hind, Charles L. *More Authors and I.* London: John Lane, the Bodley Head, Ltd., 1922 (*ALR*).

Howells, William Dean. *"Criticism and Fiction" and Other Essays.* Ed. Clara M. and Rudolf Kirk. New York: New York University Press, 1959 (*ALR*).

Jackson, Holbrook. *The Eighteen Nineties: A Review of Art and Ideas at the Close of the Nineteenth Century.* New York: Alfred A. Knopf, [1927] (*ALR*).

Knight, Grant C. *The Critical Period in American Literature.* Chapel Hill: University of North Carolina Press, 1951 (*ALR*).

Leisy, Ernest E. *The American Historical Novel.* Norman: University of Oklahoma Press, 1950 (*ALR*).

Lewis, R. W. B. *The American Adam: Innocence, Tragedy, and Tradition in the Nineteenth Century.* Chicago: University of Chicago Press, 1955.

Martin, Jay. *Harvests of Change: American Literature 1865–1914.* Englewood Cliffs, N.J.: Prentice Hall, 1967 (*ALR*).

Memorial of the Centennial Celebration of the Battle of Oriskany, August 6, 1877. Utica, N.Y.: Oneida Historical Society, 1878.

Mitchell, Edward Page. *Memoirs of an Editor: Fifty Years of American Journalism.* New York: Charles Scribner's, 1924 (*ALR*).

Mix, Katherine Lyon. *A Study in Yellow: the "Yellow Book" and its Contributors.* Lawrence: University of Kansas, 1960 (*ALR*).

Mumford, Lewis. *The Brown Decades: A Study of the Arts in America, 1865–1895.* New York: Harcourt, Brace, 1931.

Nevins, Allan. *Grover Cleveland: A Study in Courage.* New York: Dodd, Mead, 1933 (*ALR*).

Norris, Frank. *The Literary Criticism of Frank Norris.* Ed. Donald Pizer. Austin: University of Texas Press, 1964 (*ALR*).

——. *The Responsibilities of the Novelist and Other Literary Essays.* New York: Doubleday, Page, 1903.

O'Donnell, Thomas F., and Hoyt C. Franchere. *Harold Frederic.* Twayne's United States Authors Series. New York: Twayne, 1961 (*ALR*).

Parrington, Vernon Louis. *Main Currents in American Thought.* Vol. III: *The Beginnings of Critical Realism in America, 1860–1920.* New York: Harcourt, Brace, 1930 (*ALR*).

Pattee, Fred Lewis. *A History of American Literature Since 1870.* New York: Century, 1915 (*ALR*).

——. *The New American Literature: 1890–1930.* New York: Century, 1930 (*ALR*).

Quinn, Arthur Hobson. *American Fiction: An Historical and Critical Survey.* Student's ed. New York: D. Appleton-Century, 1936 (*ALR*).

Richards, Grant. *Memories of a Misspent Youth: 1872–1896.* London: William Heinemann, 1932 (*ALR*).

Rogers, Ralph Robert. "Harold Frederic: His Development as a Comic Realist." Unpub. Ph.D. diss., Columbia University, 1961 (*ALR*).

Silverman, Kenneth E. "Harold Frederic: His Themes, Techniques, and Place in American Literature." Unpub. Master's essay, Columbia University, 1958.

Stallman, Robert Wooster, and Lillian Gilkes, eds. *Stephen Crane: Letters.* New York: New York University Press, 1960 (*ALR*).

Starrett, Vincent. *Buried Caesars: Essays in Literary Appreciation.* Chicago: Covici-McGee, 1923 (*ALR*).

Taylor, Walter Fuller. *The Economic Novel in America.* Chapel Hill: University of North Carolina Press, 1942 (*ALR*).

Van Doren, Carl. *The American Novel, 1789–1939.* Rev. ed. New York: Macmillan, 1940 (*ALR*).

Walcutt, Charles Child. *American Literary Naturalism, A Divided Stream*. Minneapolis: University of Minnesota Press, 1956 (*ALR*).

Watson, Aaron. *A Newspaper Man's Memories*. London: Hutchinson, 1925 (*ALR*).

Whyte, Frederic. *The Life of W. T. Stead*. 2 vols. New York: Houghton Mifflin, 1925 (*ALR*).

———. *William Heinemann*. New York: Doubleday, Doran, 1929.

Woodward, Robert H. "Harold Frederic: A Study of His Novels, Short Stories, and Plays." Unpub. Ph.D. diss., Indiana University, 1957 (*ALR*).

Ziff, Larzer. *The American 1890s: Life and Times of a Lost Generation*. New York: Viking, 1966 (*ALR*).

Index